SOCIETY FOR NEW TESTAMENT STUDIES

MONOGRAPH SERIES

General Editor: G. N. Stanton

65

THE EPISTLE TO THE HEBREWS

For Lincoln Moody Hurst
1918–1986
A just man made perfect (Heb. 12:23)

The Epistle to the Hebrews

Its background of thought

L. D. HURST

Associate Professor of Religious Studies
University of California, Davis

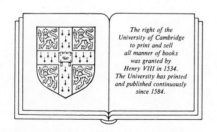

The right of the
University of Cambridge
to print and sell
all manner of books
was granted by
Henry VIII in 1534.
The University has printed
and published continuously
since 1584.

CAMBRIDGE UNIVERSITY PRESS

CAMBRIDGE

NEW YORK   PORT CHESTER   MELBOURNE   SYDNEY

Published by the Press Syndicate of the University of Cambridge
The Pitt Building, Trumpington Street, Cambridge CB2 1RP
40 West 20th Street, New York, NY 10011, USA
10 Stamford Road, Oakleigh, Melbourne 3166, Australia

First published 1990

Printed in Great Britain by
the University Press, Cambridge

British Library cataloguing in publication data

Hurst, L. D.
  The Epistle to the Hebrews.
  1. Bible. N.T. Hebrews − Critical studies
  I. Title   II. Series
  227'.8706

Library of Congress cataloguing in publication data

Hurst, David
  The Epistle to the Hebrews: its background of thought / D. Hurst.
      p.   cm. − (Society for New Testament Studies monograph series : 65
  Includes bibliographical references.
  ISBN 0 521 37097 3
  1. Bible. N.T. Hebrews − Criticism, interpretation, etc.
  I. Title.   II. Series: Monograph series (Society for New Testament
  Studies) : 65.
  BS2775.2H87   1990
  227'.8706 − dc20   89−37969   CIP

ISBN 0 521 37097 3

CONTENTS

Contents

PREFACE

This study is a revised and shortened version of a thesis accepted by the University of Oxford in 1982 for the degree of Doctor of Philosophy. George Caird acted as supervisor. Over several years he patiently read at least three drafts of each chapter, always producing many pages of handwritten criticism. My debt to him is recorded elsewhere, most obviously in the volume of memorial essays entitled *The Glory of Christ in the New Testament* (Oxford, Clarendon Press, 1987). But to this he would like me to add that our original interest in this investigation was as a kind of *Grundausbildung* for his forthcoming New International Critical Commentary on Hebrews. I still treasure a letter he wrote me in 1982 in which he stated his intention to build much of his commentary on the following work. His unheralded death in 1984 can only mean the loss of what would have been a memorable exercise in New Testament exegesis.

I would also like to thank those of my colleagues, at Davis and elsewhere, who read the thesis in whole or in part and made suggestions. To my former pupils Bill Kynes and Mike Tristram I owe a special debt of gratitude, for they helped to stimulate and refine questions which in 1978 were just beginning to be asked. The Senior New Testament Seminar at Oxford listened patiently to papers on the christology and eschatology of Hebrews and made probing criticisms.

It is perhaps especially fitting that this work should have taken its final shape while I was serving as New Testament lecturer at Mansfield College, Oxford. James Moffatt, who produced the first International Critical Commentary on Hebrews, and Caird, who was to do the second, were both at Mansfield. And anyone who wears a Mansfield tie bears constant testimony to Hebrews 1:2 – *Deus Locutus est Nobis in Filio*, as the Latinized college motto has it. I should like to express my thanks to the Senior Common Room there, particularly the Rev. Charles Brock and Dr. and Mrs. M. P. Mahony, for their friendship and support in what were sometimes difficult circumstances.

Special gratitude is also due to Prof. R. McL. Wilson, who first showed interest in this work as a monograph. His newly published, outstanding exposition of Hebrews reached me barely in time to take account of it here, however minimally. Professor Graham Stanton, the editor of this series, provided a series of careful suggestions which were matched only by his great patience in awaiting the outcome.

I should also like to thank the staff of Cambridge University Press, and in particular Mr. Alex Wright, for their patience and skill in guiding the book to a successful conclusion.

For many years my friends Harp and Barbara Junta supported me both personally and financially; without their faithful help I could not have completed this work. They are too unselfish to expect my gratitude, but I should like publicly to record it.

Finally, to my parents I owe all. Apart from life and a loving home, they gave me their encouragement and help from beginning to end. My father wished very much to see this work in print, but his long and ultimately unsuccessful battle with leukemia thwarted his intent. Making his triumphal entry on the morning of Palm Sunday, 1986, he joined the innumerable ranks of those who, following the lead of their great forerunner, have gone through the veil and penetrated the greatest mystery of all.

ABBREVIATIONS

Ancient works

Ad Autol.	*To Autolycus*
Ant.	*Antiquities*
Asc. Is.	Ascension of Isaiah
ben Sira	The Wisdom of Jesus ben Sira
B.T.	Babylonian Talmud
CD	Covenant of Damascus
De Abr.	*On Abraham*
De cher.	*On the Cherubim*
De conf. ling.	*On the Confusion of Tongues*
De gig.	*On the Giants*
De migr. Abr.	*On the Migration of Abraham*
De op. M.	*On the Creation*
De plant.	*On Noah's Work as a Planter*
De post. C.	*On the Posterity and Exile of Cain*
De somn.	*On Dreams*
De spec. leg.	*On the Special Laws*
De vit. M.	*On the Life of Moses*
El.	*Electra*
1 En.	1 Enoch
Enn.	*Enneads*
Eum.	*Eumenides*
Gen. Apoc.	Genesis Apocryphon
Hist. eccl.	*Ecclesiastical History*
Jub.	Jubilees
Leg. all.	*Allegorical Interpretation*
LXX	Septuagint version of the OT
1 Macc.	1 Maccabees
2 Macc.	2 Maccabees
Mem.	*Memorabilia*

MT	Massoretic text of the Hebrew Bible
Num. Naso	Numbers Naso
Od.	*Odyssey*
Oed. Rex	*Oedipus Rex*
Odes Sol.	Odes of Solomon
Phaed.	*Phaedo*
Praep. evang.	*Preparation for the Gospel*
Qu. in Exod.	*Questions and Answers on Exodus*
Quis rer.	*Who is the Heir?*
Quod Deus	*On the Unchangeableness of God*
1QH	Qumran Hymns
1QM	Qumran War Scroll
1QpH	Qumran Habakkuk Commentary
1QS	Qumran Manual of Discipline
1QSa	Qumran Messianic Rule
4QDeut	4 QDeuteronomy
4QFl	4 QFlorilegium
4QPB	4 QPatriarchal Blessings
11QMelch	11 QMelchizedek
Rep.	*Republic*
Sib.	Sibylline Oracles
Tim.	*Timaeus*
T. Levi	Testament of Levi
Tob.	Tobit
TR	Teacher of Righteousness
v.l.	Variant reading
Wis.	Wisdom of Solomon

Modern works

AJR	*American Journal of Theology*
ATR	*Anglican Theological Review*
AV	Authorized Version
BA	*Biblical Archaeologist*
BASOR	*Bulletin of the American Schools of Oriental Research*
BZ	*Biblische Zeitschrift*
CBQ	*Catholic Biblical Quarterly*
CJT	*Canadian Journal of Theology*
CQR	*Church Quarterly Review*

EQ	*Evangelical Quarterly*
ET	*Expository Times*
HTR	*Harvard Theological Review*
HUCA	*Hebrew Union College Annual*
IBS	*Irish Biblical Studies*
IEJ	*Israel Exploration Journal*
Interp.	*Interpretation*
JBL	*Journal of Biblical Literature*
JEH	*Journal of Ecclesiastical History*
JES	*Journal of Ecumenical Studies*
JJS	*Journal of Jewish Studies*
JSJ	*Journal for the Study of Judaism*
LQ	*Lutheran Quarterly*
JQR	*Jewish Quarterly Review*
JThC	*Journal of Theology and Church*
JTS	*Journal of Theological Studies*
MTZ	*Münchener Theologische Zeitschrift*
NEB	New English Bible
NRT	*Nouvelle revue théologique*
NT	*Novum Testamentum*
NTS	*New Testament Studies*
REB	Revised English Bible
RB	*Revue biblique*
RQ	*Revue de Qumran*
RSV	Revised Standard Version
RTR	*Reformed Theological Review*
SE	*Studia Evangelica*
SJT	*Scottish Journal of Theology*
SNTS	Society for New Testament Studies
ST	*Studia Theologica*
TB	*Tyndale Bulletin*
TDNT	*Theological Dictionary of the New Testament*, vols. I–IX, ed. G. Kittel and G. Friedrich (Grand Rapids, Mich., 1964–74)
ThLZ	*Theologische Literaturzeitung*
ThR	*Theologisches Rundschau*
ThZ	*Theologische Zeitschrift*
TS	*Theological Studies*
TSK	*Theologische Studien und Kritiken*
VuF	*Verkündigung und Forschung*
ZAW	*Zeitschrift für die alttestamentliche Wissenschaft*

ZNW   *Zeitschrift für die Neutestamentliche Wissenschaft*
ZThK   *Zeitschrift für Theologie und Kirche*

Abbreviations of the titles of the works of Philo and other ancient writers follow the pattern of *The New International Dictionary of New Testament Theology*, edited by Colin Brown (Exeter, 1975), I, pp. 31–40.

INTRODUCTION

Despite its deep severity, there is something faintly humorous about the Epistle to the Hebrews. It claims that it is "written in few words" (13:22); yet before the reader has reached the final chapter it is clear that this is one of the longest letters in the NT. Because of its canonical history the phrase "without father, without mother, without genealogy" (7:3) seems more fitting for the document than for one of its favourite characters. "The Epistle to the Hebrews" is often said to be the most "Greek" book in the Jewish–Christian Bible. Indeed, to some it might seem that the epistle itself is something of a joke – a joke played upon a church obsessed with finding complete certainty about its origins. That the most elementary facts concerning this "final word" on the Christian faith may be arrived at only through a fancy tapestry of guesswork is what punctuates the joke with its required – and exquisite – irony.

When reading modern descriptions of the epistle, it is not uncommon to encounter pejorative expressions which are extraordinary for a document which for centuries had the status of a Pauline writing. "Fantastic," "amazing," "artificial," "obscure," "outmoded," "a theological treatise in cold blood," "sheer length and nothing but length" – these are but a few one could cite from recent interpretation.

How has the epistle come upon such hard days? The answer must involve a brief survey of recent interpretation.[1] When modern critical methods gave the *coup de grâce* to Pauline authorship of the epistle, a pendulum began to swing in the opposite direction. Not only was the epistle no longer regarded as Pauline; it was now felt to have come from one so *unlike* Paul as to make doubtful the notion that he stood even in the main stream of Christian tradition. Since the writer describes the OT tabernacle and cultus as a "copy and shadow" of the heavenly things (8:5), for instance, it was natural for many to conclude that it was written by one whose primary allegiance was not to the Christian gospel but to the philosophy of Plato. By attempting to fit Christian beliefs into such a framework, he subjected the Christian gospel to enormous violence. Along with the view that the writer represents an aberrant point of view went a rejection of the traditional assumption that the danger which motivated much of the concern of the writing was a relapse on the part of the Jewish–Christian readers into Judaism. Some now suggested that Judaism in the epistle only served as an example of religion in general, and that the epistle was written to gentiles who were on the verge of lapsing either into irreligion or outright paganism. This distancing of Hebrews from the Jewish background traditionally felt to underlie the other NT writings was continued in 1939 when E. Käsemann suggested that the author wrote from a standpoint of "pre-Christian Gnosticism" which stressed the necessity of wandering in this material world until the soul finally reached its true home in the realm of the spirit. The massive commentary of C. Spicq, published in 1952, perpetuated the view that an essentially "un-Jewish" de-emphasizing of the material realm explains Hebrews. At the same time, however, the Qumran scrolls were published, and yet another explanation of the epistle was introduced. A "Qumran hypothesis" for the epistle, as made well known by Y. Yadin, seemed in its time to win the day. For some, after many disappointments and false starts, the true situation of the epistle had been uncovered by a chance discovery. Yet in a few years it was clear that not all were satisfied with this solution either; once again the question was thrown open. Other backgrounds suggested included that of W. Manson, who in 1951 had urged that Hebrews represents a "Hellenist" or "progressive" Judaism which, stressing the world mission of the Son of Man, went back ultimately to the teaching of the proto-martyr, Stephen, in Acts 7. In 1972 the Samaritans were added to the field, and a few years later it was suggested that a first-century form of *Merkabah* mysticism was at least one of the influences which determined the particular emphases of Hebrews. The latter suggestion was especially interesting, since it came from a writer who six years earlier had demolished Spicq's case, and who had therefore, one might say, earned the right to speak.

Thus the Epistle to the Hebrews continues to be a storm-center of debate in NT study. During the past century it has been read against perhaps a greater number of widely differing backgrounds than any other ancient document. By far the most common view has been to see the epistle as something of an alien presence in the NT, an intruder from a thought-world which is far from the mainstream of the

Christian tradition. To an amazing degree each of these widely differing backgrounds seems convincing when it is considered in isolation from the rest. The interpretation of the epistle is in disarray because scholarly opinion vacillates from background to background as each new publication appears. It is uncertain at present what the next step should be.

The objective of this work is to clarify the issues of the debate by examining each background separately in order to determine its strengths and weaknesses. The motivation of the study is the belief that once certain issues are isolated and clarified, and major mistakes eliminated, the problems will begin to sort themselves out. Our task will not be the process of creation *ex nihilo* described in Heb. 11:3. The necessary data have already been provided. What is needed is a bringing of order out of chaos.

The study will be divided into two parts, non-Christian backgrounds and Christian backgrounds. The agenda will not include any of the numerous questions connected with authorship, date, or identification of those to whom the epistle is addressed, except where such questions might impinge on the more pressing question of the intellectual milieu which gave rise to the ideas of the epistle.

In terms of scope, we shall confine our investigation to possible milieus for the epistle rather than sources on which it may have depended. It is not always easy to distinguish these, of course. Paul could well be *both* a milieu and a source upon which the author depended for ideas. But we shall not concern ourselves with the question of the particular sources of the gospel tradition upon which the author depended for his information about the earthly life of Jesus. Nor shall we treat studies that urge a "family likeness" to exist between Hebrews and other NT writers such as Luke,[2] since this involves more the task of classifying NT writers into theological "bloodgroups" than it does the question of which particularly identifiable milieus gave rise to the distinctive concerns of the epistle. The same may be said of similarities which are occasionally noted between Hebrews and the Johannine literature.

The need for our study is made clear when it is observed to what an extent prior decisions concerning the intellectual background of a writing will predetermine its understanding. Often the choice of a background will become the all-important "control" by which other possible understandings of the text are filtered out. A recent example of this sort is J.W. Thompson's *The Beginnings of Christian Philosophy* (1982). Throughout the work the reader is assured that the background of Hebrews lies along the trajectory of Platonic, Philonic or gnostic speculations in which the immutable realm of the heavenly is superior to the mutable realm of the sense-perceptible. If the LXX, apocalyptic or other NT parallels are mentioned, it is almost always to deny their relevance and to restate the original thesis. In his discussion of the heavenly Jerusalem of Heb. 12:22ff., for example, Thompson notes in passing that the key word μένειν occurs in Isa. 66:22. But while in the Isaiah context the term is used for the rebuilt city of Jerusalem,

> in Hebrews it is used for that which is non-material. The use of μένειν for the abiding of the supercelestial reality appears frequently in the Platonic literature ... This understanding [i.e., that of Hebrews] is set in dualistic terms which must be understood in the light of the Platonic understanding of the stability characteristic of the intelligible world.[3]

Why the passage in Hebrews "must" be understood against this background is never really *argued*. Nor would one guess from this treatment that the author of Hebrews constantly quotes the LXX and never once quotes or even alludes to[4] Plato or Philo, or that Isa. 66:18ff.LXX is one of the most important OT passages for the new heaven and earth which contains many of the same terms and ideas used in the argument of Hebrews. The theological locus of Hebrews appears to have been shifted in the direction of Plato and Alexandria before the exegetical work has been undertaken.[5]

Because of the number of quotations in Hebrews which come from the LXX, it will be a presupposition of this work that the author's study of the OT Scriptures was one of the major influences upon the formation of his argument. Often it will be seen that an emphasis in Hebrews appears in the LXX as well. This should be regarded as a weakening of the argument for the background, non-Christian or Christian, at that point. The central question to be borne in mind is this: "Is there anything in any one of these backgrounds which answers the features of the epistle better than the others?"

For the sake of convenience, throughout what follows I shall refer to the writer as *Auctor*.

PART 1

NON-CHRISTIAN BACKGROUNDS

1

PHILO, ALEXANDRIA AND PLATONISM

1 History of discussion

Since the mid seventeenth century[1] it has been argued that to understand Hebrews one needs to know the works of Philo of Alexandria. The first thorough presentation of this approach was that of Ménégoz in 1894.[2] He began a movement which so captivated critical opinion that for the first half of the twentieth century the Philonic background of Hebrews was felt to be one of the assured results of criticism. It is not difficult to list an impressive array of writers who either argue or assume the influence of Philo (and usually Plato) upon *Auctor*.[3] The Philonic trend reached its apex in 1952 with Spicq's massive commentary,[4] a *tour de force* probing vocabulary, hermeneutical techniques, psychology and special parallels with Heb. 11. Of particular significance for him was *Auctor*'s use of the argument from silence, in which the lack of any genealogy for Melchizedek is theologically important (for the same argument used by Philo in other connections, cf., e.g., *Leg. all.* I.60); the allegorical treatment of Melchizedek's name ("king of peace," Heb. 7:3, *Leg. all.* III.79ff.); and the claim that certain things are "fitting" (ἔπρεπεν) for God (Heb. 2:10, *Leg. all.* I.15). Spicq, however, did not depict *Auctor* as a thoroughgoing Philonist, since *Auctor* "repudiated resolutely" Philo's allegorical method in favour of a typological method close to Paul's. But his conclusion was that *Auctor* was a "Philonian converted to Christianity," even suggesting that *Auctor* knew Philo personally.[5]

Another full-length argument for Philonic influence was produced in 1965 by S. Sowers.[6] Sowers was mainly interested in the exegetical devices of Philo and *Auctor*, and agreed with Spicq that *Auctor* came "from the same school of Alexandrian Judaism as Philo, and that Philo's writings still offer us the best single body of *religionsgeschichtlich* material we have for this N.T. document."[7]

7

Although others have continued to present arguments for Philonic influence, it is Spicq who represents the climax of approximately sixty years of research, during which there was an extraordinarily unanimous approach to the background of Hebrews. During this time writers of immense erudition were convinced of the soundness of the case, and to many it seemed almost irrefutable. Yet there is irony in recalling that even as Spicq was assembling the ultimate case for Philonic influence in Hebrews, a group of texts was coming to light which would call it into question. Younger students who might have been persuaded by Spicq were distracted by the Qumran scrolls. A new background for the epistle was hence introduced, and the enthusiasm with which Spicq's findings were greeted dissipated quickly. Spicq himself was sufficiently impressed by the new evidence to modify his position. He now felt that the author (Apollos), having come from Alexandria, was writing to a group of Jewish priests who had been in contact with Qumran and who had fled from Jerusalem to Antioch.[8]

Spicq's case was further weakened by C.K. Barrett[9] in 1956. Barrett reacted to the old statement of Moffatt that *Auctor* had tried unsuccessfully to incorporate eschatology into his Platonism, and stressed instead the central role of eschatology in the epistle. He concluded that, although *Auctor* uses philosophical language which would have been understood by Plato and Philo, many features of his thought (for instance, the heavenly sanctuary) which have been thought to be derived from Platonic thinking were in fact derived from currents within Jewish apocalyptic.

Three years later Spicq's arguments themselves were attacked by R.P.C. Hanson.[10] Hanson, emphasizing the paucity of other surviving Alexandrian Judaic literature which is contemporary with *Auctor* and Philo, compared the two writers in terms of concepts (Messianism, eschatology, history, law) and the use of the OT. After comparing numerous passages in the two writers, he concluded that *Auctor* stands closer to Stephen's speech in Acts 7, which represents a form of Alexandrian Judaism, but of a non-Philonic variety.[11]

In 1968 F. Schröger[12] also analyzed Spicq's case and, while acknowledging certain similarities between *Auctor* and Philo, he argued that the two writers represent variant branches of Judaism – Philo an allegorizing branch, and *Auctor* an apocalyptically oriented branch similar to what one finds at Qumran.

The most thoroughgoing answer to Spicq was produced in 1970 by R. Williamson.[13] To refute Spicq would require a careful step-by-step analysis of his case, and this is what Williamson did. Examining words, phrases, ideas and Spicq's logic, Williamson argued that Spicq's claim that *Auctor* was a former Philonian was groundless.

Such a volte-face of scholarly opinion, in so short a time, suggests that there is still far from a clear grasp of the central issues. In particular it is the question of Platonic dualism on which everything seems to hinge. For Plato true reality was uncreated, eternal and immutable. Since the world of sense-perception is in flux, it compares with the archetypal realm of ideas as a fleeting shadow compares with its object (cf. *Phaedo* 80b; *Tim.* 28a–29b). One who wishes to contemplate the pattern (παράδειγμα) of the heavenly πόλις is its citizen (*Rep.* IX.592a, b). This philosophy was essentially adopted by Philo with one great modification: he identified the two creation accounts of Gen. 1 and 2 with the creation of the two realms, the ideal and the material. The creation of the ideas was for Philo the laying out of the Great Architect's plan for his creation, a plan Philo identified with the Logos (*De op. M.* 16ff.). This concept is still often assumed to explain the notion in Hebrews of creation "through" the Son (1:2), the belief "that the origin of the visible universe was at the same time the creation of the material of which the universe consists" (11:3),[14] and the notion of the two tents (8:5, 9:11,23f.). It is the last motif which has excited the most comment. Eccles[15] calls it "the clearest evidence of the influence of Hellenistic thought patterns" in the epistle. For Gilbert[16] the quotation of Ex. 25:40 in 8:5 "affords a happy opening by which the Platonic speculation enters our epistle." A linking of Heb. 8:5 with Plato goes back at least as far as Eusebius.[17] In this case the pattern shown to Moses on the mount was not simply a blueprint to be followed; it was the eternal, heavenly sanctuary which has its own significance, of which Moses' copy (ὑπόδειγμα) was only a faint shadow (σκιά). The fact that the shadow–reality dichotomy is rarely used in rabbinic texts is said to be further indication that *Auctor* stands in the Platonic tradition.[18] *Auctor* "empties eschatology of all idea of time," says McNeile.[19] This dualism involves not only *Auctor*'s two tents; it extends also to his view of humankind, for in 4:12 is found a distinction between πνεῦμα and ψυχή reminiscent of Philo (cf., e.g., *De spec. leg.* IV.122ff.; *Quis rer.* 55ff.).[20] That *Auctor* could have evolved such thoughts "independently of the Platonic doctrine" is said to be unthinkable.[21]

A dualistic reading of Hebrews thus continues to command widespread assent in the twentieth century.[22] The most thoroughgoing form of this is that of Thompson,[23] who argues that chs. 1, 7, 9, 12 and 13 of Hebrews reflect a negative view of matter (and "the flesh") based upon the Platonic material/immaterial distinction. Thompson would like to keep alive the older (pre-Barrett) approach to Hebrews.

For those dealing with this complex issue the main problem continues to lie in deciding whether, or to what extent, a "linear apocalyptic" viewpoint may be integrated with a "Platonic, vertical" framework in the epistle. There are at present at least four distinct approaches to this question: (1) that of M. Goguel[24] and J. Cambier,[25] who refuse to see a "linear apocalyptic" view in the epistle at all; (2) that of Moffatt[26] and Scott,[27] who see the linear view as resting uncomfortably side by side with a Platonic perspective; (3) that of Barrett,[28] who, although admitting the presence of Platonic thought-forms in the epistle, feels that they have been blended so skilfully with the idealist element within Jewish apocalyptic that the two viewpoints become, as it were, one; and (4) that of Hofius[29] and Michel,[30] who see the Jewish linear view as primary and providing a sufficient explanation of *Auctor*'s thought. These views have not been mutually exclusive, and often there is much overlapping and cross-referral.

By far the most common view has been that which downplays any "horizontal" element in Hebrews. For Cambier,[31] e.g., *Auctor* has transformed traditional Jewish concepts, with the aid of Platonism, into a "vertical eschatology." His corollary is that the failure of the parousia was decisive in this transformation (although Barrett, it should be remembered, demonstrated that a complete rejection of apocalyptic thinking was not necessary to counter such a problem – if problem it was). For E. Schweizer, on the other hand, the difficulty was not the parousia but how, in a Hellenist milieu, it could be said that God has encountered us in time. Thus for Cambier and Schweizer[32] *Auctor* refocuses traditional Jewish thought from event to the spatial quality the event reveals. In this eclipse even μέλλω and μένω refer, not to "when" or "how long," but to the stable character which heavenly reality reveals. Contra Cullmann,[33] who saw the Hebrew "time line" as determinative for Hebrews, the qualitative "heavenly" now replaces the temporal future. Grässer[34] sees Hebrews as a transitional stage between the two, although he is in turn criticized by Klappert,[35] who argues once again that the future-linear dimension is primary, with the Greek vertical mode used in Hebrews to reinforce the "horizontal" by providing a present hope.

Klappert's thesis is further developed by Macrae,[36] for whom *Auctor*, the Alexandrian, provides the "vertical" perspective ("faith") in order to enrich the apocalyptic viewpoint ("hope") of his readers. The epistle thus contains *both* perspectives: 8:1–5, 9:23, 9:11–12 – "apocalyptic," 9:24, 10:19–20, and (perhaps) 6:19–20, "Hellenistic."

How is the seasoned scholar of the NT, much less the beginning student, to make sense of any of this? I would suggest that the place to begin is the following. Rather than build upon writers like Thompson who are apparently trying to turn the clock back by allowing the "pre-Barrett" view to control their exegesis, we should accept once and for all that Barrett has done irreparable damage to the view that *Auctor* allows a Platonic-type dualism to *control* his thinking. Barrett, with Williamson, has established the role of history and time in the epistle. The way this is expressed, on the other hand, will require considerably more sophistication than has been in evidence heretofore. In particular we need to avoid such terms as "eschatology," "eternal," "philosophical," "true," "archetypal" and "preexistent," terms which mean too many things to too many people. By "eschatology," for example, writers often mean "apocalyptic." Rowland,[37] however, has shown how extremely complex the apocalyptic tradition is and that the two terms cannot be taken as synonymous. In what is to follow the term "eschatology" will be avoided in favour of the phrase "linear apocalyptic," by which I mean those streams of thought *within* apocalyptic which seem to stress actions posited on a horizontal time-line.

2 Unresolved issues

At least three major issues now require re-examination if the discussion is to proceed in a profitable way. These are: (1) Philo's role in Judaism; (2) Platonic, Philonic or Alexandrian language; and (3) the relation of "Hellenism" to "linear apocalyptic" in Hebrews.[38]

Philo's role in Judaism

In surveying modern writers, it is evident that when one speaks of "Philonic" or "Alexandrian" influence in Hebrews, there is no unanimity over what this means. For some it is direct acquaintance with Philo; for others it is a vaguer influence loose in the culture; for others it means that Philo is the best representative *example* of influences at work on *Auctor*; and for still others it indicates a polemical interest *against* Philo.

At this point certain things should be said about Alexandrian Judaism itself. Hanson emphasizes[39] the paucity of Alexandrian literature we have, amounting mainly to the Wisdom of Solomon, the Letter of Aristeas, Philo and the LXX. It appears that *Auctor* was acquainted with Wisdom[40] and the LXX, but to what degree Wisdom and the LXX were also in vogue in Palestine and Hellenistic Judaism at large may be impossible to determine at present. Paul also may show the influence of Wisdom in Romans.[41] It is difficult to know to what extent one is dealing with an intellectual milieu in which ideas are being tossed about in an imprecise way as opposed to a conscious reference to the Greek philosophical tradition. Wisdom shows acquaintance with notions such as the pre-existence of the soul (8:19f.), ὕλη (11:17) and ὁ ὤν (13:1),[42] but their usage is superficial.[43] The author remains fundamentally an OT Jew, demonstrating how "Greek" ideas might have percolated into the mind of a Jewish writer without controlling his or her essential viewpoint.

It is well known that the names of numerous Alexandrian individuals between Wisdom and Philo survived, but their work did not.[44] This is one ground for referring to Philo not as a towering giant but as the person whose writings survived. But Hanson wrongly assumes that other writers with ideas similar to Philo whose work is lost to us must be limited to *Egyptian* Judaism. To what extent Philo's material represents Hellenistic Judaism outside of Egypt (of which we have virtually nothing) has not yet been determined. When modern writers speak of "Hellenistic Judaism," what is meant is "Alexandrian Judaism"; we have almost nothing else. That there was also a Hellenistic Judaism in Palestine (many of the ideas in Wisdom and Philo can be paralleled in the rabbis)[45] is a suitable *caveat*. The proper question to be faced is: "Is the similarity to Philo so considerable and precise as to require that reference to explain Hebrews, or is one talking here about something much more general?" If Philo can be seen as the representative of a much broader movement of Hellenistic Judaism, therefore, and if the parallels between him and *Auctor* are not as precise as was once thought, those parallels will not necessarily determine an Alexandrian provenance for Hebrews.[46]

Platonic, Philonic or Alexandrian language

Some linguistic assumptions not dealt with by Williamson are so important they will require extensive treatment.

ὑπόδειγμα *and* σκιά[47]

A study of the important term ὑπόδειγμα is a significant omission in Williamson's study.[48] R.P.C. Hanson[49] has called its usage "a chief coincidence of vocabulary between Philo and Hebrews." For J.H. Burtness[50] the usage of ὑπόδειγμα and ἀντίτυπος shows that "there is no doubt but that he [the author] is using words which are *frequently used by Philo* and which seem to express the antithesis between heavenly realities and earthly copies."[51] The latter comment reveals what has almost invariably been taken to be a datum, namely that the term ὑπόδειγμα in Heb. 8:5 means "copy." The RSV and NEB render the key phrase of that verse as "a copy and shadow of the heavenly (sanctuary)."

Several observations are germane at this point:

(a) Contrary to these assumptions, ὑπόδειγμα is *not* a word characteristic of Philo. In the entire Philonic corpus, it is used only four times (*De conf. ling.* 64; *Quis rer.* 256; *De somn.* II.3; *De post. C.*122), as opposed to three times in Hebrews. Classical Greek usage (including that of Plato[52] and Philo[53]) preferred παράδειγμα to ὑπόδειγμα.

(b) There is no instance in known Greek literature where ὑπόδειγμα can be demonstrated to mean "copy." It is an astonishing feature of the interpretation of Hebrews that to this day the translation of ὑπόδειγμα as "copy" has remained virtually unchallenged. In all its known occurrences a ὑπόδειγμα, as with the shorter form δεῖγμα, is a "sample," "suggestion," "symbol," "outline," "token" or "example,"[54] usually "something suggested as a *basis* for imitation or instruction"[55] – a basis for something which comes later. A δεῖγμα, in addition to being a "sample," may be a "prefiguration of a cosmic or eschatological secret."[56] The verbal form ὑποδείκνυμι, furthermore, means "to display," "to show," "to point toward." It *never* means "to copy." The only occurrence of ὑπόδειγμα in Hebrews apart from its connection with the heavenly sanctuary bears this meaning: it is a moral *pattern* of disobedience which may be imitated (or "copied") by later generations (4:11). In three out of four occurrences in Philo the term bears this meaning, i.e., that of a moral example to be imitated. This element of futurity is also found in ben Sira: "Enoch pleased God and was taken off to heaven, an example (or sample – ὑπόδειγμα) of repentance for the future (ταῖς γενεαῖς,' 44:16), and particularly in the Fourth Gospel (Jesus, in washing the disciples' feet, gives them a ὑπόδειγμα, 13:15). "This is more than an example," says H. Schlier[57] of the John 13 text; "it is a definite prototype." That a term used by the Fourth Gospel for "a prototype" (that which comes *first*) is used in Hebrews for the earthly tent should be borne in mind when looking at Heb. 8:5 and 9:23.

This information puts us in a better position to evaluate the RSV and NEB translation of ὑπόδειγμα in Heb. 8:5 and 9:23 as "copy." This single word has perhaps played more of a role in the "Platonizing" of Hebrews than any other factor. For Plato the earthly sense-perceptible world is a "copy" (μίμημα[58] or εἰκών[59]) of the eternal Ideas – the pattern (παράδειγμα). Philo similarly likens creation to the practice of an architect who makes "copies" (μιμήματα) of a previously constructed pattern. The assumption in commentaries on Hebrews has been that ὑπόδειγμα in 8:5 and 9:23 is *Auctor*'s version of the same viewpoint.[60] The older English translations of the NT,[61] on the other hand, did not render ὑπόδειγμα as "copy." Most chose terms connected with the idea of "example" (following perhaps the Vulgate's *exemplar*, which may mean "original" *or* "copy"). The RSV (unfortunately followed here by the NEB) would have done better to stay with the idea of "example" rather than adopting the one-sided term "copy."

This would indicate that the RSV and NEB translation of Heb. 8:5 and 9:23 involves a serious error. ὑπόδειγμα normally means the precise *opposite* of "copy," "likeness," or "imitation" – it is something *to be* copied, "a basis for imitation or instruction."[62] E. Lee[63] has correctly pointed out, although without argumentation, that in Heb. 8:5 the idea is neither that of example nor copy, but a *"glimpse* as distinct from a vision, a partial suggestion as distinct from a complete expression"; W. Barclay[64] views it as a "specimen, or still better, *a sketch plan.*" A crucial text in the latter regard is Ezek. 42:15LXX: there the angel guiding the prophet "measured the ὑπόδειγμα of the house round about." This passage is important for Hebrews, since (a) it involves a new temple, "a prophetic vision of the new house of God,"[65] and (b) it is the only occurrence in the LXX of ὑπόδειγμα in the specialized, "structural" sense of "pattern" or "outline" (as opposed to a moral example). In Ezekiel it is the *outline* (again, note the inadmissibility of "copy" as a viable translation option) of the new temple which is measured by the angel. Are there any grounds for supposing that *Auctor* has taken the term from his LXX text of Ezekiel and has connected it with Moses' vision in Ex. 25, with the result that the ὑπόδειγμα (outline) is what Moses produces in accordance with the vision?

Before an answer to that question is attempted, it is necessary to pose a prior question: Why have translators so persistently rendered ὑπόδειγμα in Heb. 8:5 as "copy"? The answer appears to consist in two presuppositions: (a) *Auctor* in this verse demonstrates a linguistic and philosophical indebtedness to Plato (an assumption going back at least as far as Eusebius).[66] Thus Heb. 8:5 has been read continually through the eyes of Plato, with the consequence that the author has not been allowed to speak for himself. (b) *Auctor*, in reading his text of Ex. 25:40, has focused his attention primarily on the words ποιήσεις κατά – "make according to." The assumption in this case, while never articulated, is that the "copy" idea (gained, incidentally, only *by extrapolation* from Moses' making his tabernacle "according to" something else in 8:5) may be allowed to cast itself back upon the ὑπόδειγμα of 8:5a. But 8:5a and 8:5b should not be so easily run together, nor is it certain that the author centers his interest in Ex. 25:40 upon the "make according to" element of the verse. It is here that the evidence of the LXX leads one into the realm of justified speculation. Rather than focusing on the "copy" idea, it is possible that the author is primarily interested in three terms in the Exodus 25 passage which remind him, via *gezerah shewah*, of the other great text concerning a "heavenly" sanctuary: Ezek. 40–8. As one reads those chapters, it is difficult not to notice elements which also figure prominently in Ex. 25:40: Ezekiel is given his vision of the city-temple on a *mountain* (ὄρος) and is warned to lay up in his heart *all things* (πᾶς) *shown* (δείκνυμι) to him (Ezek. 40:2–4). In this case "mountain," "all things" and "show" would be link words or "magnets" which would have the effect of drawing the attention of a writer such as the author of Hebrews from Ex. 25:40 to Ezek. 40–8. That the rare occurrence of ὑπόδειγμα in a structural, "architectonic" context – unique in the LXX to Ezek. 42:15 – appears to repeat itself in Heb. 8:5, again in connection with an ideal sanctuary seen on a mountain, is a powerful piece of evidence pointing to the conclusion that the author is familiar with the Ezekiel story. He may be quoting Exodus, but what is really in his mind is Ezekiel's city-temple. Just as the angel measures the perimeter of the new sanctuary in Ezek. 42:15, so Moses produces an "outline" of the heavenly τύπος shown to him on the mount.[67] Many years ago G. Buchanan Gray[68] argued that the Exodus story, by virtue of its allusive and general nature, assumes as its basis the more graphic account of Ezekiel's vision of the new temple. To examine Gray's case would take us beyond our brief, but at least it must be said that in the course of his discussion he proves that there is an undeniable "family likeness" between the two stories. It is also possible that in Jewish apocalyptic Ex. 25 and Ezek. 42:15 were fused.[69] This would not mean, of course, that the author of Hebrews would be without his own distinctive contribution. By identifying the "outlining" activity of the angel of Ezek. 42:15 with the action of Moses as he produces his "outline" of the heavenly things shown to him, one finds an original and imaginative answer to the dilemma of how the tabernacle could be of divine origin and yet fail to accomplish its purpose – an answer wholly independent of the Platonic/Philonic solution.[70]

Rather than any "copy," therefore, it would appear that Moses' ὑπόδειγμα is a lightly traced outline, pattern or blueprint,[71] a preliminary sketch to be followed. The idea is also found in 1 Chron. 28:11f., 18f. – there David gives Solomon the παράδειγμα (etymologically related to ὑπόδειγμα) of the temple – the "plan" or "pattern" – which is to be followed.[72] It is thus difficult to deny on linguistic grounds that this meaning is primary in *Auctor*'s choice of ὑπόδειγμα in Heb. 8:5. But does this mean that God later "copies" something from Moses' "pattern"? This is unlikely to be the point. The idea is probably closer to the procedure of an artist or sculptor, who, before the work of art is begun, produces a light sketch or mould which is later to be filled. Thus God, in "the last days" (1:2) when "the good things to come" (10:1) have arrived, fulfils (literally "fills full") Moses' sketchy outline of future (heavenly) things. Such an interpretation would mean that the heavenly things do not cast their outline *beneath* them (the "Platonic" model), but that future events and entities cast their outline *ahead of* them (the "apocalyptic" model).[73]

This understanding is enhanced by the coupling of ὑπόδειγμα with σκιά in 8:5. σκιά definitely has the "horizontal" nuance in 10:1: there the law has a σκιά of "the good things *to come*" (τῶν μελλόντων ἀγαθῶν). We have already noted the curious opinion that the two passages (8:5 and 10:1) in which one finds the term σκιά demonstrate *two different usages* of the term corresponding to the two rival conceptual modes (vertical – Platonic, 8:5; horizontal – apocalyptic, 10:1).[74] Yet the idea that σκιά in 8:5 must be "vertical" has doubtlessly been based on its combination with the Platonic-sounding "copy" in many translations of Heb. 8:5 and 9:23.[75] Even those who have argued against Platonic/Philonic influence at 8:5 have felt the need to concede its language to be "philosophical," making the point of issue the *use* to which the language is put.[76] Yet once it is seen that ὑπόδειγμα in 8:5 is not philosophical but architectural, the burden of proof shifts; it rests upon those who claim that σκιά is used in *different* senses in 8:5 and 10:1.

The usage of σκιά for an object's insubstantiality goes back as far as Homer (*Od.* X.495), Aeschylus (*Eum.* 302), and Sophocles (*El.* 1159).[77] It is, of course, used by Plato in the famous cave passage (*Rep.* VII.515–17),[78] but what is significant is that it is hardly peculiar to Plato. It has the "insubstantial" nuance in Paul's letter to the Colossians (2:17), a passage not normally thought to be Platonically influenced. The LXX provides numerous instances where σκιά (translating the Hebrew *tsel*) denotes that which is both transient and insubstantial, qualities which the author would undoubtedly want to attribute to the OT cultus.[79] Wisdom uses σκιά in this sense twice (2:5 and 5:9). The latter passage, speaking of material wealth and pride as a passing σκιά, would come with force to one writing to those in danger of clinging to material goods (Heb. 13:5) and to a natural pride in their Jewish cultus and heritage, elsewhere depicted as "near to disappearing" (8:13; note the language of Wis. 5:10ff. for the disappearance of ships and birds). Moffatt's[80] understanding of ὑπόδειγμα καὶ σκιά as a hendiadys – "a shadowy outline" – is acceptable, but his belief that this owes something specifically to Plato or the other Greek philosophers must be regarded as no longer tenable. The possibility exists that the author of Hebrews deliberately coupled ὑπόδειγμα with σκιά in order to guarantee that the latter would have a *forward* nuance identical to its usage in 10:1 (and Col. 2:17) and quite unlike its usage in Plato.

ἀντίτυπος

The RSV translation of ἀντίτυπος as "copy" in Heb. 9:24 is *prima facie* more defensible than in the case of ὑπόδειγμα, since it *may* mean "copy" as well as "original." Yet the term is rare in Judaism – it is used only once in the LXX (*v. l.*, Esther 3:13d), three times in Philo[81] (*De plant.* 133, *De conf. ling.* 102, *Quis rer.* 181), and twice in the NT (Heb. 9:24; 1 Pet. 3:21). In both Esther and Philo it means "resistant," "inimical." While in classical Greek it may bear this meaning, it also occasionally means "echo," "corresponding," "opposite," "reproduction," or "copy." Neo-Platonism (e.g., Plotinus, *Enn.* II.9,6) uses it in the last sense to denote the world of sense-perception as opposed to the heavenly realm of Ideas, the αὐθεντικόν,[82] and it is probable that the RSV committee saw this usage underlying Heb. 9:24. However, as Goppelt[83] observes, in the NT the usage of ἀντίτυπος was "redeveloped on the basis of the specific use of τύπος." Thus one must look at the only other NT instance of the term, 1 Pet. 3:21. The initially striking feature of this text is that the order is reversed from that of Hebrews; the antitype (baptism) is the NT fulfilment of the OT prefiguration (the flood). This has little significance, of course, since it is the type−antitype correspondence set within a framework of *Heilsgeschichte* which is of interest for the interpretation of Hebrews. The translation of 1 Pet. 3:21 continues to be a source of debate (cp. RSV, "Baptism, which corresponds to this," with NEB, "This water prefigured the water of baptism"); yet what emerges with clarity is the difficulty of taking the type−antitype relationship there in the sense of original−copy. P. Lundberg[84] has argued that in Hebrews and 1 Peter ἀντίτυπος is used in its two possible meanings, each indicating a different conceptual mode: for the Platonist author of Hebrews, it denotes spatial categories, the inferior sense-perceptible cultus (antitype) being contrasted with the higher world of the ideal (type); for the primitive Christian typologist who wrote 1 Peter, it denotes a time framework of past (type) and present (antitype). Yet in the light of the above evidence, this is now worth questioning. While it is true that the pejorative element in the usage of ἀντίτυπος in Hebrews is missing in 1 Peter, once the idea that ὑπόδειγμα in Heb. 9:23 means "copy" is exploded, it becomes possible to see 1 Peter *and* the author of Hebrews using the ἀντίτυπος in a framework of past and present.[85] ἀντίτυπος in Heb. 9:24 could be, simply, "counterpart," "opposite," "that which is sent back," or "that which corresponds to."[86] The existence of such simple translational options exposes the Platonic "copy" of the RSV and NEB as tendentious. The substantive of the verb "prefigure" (1 Pet. 3:21) is an equally viable option for Heb. 9:24, and this would correspond to and complement the usage of ὑπόδειγμα in the previous verse, the idea now being: "Christ has entered, not a sanctuary made with hands, a *prefiguration* of (or pointer to − REB) the true one, but into heaven itself ..." The RSV, by understanding ὑπόδειγμα as "copy" and ἀντίτυπος as "copy," has allowed each to throw the burden of proof upon the other. That there is no warrant for the term "copy" *anywhere* in the argument of

Hebrews is further suggested if one remembers that Wisdom, a book with which the author may well have been familiar,[87] uses the term μίμημα in comparing the temple with "the tent prepared from the beginning."[88] This makes the author's apparent avoidance of μίμημα or εἰκών in his discussion of the earthly tent all the more striking. It is, of course, tantalizing to ask why he would have avoided such terms in favour of ὑπόδειγμα and ἀντίτυπος. A possible answer is that he had no use for popularized Platonic notions of the earthly as a "copy" of the heavenly because he wished to identify the heavenly tent firmly with the good things *to come*; it would have been inappropriate, therefore, for Moses, the representative of the Old Covenant, to have made a "copy" or "replica" of something which properly belongs to the future, the New Covenant.

In his treatment of ἀντίτυπος Selwyn[89] calls attention to Melito's Passion Homily, which uses the term in the sense of "a preliminary mould." In several ways the passage is strikingly like Heb. 9:24,[90] and it is more than possible that in Hebrews, as in Melito, the earthly tent is seen as a preliminary mould or pattern, constructed in this case by Moses on the basis of his vision of future things.[91] In this case Heb. 9:24 would be paraphrased: "Christ has not entered any sanctuary made with hands, the preliminary mould [which, like the "shadowy sketch" of the previous verse, has no independent value]; he has entered the work itself."[92] Again ὑπόδειγμα and ἀντίτυπος in 9:23f. seem to refer to that which prefigures and corresponds to something to come later. As in Rom. 5:14 Adam is a type of the Christ *to come*, so in Heb. 9:24 the earthly tent appears to be the antitype (or prototype) of the sanctuary to come.[93] Thus the rendering "copy" for ἀντίτυπος is only one option among several, and its unquestioned acceptance has undoubtedly pushed the argument of Hebrews at this crucial place towards Plato and away from other NT writers when it was far from necessary.[94]

εἰκών *and* πρᾶγμα

Moffatt,[95] citing Plato (*Crat.* 306e), claims that εἰκόνα τῶν πραγμάτων in Heb. 10:1 is "Platonic." However, according to *Crat.* 306e and Philo (e.g., *Leg. all.* III.96, *De Abr.* 3f.), εἰκών is associated not with the heavenly realities but with the earthly copies. Plato uses εἰκών interchangeably with σκιά and μίμημα (*Tim.* 29b, 48e–49a, *Rep.* VII.515–17). Had *Auctor* "read Plato and other philosophers," as Barrett thinks possible,[96] this nuance would probably have carried over to him. Yet for *Auctor* εἰκών falls on the heavenly side of the ledger *as opposed to* the σκιά.[97] While in isolation the phrase "image of the things" does look Platonic, its juxtaposition with σκιά tells against any direct knowledge of Plato's works.[98] While it is true that Philo (*De somn.* I.79) also uses εἰκών synonymously with ἰδέα to mean "form" or "invisible image,"[99] it is more likely that in 10:1 *Auctor* reflects Jewish Christian usage, in which εἰκών is something positive (Gen. 1:26 LXX; cf. Heb. 1:3a).[100] Or (as a third possibility) *Auctor* may simply reflect current idiom in which Plato's original terms are now, in popular form, tossed about imprecisely. The term πρᾶγμα for "thing," "matter" or "event" is common in the vernacular of the first century,[101] and its coupling with εἰκών in 10:1 is hardly extraordinary.

ἀληθινός

It has been assumed by many that ἀληθινός, used by *Auctor* in 8:2 and 9:24, relates specially to Plato's *Rep.* VI.499c, and means the "real" world of the eternal archetypes as opposed to the "unreal" world of earthly copies. "The adjective ἀληθινός is of course used in the Platonic sense of a 'true form' or pattern of an earthly thing," claims Sowers,[102] who follows Bultmann[103] in emphasizing its reference to "that which is *eternal*."[104] Bultmann refers to Philo, Plotinus, the Hermetic writings and the Fourth Gospel in support.

It should be noted, however, that the term in Hebrews occurs within a polemical context in which the writer is fighting against the interpretation of the symbol as ultimate rather than the thing to which it points. There is no contrast involved between the earthly and heavenly tents as two kinds of *tent*, phenomenal and ideal. Just so in the Fourth Gospel (6:32) ἀληθινός occurs, not in terms of two kinds of bread, but in terms of *law interpreted as bread*. In such "fighting" contexts the term "true" has already been given a specialized definition: it is the reality to which a symbol points. Rather than looking to Platonic parallels at this point, we should see the thought of *Auctor* as closer to two highly polemical Pauline texts, Rom. 2:28f. and Phil. 3:3. In the former passage

> He is not a real Jew who is one outwardly, nor is true circumcision something external and physical. He is a Jew who is one inwardly, and real circumcision is a matter of the heart, spiritual and not literal. (RSV)

Although the term ἀληθινός does not occur in the Greek, the idea appears to be the same as that of Heb. 8:2 and 9:24 – the *symbol* is not the reality to which it points. In Phil. 3:3 Paul, in a similarly polemical context, says "we are the true circumcision, who worship God in spirit ... and put no confidence in the flesh." Again, ἀληθινός does not appear in the Greek, but it is implicit in the point (well founded in the OT – cf. Deut. 10:16; 30:6; Jer. 4:4, 9:23ff., etc.) that fleshly circumcision is not the ultimate; it only points to the true thing, circumcision of the heart.[105] The Fourth Gospel, Paul and *Auctor*, in other words, all reflect an inter-Jewish debate concerning the interpretation of certain OT legal institutions. In such contexts words are often given a "tactical definition,"[106] triggering an instantaneous response from the listener, a response which has little or nothing to do in this case with Platonic distinctions between phenomenal and ideal.

"Hellenism" and "apocalyptic"

As noted, this is probably the greatest impasse in the current interpretation of Hebrews. The view of Eccles[107] that "the clearest evidence of the influence of Hellenistic thought patterns" lies in *Auctor*'s heavenly tent and the view of Barrett[108] that the heavenly tent of Hebrews "is not the product of Platonic idealism, but the eschatological temple of apocalyptic Judaism" illustrate the problem. If the cleavage is to be narrowed, it is necessary to pose a number of sub-questions.

The vertical dimension in antiquity

The idea that Hebrew thought deals in time and Greek thought deals in space[109] has had much influence on the interpretation of Hebrews. Fortunately the caricature has recently been attacked,[110] and it may now be said that a dichotomy by which a "horizontal" (temporal) framework is Jewish and a "vertical" (cosmological) framework is Greek is a fiction of modern scholarship. Thus, even if Hebrews could be shown to contain a "vertical" correspondence between heaven and earth, there is nothing in such a view which would compel one to think that *Auctor* has stepped out of mainline Jewish thought to the point where it is necessary to posit a specifically Alexandrian or philosophical orientation. There are several indications pointing in this direction: (a) The notion of a divinely planned earthly temple goes back as far as Gudea of Lagash (c. 3000 B.C.) and is seen in the Code of Hammurabi.[111] Nineveh and Asshur (and their temples) were built according to heavenly patterns. (b) A great deal of "vertical" language exists in the OT (cf. Gen. 11:5, 28:12, Ps. 24:4, 102:19, etc.). It is sterile to argue whether or how much such OT statements are indebted to Babylonian influence or whether NT statements indicating a heaven–earth correspondence come from the Babylonian/OT.branch or the Hellenistic branch.[112] It is not a choice between stark alternatives. That there is some Greek influence in these texts is undeniable, but it appears to have come into ground already prepared for it in which there was no great contrast between the two. Thus NT writers who deal in "above" and "below" have not *a priori* stepped out of the Hebrew world into that which is exclusively Greek. Also, the introduction by Christianity of the notion of two ages overlapping would make it virtually impossible to avoid speaking in terms of "above" and "below." Paul Minear has shown how in a thoroughly Jewish–Christian apocalyptic work such as Revelation one can find spatial categories which have nothing overtly to do with Platonism, and which, as neither timeless nor time-bound, do not conform to the usual caricatures of "Greek" and "Hebrew" thought: "His city is devoid of neither time nor space, since it binds together acts of obedience and sovereignty. Yet that city is neither bounded by space nor regulated by time. It comes down 'from heaven from God,'"[113] Similarly, for *Auctor* the cross is devoid neither of time nor space – it takes place "once and for all," "at the consummation of the ages" (9:26) and "outside the gate" (13:12). Yet it is neither bounded by space nor regulated by time – it is offered in the heavenly realm (9:12). The future things are still to come, but they are also present; the two ages, as it were, *overlap*. The idea of heavenly and earthly things overlapping could be one point where a certain amount of Greek influence has come into play; but in this case *it was the introduction by Christianity of the idea of two ages overlapping* which had already provided the ground into which it came. Minear is correct to suggest that such a phenomenon is more widespread in the NT than has often been thought. In Col. 3:1–4 one finds the dichotomy of "the things that are above" and "the things that are on earth" set within an eschatological framework (note "you will appear with him in glory"). The more widespread this trend can be shown to be, the less likely becomes any *conscious* dependence in Hebrews upon Platonic categories.

The vertical dimension in Hebrews

With the above consideration in mind one must look to the most "vertical"-sounding passage in Hebrews – 8:4ff. Here one is confronted with an initial question: What is the meaning of the present tense of λατρεύουσιν in 8:5a? This certainly does seem "vertical." But if the "they" of "they serve" are the priests of the entire Jewish age (a likely supposition), all that is being said is that from the beginning they have served not the finished work (which has finally arrived and which Jesus has entered) but merely the preliminary sketch (which is now due to be discarded). This would not in fact be a vertical framework; it is a horizontal mode of "then–now," the earthly priests serving[114] the sketch meant for "then," Christ serving the finished work meant for "now."

But this in turn raises another difficulty. What is to be done with the apparent "vertical" mode of 8:5b (Ex. 25:40)? Did not the τύπος already exist in Moses' time, and is not the τύπος the counterpart of the ἀντίτυπος of 9:23? Here it is crucial to ask what *Auctor* understands by τύπος in his text of Ex. 25:40. Like its opposite, ἀντίτυπος, a τύπος may be a "pattern," "blueprint," "original" or "copy." Because this is the only occurrence in the epistle of τύπος, it is usually assumed that it is the precise counterpart of ἀντίτυπος – Moses saw the "original" or "archetypal" sanctuary.[115] Yet even if it is granted that for *Auctor* Moses saw the heavenly tent, and not just a pattern (the original meaning of Ex. 25:40 undoubtedly being the latter),[116] is "actual" pre-existence required?[117] Ezekiel, given his prophetic vision of a temple-city in explicit architectural detail, hardly required such an idea. Biblical writers often depict future entities as apprehended in the present because they already exist *in God's purposes*. Thus for *Auctor* (11:1, 7, 13) OT men and women of faith are those who "see" the future as though it were present.[118] In 3:5 Moses is a μαρτύριον of things to be spoken in the future, and this gives us strong grounds for concluding that *Auctor* took Ex. 25:40 to mean that Moses, a person of faith, "sees" the future sanctuary, one of "the good things to come" (10:1). Then, like Ezekiel, he makes a shadowy outline of what he saw.[119] John of Patmos (also bearing an affinity with the Ezekiel account) similarly depicts, through prophetic vision, things to come. Are they for him *already* in heaven, or are they entirely in the future? Such questions may ultimately be unanswerable. Yet 1 Pet. 1:4f. shows how common is the idea within Jewish–Christian circles *which have no demonstrable contact with current philosophical systems* that things may "exist" in heaven while awaiting a manifestation in history.[120] Heb. 8:5b (Ex. 25:40) could be said to contain both the horizontal and the vertical mode, but this needs careful definition. Both are ways of relating the transcendent to the earthly, and in a mature theological perspective both are necessary. Based upon the evidence above for ὑπόδειγμα and σκιά, Heb. 10:1 and 8:5a provide the horizontal, with Heb. 8:5b – Moses' vision on the mount – forming the point where the vertical and horizontal *intersect*. The τύπος on the mount may well be "vertical" because, even in Moses' time, it existed within God,[121] and "horizontal" because it is yet substantially future. It would be impossible to reduce the two to a single "frame" which does justice to both without at the same time giving one or the other primacy. *Auctor* certainly knows the value of both. A claim that Moses made a shadowy outline of the heavenly things to come (temporal) is based upon the fact that, even in OT times, the τύπος existed within God because it was destined by him to be the place of Christ's self-offering. NT writers who are sensitive to the problem of integrating time and eternity need no recourse to Plato's solution. John of Patmos can thus speak of something (whether a name written or a lamb slain – the meaning is uncertain) accomplished "from the foundation of the world" (Rev. 13:8) in a thoroughly Jewish context. This makes it easier to understand that apocalyptic writers and rabbis may have thought in terms of "a tent prepared from the foundation of the world" while at the same time holding that the historical manifestation is put off to the future. Interpreters of Hebrews who try to emphasize the vertical (existence within God's purposes) to the exclusion of the horizontal (the good things to come), or *vice versa*, are in effect doing something which is futile, unnecessary and damaging.

Auctor's "true tent"

The attempt to identify *Auctor's* heavenly tent has followed two main approaches: (a) those scholars who view the heavenly tent as a metaphor for something else, such as (1) the whole cosmos;[122] (2) heaven;[123] (3) the eucharistic body of Christ;[124] (4) the glorified body of Christ;[125] (5) the church as the body of Christ;[126] or (6) an event or events, such as the death of Christ on earth and his ministry in heaven (see below); and (b) those scholars for whom the heavenly tent is not reduced to mean something else, but for whom there is in heaven *an actual tent*, which in essence was what Moses was permitted to see on the mountain (whether in blueprint or in substance). This second group itself may be sub-divided: (1) There are those such as Farrar[127] who interpret the tent Platonically ("the ideal or genuine Tabernacle is the *eternal uncreated archetype* as contrasted with its antitype [or 'imitation'] made with hands"). (2) There are those such as

Windisch,[128] Barrett[129] and Michel[130] who claim that the heavenly tent is the eschatological sanctuary of Jewish apocalyptic (although for apparent tensions in Barrett's position, see below).

These are hardly new choices. In the Graeco-Roman world there was a clearly defined movement towards spiritualizing the idea of temple (e.g. Philo), while at the same time others continued to place the emphasis upon an actual temple (whether "new," "heavenly" or both).[131] Accordingly, views of a "heavenly" temple followed one or the other line: for some it must be a symbol for something else (e.g., the cosmos); for others it meant that there was an actual temple *in heaven* which corresponds in most or all details to the earthly temple.[132] Today one is faced with the choice of which background best interprets Hebrews. Should *Auctor*'s "true tent" be reduced so that it is a metaphor for something else (as in the case of Philo and other "Hellenistic" Jews)? Or, when one is told that Jesus has entered a tent which is "not of this creation" (9:11), are we to assume that heaven itself contains its own sanctuary? The choice will ultimately determine which background, the Philonic or Jewish–apocalyptic, explains the true tent of Hebrews. In order to evaluate which option is the more likely, further issues will need to be clarified.

(a) A "reductionist" approach to the heavenly sanctuary is often assumed without argument. For many it is unthinkable that what corresponds to *Auctor*'s earthly tabernacle could be located in a *place*, even if that place is within heaven.[133] In this case Moses' tent is really a symbol of a symbol ("the earthly tent stands for the heavenly tent which stands for ..."). Such an approach is more conducive to a background of Philo than to the apocalyptic or rabbinic traditions. While Philo's view of the true temple is difficult to define (his writings reflect both Platonic and Stoic influences), it is the Stoic spiritualizing tendencies which predominate. Thus the "pattern" on which the earthly temple is modeled can be either the soul[134] or the universe (cf. *De somn.* I.215), although Philo favours the latter (cf. *De spec. leg.* I.66, where the whole universe is God's temple, with "the most sacred part of all existence, even heaven" as its sanctuary (also *De vit. M.* II.101f.; *Qu. in Exod.* II.91f.)). Within this sanctuary or upper part (νεώς) are placed immortal beings (*De somn.* I.34), with angels for priests (*De spec. leg.* I.66) and the Logos for high priest (*De somn.* I.215). While such cosmic symbolism is often associated with Philo, it is also found in Josephus (*Ant.* III.123, 180ff.; *War* V.212f.), with details so different as to indicate that the interpretation was both widespread and independent.[135] A number of writers (including

Gray,[136] Eccles[137] and Montefiore)[138] have argued to varying degrees for such a cosmic allegorizing in Hebrews.

Yet a "spiritualized" interpretation of the true sanctuary in Hebrews inevitably rests on four passages which are notoriously ambiguous. These should be treated in order.

(1) 9:8. Here it is said that the first tent is a "parable of the present time," a comment often taken to indicate a spiritualized or cosmic temple. Sowers[139] looks to Philo, for whom the holy of holies is "heaven" and the Jewish priest's entrance is "the mystic soaring of the mind into heaven" (*De somn.* II.231–33; *De gig.* 52; *De mig. Abr.* 104). Macrae,[140] on the other hand, along with Montefiore,[141] interprets the passage as combining "an apocalyptic time scheme with the Hellenistic mode of heavenly temple symbolism" in which the inner shrine equals "heaven" and the outer shrine equals "this age." For these writers Moses' tent has a dual function: It is a "parable" or "symbol" of heaven and earth *and* the old and new ages.

What is usually left unsaid in such discussions is that the interpretation of 9:8ff. is beset with problems. The reason for this is twofold: (a) The meaning of πρῶτος in ch.9 is highly ambiguous. In v.1 it is used for the first and second σκηνή, whereas in vv.2, 6 the first and second σκηνή must mean the outer and inner tent. Which idea controls the use of πρῶτος in v.8? Is it the entire Mosaic structure, or only the outer court? Sowers, Montefiore, Macrae, Westcott, Nairne, Peake, Buchanan, McKelvey and Michaelis[142] all assume the latter; Moffatt, Cody, Bruce and Héring, among many others, opt for the former. Westcott feels it outrageous to suppose that *Auctor* suddenly changed his meaning from vv.6f. to v.8; Héring, on the other hand, claims that "this takes no account of the facility with which our author sometimes manipulates expressions with various senses." On Westcott's reckoning, as long as the outer court is recognized as the proper place of priestly activity (i.e., "has its standing"), the people remain barred from the goal of worship; in Héring's, the ascension of Christ into the true sanctuary robs the entire old center of worship of its "standing." In theory either interpretation is possible. But is there not something forced about the Westcott logic in this case? Elsewhere when *Auctor* juxtaposes the old with the new, he deals with whole entities – priesthood (7:11), earthly sanctuary (9:24), covenant itself (8:13). This would suggest that in v.8 he is doing the same, looking back to the usage of 9:1 and signifying the passing away of the whole structure, the "first tent." This understanding of 9:8 involves no necessary relation to the cosmic temple symbolism of Philo. (b) The meaning of the phrase "which is a parable for the present age" is equally ambiguous. As with μέλλω in 2:5, is it present from the standpoint of *Moses* ("the time then present" − AV) or of *Auctor* ("the time now present" − RSV, NEB)? In the former it would mean that the barrier between the two tents (or the entire tent itself) symbolized Jewish lack of access to the presence of God; in the latter it is a symbolic pointer ("prefiguration") to the future work of Christ as the high priest who achieves *real* access. It should be observed, however, that in neither case is the existence of a sanctuary *in* heaven precluded.

(2) 9:11. The interpretation of this verse is so contentious it would be hazardous to build *any* theory on it. The old view of Oecumenius that the "greater and more perfect tent" is the body of Christ, the sacrifice of which allows him (διά) to enter the presence of God (9:12), has been universally rejected by all except Roman Catholic scholars.[143] An equation of the true tent with the church[144] is equally difficult. A more serious proposal concerns the apparent division, if the διά of 9:11 is taken *locally*,[145] of the true tent into two sections. This could be used, however, to argue in two directions: (a) It could show that the true tent is *spiritualized* as the heavenly world in general. No actual tent *in* heaven is meant. Christ passes through the outer tent (the cosmological "heavens" of 4:14) and enters the holy place (the "axiological"[146] heaven of God's presence, 9:12). The true tent is thus a symbol for the upper regions. This approximates Philo's cosmic allegorizing of the temple, in which the outer precincts represent the sense-perceptible (αἰσθητός) realm (including "the heavens"), while the holy place is the unchanging heavenly realm of ideas where God properly dwells (*Qu. in Exod.* 91−96).[147] (b) The twofold division of 9:11 indicates that for *Auctor* there exists in heaven an actual tent which corresponds structurally to the twofold tent built by Moses.[148] Thus "the heavenly sanctuary, too, has a front part which is greater and more perfect as compared with the tabernacle, but which is still to be distinguished from the true sanctuary, the holy of holies."[149]

These two clear-cut possibilities are unfortunately complicated by a third option. If the διά is taken instrumentally[150] instead of locally, the idea of 9:11 is much more general. Christ enters the presence of God, not *by means of* any earthly tent, but *by means of* the true tent.[151] This would provide no precise information as to what the true tent is or which tradition *Auctor* reflects. Since the commentators are still fighting over the proper way to understand it, Heb. 9:11

must remain shaky ground upon which to mount any particular case for the foreseeable future.

(3) 9:24. This text is commonly used as proof that for *Auctor* the heavenly tent = heaven: "For the first time the heavenly sanctuary is identified with heaven itself, a key point for understanding our author's argument."[152] Bruce[153] draws a parallel with Rev. 4–7, where "heaven itself is the temple of God." Barrett,[154] who traces the true tent of Hebrews to the eschatological temple of Jewish apocalyptic, does not make this equation (although he does say that the sanctuary has existed eternally *in* heaven).

The problem of whether a heavenly temple is *in* heaven or is to be equated *with* heaven is not confined to the interpretation of Hebrews; it confronts one in the Near Eastern texts.[155] An equation of the heavenly tent in Hebrews with "heaven itself" is based solely on the assumption that in 9:24 *Auctor* intends this phrase to be the precise definition of the heavenly tent. It is more probable, on the other hand, that instead of defining what the tent is, the phrase indicates the general realm in which Christ ministers *as opposed to* the earthly priests. *Auctor* may well be looking back to his earlier statement in 8:4: "Now if he were on earth he would not be a priest." "On earth" and "heaven itself" are thus synecdoche, in which the whole ("earth," "heaven") stands for the part (the earthly and heavenly sanctuaries).[156] This means that 9:24 is a dubious text to use against the existence for *Auctor* of a sanctuary *in* heaven.[157]

(4) 10:20. As W.G. Johnsson[158] has put it, if "flesh" defines "curtain" in 10:20 so as to read "through the curtain, that is, through his flesh" (RSV), one will have "unambiguous evidence of a 'spiritualizing' intent on the part of the author" regarding the heavenly tent. So claims Moffatt: "He *allegorizes* the veil here as the flesh of Christ."[159] The difficulty is that there is no consensus as to how 10:20 should be translated. Does τοῦτ' ἔστιν τῆς σαρκὸς αὐτοῦ attach to ὁδός or καταπέτασμα? Various grammatical and theological points continue to be argued. The grammatical problem of taking "flesh" with "way" (i.e., the distance between the clauses and *Auctor*'s apparent habit in τοῦτ' ἔστιν clauses elsewhere of matching his cases)[160] must be regarded as powerful. Yet the theological implications of taking "flesh" with "curtain" may in the end be more formidable. Westcott[161] notes that this would involve taking the "flesh" of Christ as "a veil, an obstacle, to the vision of God in a place where stress is laid on His humanity (ἐν τῷ αἵματι Ἰησοῦ)." But the problem is far greater; it requires the grotesque

corollary that Christ's flesh *is a barrier which he himself had to penetrate, and which he helps others to penetrate.* Although the evidence is therefore ambiguous, it remains difficult for many to overcome the theological and logical dilemma of taking "flesh" with "curtain." In any case 10:20 is far too uncertain to be used to argue for any "mystical–allegorical"[162] approach by *Auctor* to the heavenly tent.

A notably elaborate spiritualization of the heavenly tent in Hebrews is that of U. Luck.[163] For him the heavenly tent involves both Calvary and the priestly ministry in heaven (hence spanning "heaven" and "earth"). Luck's view has been accepted by some English-speaking writers.[164] Floor,[165] e.g., claims that "the church on earth forms together with the 'throne of grace,' or the inner sanctuary, the true tent into which believers can enter ..." Again, this would come close to Philo, for whom the true tent is composed of two parts, earth (the outer court) and heaven (the holy place), making *Auctor*'s view an interesting modification of the cosmic temple. But inevitably much of Luck's exegesis depends upon his interpretation of the four ambiguous passages above. To this it should be added that it is extraordinarily difficult for anyone to relate what happens in the heavenly tent to what happens at the cross. Simply stated, the problem is this: if the atonement is transacted in the heavenly sanctuary "once and for all," one is dealing *at that point* with time and not eternity. But what relation is there between this and the cross? Does Christ die on earth and then, *subsequent to his exaltation*, make the sacrifice in heaven? While this question is difficult to answer, the fact that for *Auctor* the death occurs outside the camp – and hence outside the tent (13:12f.), with the blood subsequently brought in – makes it unlikely that in *Auctor*'s understanding the true tent can be equated *even partly* with the sacrifice on earth.

Those approaches which view the heavenly tent in Hebrews *as a symbol for something else* therefore fall short of proof. Consequently one must look to the second possibility, that of an actual sanctuary *in* heaven.

Here it should be said at the outset that a thoroughgoing Platonic approach is impossible. Farrar's statement that for *Auctor* the heavenly tent is an "*uncreated* eternal archetype" which was copied by Moses is ruled out by 8:2. At some point the true tent is "pitched" (ἔπηξεν, cf. Num. 24:6LXX) by God. This could have been said by Philo, but not Plato. Thus the second option, the apocalyptic tradition, must be examined.

It is not difficult to trace the Jewish belief in a new temple to its origins in the failure of the earthly temple.[166] Dan. 8:14, 2 Macc. 2:4–8 and Tob. 14:5 show the hope for a new and more glorious sanctuary to come. According to Jub. 1:17, 28, God himself will build it in Zion, while in Sib. 3:290 and Targ. Isa. 53:5 it is built by the Son of Man and the Messiah, respectively.[167] Eventually this hope for a new temple became fused with a growing interest in a heavenly temple. Perhaps under the influence of such texts as Isa. 6 and Ezek. 1, God is now assigned his own temple in heaven. The earliest such reference is generally thought[168] to occur in T. Levi: "And thereupon the angel opened to me the gates of heaven, and I saw the holy temple, and upon a throne of glory the Most High" (5:1). Ch. 3 describes a heavenly cultus, complete with holy of holies and angels who minister (λειτουργοῦντες) and perform expiation (ἐξιλασκόμενοι) for the sins of ignorance of the righteous. In the Book of Wisdom pre-existence may[169] also be ascribed to the heavenly sanctuary: "You have given command to build a temple on the holy mountain, and an altar in the city of your habitation, a copy (μίμημα) of the holy tent which you prepared from the beginning" (9:8). This interest in a heavenly sanctuary was taken up by apocalyptic and fused to the notion of the new Jerusalem. According to 4 Ezra, "The city that is now invisible shall appear" (7:26); it "shall come and be made manifest to all, *prepared and builded*" (13:36; cf. 8:52, 9:26–10:57). Now the site of the old Jerusalem is no longer indispensable to the future salvation.[170] In 2 Baruch, likewise, a "Jerusalem above" also appears to be "the Jerusalem to come" (4:1–7, 32:4). It is the city which was

> prepared beforehand here from the time when I took counsel to make Paradise, and showed to Adam before he sinned ... and again also I showed it Moses on Mount Sinai when I showed him the likeness of the tabernacle and all its vessels. And now, behold, it is preserved with me, as also Paradise.
> (4:3–6)[171]

This text is interesting for several reasons: (1) It seems to reflect Ezekiel's vision of the temple-city, except that *Moses* is shown both the city and the tabernacle[172] (a transfer similar to what I have suggested has happened in 8:5a).[173] (2) Ezekiel said nothing about pre-existence; some form of this, however, is attributed both to the city and the sanctuary. (3) The "city," "the tabernacle" and "Paradise" all seem to be independent but related entities; they are prepared by God before or at creation[174] (they were shown to Adam);

yet they are in some sense "preserved" with God for a future time. Here one has access to another thoroughly Jewish text which may shed light precisely upon those features of Hebrews which have previously been described as "Platonic." 2 Baruch, Wisdom and 4 Ezra thus indicate a process at work in which "Old Testament texts which state that the tabernacle and the temple of Jerusalem were built according to a pattern are now taken to imply the existence of a heavenly archetype."[175] As time went on, this heavenly counterpart became increasingly realistic.

Belief in a heavenly sanctuary was perhaps further stimulated by popularized Platonic notions wedded to early Jewish interpretations (or misinterpretations) of texts such as Isa. 6 (which were now felt to refer to a temple *in heaven*). But this would be very difficult to *prove*. Macrae hesitates "to minimize the extent of hellenistic influence upon all forms of ancient Judaism, including the apocalyptic tradition."[176] McKelvey, on the other hand, observes more cautiously that "the literature of Palestinian Judaism bears little if any trace of Platonism."[177] The central point we need to observe is that in the apocalyptic tradition one has access to literature which comes from roughly the same period as Hebrews but which speaks of a "pre-existent heavenly Jerusalem" in a milieu which at that time was probably having little or no direct contact with Platonism.

To all this should be added the most important piece of evidence. Ethiopian Enoch speaks of a new Jerusalem and temple (14:16–18, 20, 26:1f.; chs. 85–90), but in 90:29 it is clear that they do not *actually* pre-exist: "All its pillars were *new*, and its decorations were new and greater than those of the old house which He had pulled down." According to Fohrer and Lohse,[178] "the new Jerusalem is not depicted as a pre-existent city, but there is reference to its origin in the act of God alone." In other words, that it is built by God, not human beings, does not necessarily mean that it already actually exists in heaven; its creation is put off to the future. This shows that during this period (1 Enoch, except for the Similitudes, is normally viewed as pre-Christian), there was something of a ferment in which opinions differed as to how the heavenly city and temple should be understood: before their consummation, do they "pre-exist," or are they entirely "new" entities? "On the one hand Jerusalem at the end of the days is the city of David built again with glory and magnificence, on the other hand Jerusalem is thought of as a pre-existent city which is built by God in heaven and which comes down to earth with the dawn of a new world."[179] It could be said that 4 Ezra and 2 Baruch are examples of an early Jewish apocalyptic strain in which the motif of the heavenly and earthly city is developed according to a "vertical" frame; 1 En. 90:29, on the other hand, reflects what may be termed an entirely "horizontal" approach to the heavenly[180] Jerusalem. *That these differing approaches existed even within the apocalyptic tradition at the time when Hebrews was written* is of enormous significance for our investigation.

The rabbis also believed in a heavenly Jerusalem and temple which parallel their earthly counterparts (B. T. Taanith 5; Gen. Rabbah 55:7; Mekilta to Ex. 15:17).[181] This may extend even to the vessels of the two sanctuaries. But even after A.D. 70 the rabbinic tradition, unlike the apocalyptists and NT writers, could not bring itself to see the earthly Jerusalem actually being superseded by the heavenly city. The first occurrences of such a view are found in the later midrashim,[182] where the heavenly Jerusalem finally comes down to earth. Yet McKelvey[183] uses the midrashim as further evidence of views current in the first century, and Barrett[184] cites Paul and John of Patmos – the other two NT writers besides *Auctor* who speak of a "heavenly Jerusalem" – as proof that the notion of a heavenly Jerusalem was early. Paul speaks of the "Jerusalem above" as existing already (Gal. 4:26) – it is our "mother"; for John of Patmos it "comes down out of God" after the destruction of the old heaven and earth (Rev. 21:1f.). Hebrews reflects both ideas. God has built the city (11:10) and prepared it for the saints (11:16); in one sense it can be approached now (12:22, "you have come"). On the other hand, it is still "to come" (13:14).

There is another approach to Hebrews which requires comment at this point – the attempt to "rescue" it from the naïveté of the apocalyptists and the "crass" literalism of the rabbis:

> We must not imagine that our generation is the first to appreciate the necessity of "demythologization" or to realize the inadequacy of the image of "God up there" ... The Writer to the Hebrews is the last person in the NT to be suspect of envisaging the sanctuary and throne as a superior but equally material counterpart of the wilderness tent.[185]

Such asseverations are normally accompanied by an insistence that the heavenly tent could never have been envisaged by *Auctor* as a *locality*.[186] But this approach, in addition to using the question-begging word "material," is unfortunate in two respects: (1) Linguists today observe that it is possible to visualize an entity as concrete or local without necessarily *conceiving of it* that way. 1 Kings 8:13, e.g., depicts Solomon as, in a sense, "visualizing" the temple as God's dwelling, "a habitation for you forever," all the while knowing that God transcends all limits of space and time (v.27). Plato's language about the heavenly world of Ideas (ὑπερουράνιος τόπος) likewise seems at times to imply that it exists in some "place" (ἔν τινι τόπῳ, *Tim.* 52b, c), but this is only "because of our finite understanding."[187] John of Patmos is hardly different. He depicts events and entities in "local" terms on earth and in heaven without confining them in absolutely local terms.[188] (2) Linguists also point out that it is possible to employ images *without any need to visualize them*. All images involve comparison, but sometimes the point of the comparison is non-visual.[189] Unlike John of Patmos, *Auctor* is not a particularly visual writer. He actually has an anchor ("hope") entering into the holy of holies (6:19), a telltale sign that he has little regard for the visual impact his language about the heavenly tent might be making. To put it one way, he is simply verbalizing. Yet this does not mean *a priori* that his images cannot be those of the rabbinic or apocalyptic traditions. For him the point of comparison with these images may be *function*, not appearance. Both the earthly and heavenly tents are the place where the presence of God is centralized. The heavenly Jerusalem of Rev. 21, with its lack of any temple, is the exception which proves the rule[190] that within certain streams of Jewish apocalyptic even heavenly cities require a functioning temple or shrine – they require a place for both sacrifice and a central-ization of the presence of God.[191] Apart from certain clues given by *Auctor* (see below), it is difficult to determine whether the "true tent" of Hebrews is the shrine of the heavenly city or whether for him it is an independent entity. The crucial point is that *Auctor*'s heavenly tent could consist of verbal symbols borrowed from the apocalyp-tic/rabbinic traditions, without any need to visualize them or to translate them into symbols for yet something else.

An 'Eternal' tent in Hebrews?

This question has already partly been treated, but there are further considerations made necessary by recent treatments of the eschatology of Hebrews. As has been seen, for Barrett the true tent is not the product of Platonism but is the eschatological sanctuary of Jewish apocalyptic. Consequently his claim that "the new high priest requires a new sanctuary"[192] and that the sanctuary exists in heaven in order that it may be manifested on earth[193] seems straightforward in the light of that background. The picture is blurred, however, when it is said that "the true tabernacle exists *eternally* in heaven, whither Jesus has ascended (7:1), but the ministry exercised within it took its origin in the fulfilment at the appointed time of O.T. prophecy …"[194] Does Barrett at certain points give back with one hand what he takes with the other? This question gains strength in the light of other statements he makes. For him "the heavenly tabernacle and its ministrations are from one point of view eternal archetypes, from another, they are eschatological events."[195] *Auctor*, further-more, uses "philosophical language" and has written a "Christian approach to philosophical discourse"[196] in terms which would have been "understood" by Plato and Philo.[197] He may even have read "Plato and other philosophers."[198]

Such comments create more unanswered questions.

(a) What is meant by "from one point of view [they are] *eternal archetypes*"? This *could* mean that the sanctuary pre-existed within the purposes of God. Elsewhere this seems to be Barrett's meaning − he states that *Auctor* is developing the "idealist" element in Jewish apocalyptic (an illuminating explanation). But that this development is accomplished in a way that Plato or Philo would have "under-stood" (see below) or that *Auctor* would have felt his language to be "akin" to theirs are more shadowy assertions. When stating the argument of Hebrews it is common practice to use loaded terms such as "copy," "archetype" and "eternal," terms which have inevitable associations with Plato[199] and which serve only to prejudice the argument. αἰώνιος, e.g., is used six times in Hebrews: 5:9 (of "salvation"), 6:2 (of "judgment"), 9:12 (of "redemption"), 9:14 (of "spirit"), 9:15 (of "inheritance") and 13:20 (of "covenant"). Except for possibly 9:14,[200] all these refer, not to any "timeless" sphere involving pre-existence, but to realities which come in time and are everlastingly valid. Neither the heavenly city nor the sanctuary, furthermore, is referred to by *Auctor* as αἰώνιος. "Eternal" may thus be a misleading word to use for them.[201] But even if such vocabulary is retained, we are not necessarily confined to a "Platonic" nuance. Truth which exists in the mind of God is, in theory at least, "eternal." When, as we have seen − in a work not generally thought to have been influenced by Platonism − John of Patmos speaks of something existing "from the foundation of the world" (Rev. 13:8), it is obvious that what is meant is an entity which "pre-exists" only within God's purposes. Earlier such a doctrine of predestination may have developed within Judaism with the help of some "Platonic" influence;

but clearly by the time John wrote it was a thoroughly "Jewish" idea. Thus for the Jew "eternal" could mean, simply, "predestined."

Such reflections mean that the language used in discussions of the eschatology of Hebrews needs to be sharpened if further distortions are to be avoided. Barrett claims that Hebrews contains *both* Platonic philosophical influences (albeit transformed) and primitive Jewish eschatology, but that the eschatological imagery is primary, "as it must always be in any Christian approach to philosophical discourse." "The eschatology, though rough, crude and intractable,"[202] is essential. Yet there is no guarantee that such "rough, crude and intractable" eschatology (which includes, presumably, "the primitive sanctuary of Jewish apocalyptic") would have been understood at all by Plato or Philo. It is more likely that they would have *mis*understood *Auctor*, i.e., they would have read his eschatology in the light of their own philosophical categories, as numerous subsequent interpreters of Hebrews over the centuries have done. Williamson[203] points out that theologians have often read Christianity into Plato. But the reverse must also be considered: Plato (and Philo) would almost undoubtedly have read Platonism into Hebrews.

(b) At points Barrett's language is imprecise. He says, e.g., that "the heavenly tabernacle *and* its ministrations are from one point of view eternal archetypes, from another they are eschatological events."[204] As with Luck, this seems to include the heavenly tent as, from one point of view, an "event." But elsewhere Barrett *distinguishes* the tabernacle from events which occur within it. This is no pedantic point. It is such logical lapses which lead to confusion regarding the referent of *Auctor*'s language.

(c) There is no basis for distinguishing, as does Barrett, the heavenly tent from eschatological events *within* it by claiming the former to be "eternal." Once "eternal" is defined as "within the mind of God," "tent" *and* "events within it" are "eternal."

Although Barrett has done much to redress the balance of opinion on Hebrews toward elements within Jewish apocalyptic and away from Platonism, we need to ask whether he went far enough. Williamson, though appreciative of Barrett's contribution, senses major difficulties. In particular he reacts to Barrett's claim that *Auctor* "may well have read Plato and other philosophers,"[205] and elsewhere insists (contra Barrett) that "the activities of the heavenly tabernacle could not *become* 'eternal archetypes' until they had first *occurred* as 'eschatological events.' "[206] Yet *both* statements by Barrett and Williamson are in need of scrutiny. In each much depends upon how the slippery English terms "eternal" and "archetype" are construed. As noted above, the former may carry within it notions of pre-existence; or it can mean, simply, "everlasting." "Archetype" is similarly slippery. Like the Greek ἀρχέτυπος or ἀρχέ-τυπικῶς,[207] it may mean either "prototype" – the original pattern from which copies are made – or a perfect example or standard. In the latter an entity may be an archetype *without being a prototype*.[208] In Eusebius ἀρχέτυπος may be actually contrasted with πρωτότυπος.[209] This is possible because ἀρχή, in addition to meaning "beginning" or "firstfruits" (that which precedes), can mean "rule," "sum-total," or "head."[210] What Barrett means by "eternal archetypes" seems clear. He explicitly says that *Auctor* uses "philosophical" language akin to that of Plato and Philo in order to highlight the idealist element within Jewish apocalyptic, and that the Greek philosophers would have understood him. The truths to which *Auctor*'s shadows point, in other words, are truths which exist *eternally* in the mind of God.

When Williamson speaks of things in Hebrews *becoming* "eternal archetypes," on the other hand, he has clearly changed Barrett's meaning. If "archetype" is given Barrett's quasi-Platonic, philosophical nuance, the statement is simply not true. There is no way an entity may *become* an archetype which would have been understood by Plato and the philosophers, least of all by occurring in time as an "eschatological event." Neither can Williamson's statement refer to pre-existence within the mind of God (as does Barrett's), for it is equally untrue to say that such existence cannot be spoken of until the event occurs "in time" – there is no point logically at which something may "become" an entity within God's mind. Williamson must be thinking of archetype as "ideal examples." In this case his statement makes sense: "The activities of the heavenly sanctuary could not become permanently ideal examples of sacrifice and obedience until they had occurred once and for all in time." But in order to get this he had to change Barrett's meaning, for Barrett clearly uses the term in question to admit a strand of semi-Platonic idealism into the scope of *Auctor*'s thinking.

Williamson's corrected version of Barrett, however, relates only to the *events* within the heavenly sanctuary; it leaves unresolved whether the sanctuary itself bears any relation to Plato's "archetypes." A way forward is therefore needed, and I would suggest the following. Rather than assuming – as does Sowers[211] – that "certain features of the earthly cult reflect prototypes in heaven while the sacrifices *within them* foreshadow features of Christ's work accomplished later in history," one should see the true tent in Hebrews as a basically *functional* entity. The sanctuary and the events within it, in other words, are *not to be separated*. And it is difficult to speak of anything (whether sacrifice or tent in which the sacrifice occurs) which is so linked with humanity's sinfulness and its purgation as actually "eternal." *Auctor* says that the earthly sanctuary was made on the pattern of what Moses saw (Ex. 25:40), *but for him this may have included not only the physical structure, but everything which goes on there – the sacrifices*. Therefore, before it is asked what the heavenly tent "is," or whether, as with 4 Ezra and 2 Baruch, it "pre-exists," the proper question is what, according to *Auctor*, the *sacrifice* of the heavenly tent really is. And here the answer can be in little doubt: It is the self-offering of Christ. If the sanctuary is thus viewed as a *functioning* institution and not just as an object, it becomes extremely difficult to suggest that *Auctor* thought that there was an "eternal archetype" – whether "heaven itself" or something *in* heaven, beginning before Moses and going on afterwards – in which a heavenly sacrifice was eternally being offered or made effective. Once one is prepared to say with Sowers[212] and others that there is no eternal sacrifice going on within the sanctuary, and admit that the "true tent" of Hebrews may be the functioning sanctuary of apocalyptic, it is but a short step to say that there is no actually "eternal" sanctuary in Hebrews. The one sense in which *any* functional entity which exists in consequence of human sin and finiteness could be said to be "an eternal archetype" would be within the destining purposes of God; but as noted, by the time *Auctor* wrote this idea was thoroughly Jewish.

Two further observations should help to clarify this problem.

(a) In addition to being "pitched" (8:2), the tent is said to have been *entered* at some point by Jesus. It has been observed[213] that this could not have been said by Philo, with his low regard for time and history. Within the apocalyptic tradition, however, the new temple no doubt could be entered by human beings, if only when ultimately that temple descends to earth. The unique contribution of *Auctor* would be his adjustment of this tradition so as to make the entry by human beings (Jesus) an event which has *already taken place*. In other words, its ultimate involvement in the affairs of humankind has begun "in these last days" (1:2).

(b) There appear to be at least *four* traditions in Judaism[214] regarding "when" the heavenly sanctuary could have been "built" by God: (1) before the creation (Pesahim 54a, Nedarim 39b, Wis. 9:8);

(2) at the creation (Philo),[215] Bereshith Rabbah 1.4,[216] Wis. 9:8);[217] (3) when the earthly sanctuary was built – whether Moses' tent (Num. Rabbah 12)[218] or the temple (Pesiqta Rabbati 5, Num. Naso 12.12); (4) and at the end of the age (1 En. 90:28f.). The rabbinic references are late, but they may enshrine earlier traditions which show that in the first century questions about the origins of the heavenly temple were being asked. That such questions may never have occurred to *Auctor* needs no stating; but that such varied opinions existed demonstrates that there is more than one viewpoint from which we must choose today if we are to determine the kind of notions which surround the heavenly tent of Heb. 8–9.

The true tent of Hebrews and the new temple within Jewish apocalyptic

The groundwork for this topic has been laid by emphasizing the ambiguity of such texts as Heb. 9:8f., 11, 24 and 10:20, and by looking briefly at the evidence of the apocalyptic tradition. It remains now to look at several indications within the epistle itself upon which a case could be mounted that convincing *Auctor* stands firmly within the apocalyptic tradition, and that he is in line with the viewpoint represented by 1 Enoch 90:28f. that the heavenly Jerusalem and sanctuary are *new* entities built by God at the end of the age.

(a) Heb. 9:23. A clue to this direction is provided by the singularly peculiar logic of Heb. 9:23: "Thus it was necessary for the copies (ὑποδείγματα) of the heavenly things to be purified with these rites, but the heavenly things themselves with better sacrifices than these" (RSV). This text has caused interpreters enormous problems. Why do the "heavenly things" need "purification" at all? Moffatt[219] has called the idea "fantastic"; Montefiore[220] thinks it "an unhappy comparison"; Dods[221] calls it "poetry," not "theology." Attempts to relate the heavenly cleansing to the expulsion of Satan from heaven,[222] the notion of reconciliation found in Col. 1:20,[223] or the cleansing of human beings' consciences[224] have not been convincing. What needs to be noted is that the context of 9:23 is not the annual day of atonement ritual, but the initial purification of the newly built tabernacle at the inauguration of the first covenant. Heb. 9:6–14 does deal with the continuous atonement cycle; but the subject shifts at v. 15 to the manner in which a covenant is *ratified*; 9:15–18 describes the relation of the death of the victim to the institution of the covenant, while 9:19–20 reflects the aspersion of the altar (here substituted with "the book") and the people recorded in Ex. 24:6–8.

The sprinkling of the tent and vessels of 9:21 seems to be drawn primarily from the consecration of Lev. 8:10f., 23f. (cf. Ex. 29:12, 40:9−11) rather than the annual atonement ritual of Lev. 16, only the sprinkling is now extended to the tabernacle and all its furnishings. Josephus (*Ant.* III.206) also records the belief that at its inauguration Moses purified the tent and its vessels not only with oil but "with the blood of bulls and rams." Similarly, *Auctor* seems to say that, "just as it was necessary for the first tent to be inaugurated with blood, so it was necessary for the second tent." That the term καθαρίζω can be used interchangeably with ἁγιάζω so as to mean "inaugurate" (cf. ἐγκαινίζω, 9:18)[225] is proved by Ex. 29:36 and Lev. 8:15 LXX, and especially by Josephus. The latter, in another passage clearly describing the inauguration (*Ant.* III.197), states that "he [Moses] sanctified (ἥγνιζε) both the tabernacle and the priests, accomplishing in such a way their purification (τὴν κάθαρσιν) ... He anointed both the priests themselves and all the tabernacle, thus purifying (κεκάθαρκε) all."[226] One may speculate as to why for these writers the first tent needed purifying at the inception of the covenant. The most likely answer is that it had been built by sinful human hands. Here, of course, *Auctor*'s analogy breaks down, for the heavenly tent, *not* built by human hands (9:11), would require no such rite. But this would be to press for an unnecessary logic. In my exegesis, furthermore, v. 22 needs to be viewed as neither parenthetical[227] nor the introduction of a new subject.[228] The sacrifice of 9:15ff. is at the same time an inaugurative sacrifice *and* an atonement sacrifice. The death which is the initiation of the covenant (v. 18) has as its goal the forgiveness of sins under the first covenant (v. 15).[229] In Hebrews the maintenance of the covenant is *subsumed* in its inauguration. N. H. Young[230] is one of the few scholars to appreciate this, although he applies the inaugurative aspect only to the new age, not to the sanctuary itself. This results from his equation of the true sanctuary with "heaven itself, the presence of God" (and to his decision elsewhere[231] that the veil of the tent in Hebrews is the flesh of Jesus). Yet it is more likely that what *Auctor* has in mind in 9:23 is the inauguration of the new temple (and *hence* new age) of Jewish apocalyptic. Such a view should be kept in mind in the light of Barrett's suggestions for the role of apocalyptic in Hebrews.[232]

(b) Heb. 9:8. The possibility that *Auctor* thought of the true tent as the *new* tent is also raised by the language of 9:8. If *Auctor* in fact thought of the true tent as the "eternal prototype" of the earthly, it is doubtful that he could have referred to the earthly tabernacle as the "first" tent; it would more likely be the "second" tent.[233] As was seen above, there is ambiguity with reference to *Auctor*'s use of πρῶτος in ch. 9; but if "the first tent" in 9:8 refers to the entire tabernacle structure, such a first tent–second tent schema would be unprecedented in any Philonic milieu. In this light it is interesting that Köster,[234] discussing Heb. 8:1ff., can actually speak of "the prototypical *earthly* sanctuary." This is a better depiction of the argument of *Auctor* than speaking of *heavenly* prototypes. A closer parallel than Philo to this kind of thought is 1 Cor. 15:45–47. There Paul describes that which is "heavenly" as *second* rather than first. The "animal body" (NEB for τὸ ψυχικόν) is juxtaposed with the "spiritual body" (τὸ πνευματικόν), but the latter has not existed from all eternity, nor is "out of heaven" synonymous with "eternal"; "the man from heaven" is an eschatological entity. The point of departure of the physical and heavenly is not their natural status, but the relationship which each bears to "earth" and "heaven," respectively.[235] That which is "heavenly" (8:5, 9:23, 12:22) in Hebrews may be similarly conceived as "second" in time as compared with its prototypical "earthly" (9:1) counterpart – its ἀντίτυπος.[236]

If for *Auctor* the heavenly tent was the second tent, rather than some eternally existing entity, it would explain why for him it needed its own inaugurative ceremony – its own purification with blood. The apocalyptic tradition provides a cogent background for such a thought; Plato or Philo do not.

(c) Heb. 13:14. We have examined several of the apocalyptic and rabbinic texts which speak of a heavenly Jerusalem which is to come to earth. Barrett likewise suggests that the heavenly temple in Hebrews "is in heaven primarily that it may be manifested on earth," but he adds that *Auctor* "conceives its earthly manifestation *in a new way*." His explanation of this is that "the decisive act – the death and ascension of Christ – is already *past*, and the normal pattern of eschatological belief is thereby disturbed."[237] Yet this provides little basis for an "earthly" manifestation of the temple-city. What does the term μέλλουσιν in 13:14 indicate? Or, put another way, if the earthly manifestation is already "past," and if the city already "exists" (12:22), in what sense are these entities yet "to be"? The most Barrett will grant is that, according to the apocalyptic tradition (which he has claimed underlies Hebrews), "this heavenly city will *in some way* be manifested as the Jerusalem of the age to come."[238] His references to 4 Ezra (cf. 7:26, "then shall the city that now is invisible appear," and 13:36, "Sion shall come and shall be made manifest to all men, prepared and builded'') are relevant in this regard, containing terms similar or identical to those found in Heb. 11:1, 10,16, and 22. But since Barrett views the idealist element in Hebrews as developed in quasi-Platonic and philosophical terms, he is unwilling to go so far as to suggest that *Auctor*, in line with the rest of the apocalyptic tradition, feels that there is *still to be* an ''earthly'' manifestation of the heavenly things, however ''earthly'' is defined. Yet, while there are no explicit statements of this kind of Hebrews, it should be borne in mind that the more familiar an idea is, the more allusively an author will treat it. Hofius[239] presents parallels between Hebrews and 4 Ezra, concluding that *Auctor* expected the heavenly city in terms similar to the author of that work, i.e., a future earthly manifestation will occur; and Michel[240] cites Rev. 21:1f. as a parallel in his discussion of ''the world to come'' of Heb. 2:5.

The manifestation of 13:14, of course, concerns the city. That it involves as well the eschatological temple cannot be proven, but that the heavenly city of 12:22 is called ''Mount Zion'' points in this direction. McKelvey[241] asks (with reference to 1 En. 25:3), ''how could a Jew think of a descent of the heavenly Mount Zion without having in mind a descent of the heavenly temple?'' The reference to Mount Zion in Heb. 12:22 may compel a similar question: How could a Jew think of the heavenly city *as* Mount Zion without thinking of a heavenly temple?[242]

3 Conclusion

Other passages in Hebrews have been singled out for special treatment by those who read the epistle against a Platonic background,[243] but the foregoing should enable us to reach a general conclusion. Although Spicq assembled what must be seen as the climax of a half-century's case for the Philonic background of Hebrews, his plea for direct dependence must be judged to have failed. The Qumran texts show that many of the ideas thought to be peculiar to Hebrews and Philo circulated in at least one other background. The work of Hanson, Barrett and Williamson ended any thoroughgoing form of the Platonic/Philonic approach to Hebrews. More modified forms of it, however, continue to flourish. Philo and Wisdom probably demonstrate a much broader movement of Hellenistic Judaism than that limited to Egypt. It should not be denied that ''Greek'' influence has contributed at some point to the ideas found in Hebrews, but the contribution probably was made before *Auctor* wrote, and it was made at points where it cannot be easily isolated or detected. The linguistic similarities between Plato/Philo and Hebrews have been exaggerated, as Williamson has shown, but of five additional terms examined (ὑπόδειγμα, σκιά, ἀντίτυπος, ἀληθινός, εἰκών) which have played a dramatic role in the Platonic interpretation of Hebrews, none were seen to have a distinctly Platonic, Philonic or philosophical nuance. There could be said to be a cumulative argument for a Philonic allegorizing approach to the heavenly sanctuary in Hebrews. Barrett, however, has stressed the role of apocalyptic influences in Hebrews, and the ambiguity of the four crucial texts considered (9:8f., 11, 24 and 10:20), together with certain other indications in the epistle, provides an equally plausible cumulative argument in the direction of certain currents within Jewish apocalyptic. With regard to his suggestion for a *conscious* blend of apocalyptic motifs with Platonic idealism, Barrett may have gone beyond the evidence. There is a cumulative case to be made that for *Auctor* the heavenly sanctuary is the new sanctuary, built (8:2) along with the city, by God at the end of the age (now come, Heb. 1:2) and inaugurated (9:23f.) by the supreme eschatological sacrifice. Since the climax of history has now occurred in Jesus, he is the first to enter the sanctuary of the new age. Whether for *Auctor* before this time the city and sanctuary actually "pre-exist," or whether this is simply a way of talking about pre-destination, may be difficult to determine, but there are indications that the latter should not be ruled out. In such a case the sanctuary was seen by Moses (8:5; Ex. 25:40) in blueprint, in prophetic vision (cf. Ezek. 42f.), or through the faith which "sees" God's future (11:1ff.). There is a sense in which the city, even from the Christian viewpoint, is still future, and at the consummation some form of additional manifestation, as in Rev. 21, will occur. In all of this there is nothing *distinctly* "Platonic," "philosophical" or "noumenal"; much of it is drawn from the OT. Enough indications exist to point to a reasonable conclusion that *Auctor* developed certain OT ideas within the Jewish apocalyptic framework, while Philo developed the same themes within a Platonic framework. Both writers, in other words, probably go back independently to a common OT background. The Platonic/Philonic background for Hebrews is therefore "not proven," and as such it must give way to an examination of other possible backgrounds.

2

QUMRAN

1 History of discussion

When the discovery of the Qumran sect and its writings resulted in numerous fresh speculations regarding the nature of the NT writings, it was not surprising to find that Hebrews was, in its turn, affected.[1] Scholars have seen varying degrees of importance of the sectarian writings for the epistle, ranging from decisive to virtually none at all.

As noted above, the first serious treatment of Hebrews and Qumran was that of Yadin[2] in 1958. According to Yadin, the discussion of whether the recipients were Christianized Jews or Christianized Gentiles must be abandoned for a new hypothesis: before their conversion to Christianity, they had been members of the Qumran sect, which Yadin identified with the Essenes, who entered the church "carrying with them some of their previous beliefs."[3] Yadin summarized the principal points of contact between Qumran and Hebrews: (a) The Qumran sect assigned a superior status to angels, which Hebrews combats in chs. 1 and 2.[4] (b) The sect held to a belief in two Messiahs, one priestly and one lay, which forms the backdrop of *Auctor*'s portrayal of Jesus as combining both offices in one person.[5] (c) Heb. 1:1, which juxtaposes the revelation of Jesus with that of the prophets, "is obviously directed against the belief ... that in the eschatological era a prophet should appear − a prophet who is not to be identified with the Messiah himself."[6] This figure, according to Yadin, is the Mosaic prophet of Deut. 18:15f., which accounts for much of the concentration on Moses in Hebrews.[7] (d) The high degree of pentateuchal quotations in Hebrews is the result of the sect's concentration on its wilderness calling and identity.[8]

Yadin's study was followed by that of Hans Kosmala,[9] who, unlike Yadin, postulated astonishingly that the readers of Hebrews were Qumranites who were not yet Christians when Hebrews was written, but were in process of being catechized as part of the

Christian mission to the Essenes.[10] According to Kosmala, central to the theology of Hebrews and that of the Essenes is the prophecy of Malachi, which has a priestly tendency identifying Elijah with the high priest of the end time.[11] While taking Yadin's theory of a direct relationship between Qumran and Hebrews to an extreme, Kosmala reworked Yadin's premise drastically. Integral to his scheme is the notion of the progressive growth of the readers' "confession" (ὁμολογία), characterized by the use of three terms: κατανοέω (3:1), κατέχω (3:6, 14) and κρατέω (4:14). The first is a general invitation to speculation and the second an admonition not to jettison already-held Messianic beliefs, while the third encourages them to grasp a new belief in Jesus as Messiah.[12] Crucial to Kosmala's theory is the elimination of such passages as Heb. 5:11–14 and 6:6b as interpolations.[13]

Thus a new trend in the interpretation of Hebrews was begun, and to the present day the "Qumran hypothesis" continues to exercise a vigorous popularity in NT studies.[14] There are, however, numerous writers who have rejected Qumran as a background for Hebrews. This reversal is largely due to the almost simultaneous findings of F.F. Bruce[15] and J. Coppens.[16] Bruce showed that the parallels drawn by Yadin and Kosmala are susceptible of other, more plausible explanations, while Coppens posited a two-source theory for Hebrews, one dogmatic and the other paraenetic, with only the latter showing signs of Qumran influence.[17] While themselves vulnerable, the force of these observations, together with those of Braun in 1966,[18] was enough to influence many away from Qumran.[19] To this group must be added writers who, without explicitly denying Qumran connections, have written on Hebrews since 1962 without allowing their interpretations to have been influenced by Qumran considerations.[20]

Opinion thus continues to be divided over the degree to which Qumran should be considered in interpreting Hebrews. In addition to Yadin and Kosmala should be added the excitement generated by the publication of the Melchizedek fragment from Qumran Cave 11 and its implications for Heb. 5–7. It thus remains to attempt an analysis of "the great debate,"[21] with particular reference to the arguments of Yadin, which continue to enjoy the most longevity.[22]

2 Points of contact

Angels

"The part played by angels in Hebrews is one of the principal features which have suggested a relation between it and the Qumran community."[23] Yadin emphasizes that at Qumran angels enjoy a quality of sonship[24] and dominate eschatology (cf. 1QM 13:9–10, 17:6–8; 1QS 3:21; 1QH 10:8 and 1QH 3:21f. – cf. 1QS 11:7–8 – where Michael, the Prince of Light, assists the saints and enjoys supreme authority), claiming that the readers of Hebrews were given over to angel worship. Michael is to have control over the world to come (2:5), "far above the control which might be exercised by both the human Messiahs."[25]

This hypothesis needs serious questioning. *Auctor*'s concern with angels in chs. 1–2 does not appear to be a polemic but an attempt to prove the superiority of the new covenant to the old. His association of angels with the Torah (2:2) is the linchpin which connects the angels of Ps. 8 (cf. 2:5ff.) with ch. 1. If Jesus is mediator of a superior covenant, he must be superior to those covenant-mediators with whom the readers are familiar (angels, chs. 1–2; Moses, chs. 3–4; Aaron, chs. 5–7). It should be further mentioned that while Ps. 104:4 is quoted in both literatures, it is the MT which is quoted at Qumran, representing a significantly different reading than the LXX of Heb. 1:7.[26] Would not *Auctor*, if he were combating notions of Qumran angelology, have quoted a text closer to the version at Qumran, as is apparently the case in the previous verse (1:6, Deut. 32:43)?[27]

Thus we should view with suspicion G. Milligan's[28] references to Job. 1:6, 38:7, Ps. 29:1 and 89:6, from which he concluded that, since it cannot be denied that angels *as a class* are called "sons of God" in the OT, *Auctor* must mean that no *individual* angel has enjoyed the title "son" (an argument which, incidentally, would fall neatly in line with Qumran's concentration on Michael). Milligan failed to note that in Job 1:6LXX and 38:7LXX *ben* is transmuted to ἄγγελοι. It is unclear, furthermore, what the referent of "sons of gods" is in the MT of Ps. 29:1, while the MT of Ps. 89:6 does not use the term "son"; it speaks of "the assembly of the holy ones." Ps. 28:1LXX (29:1MT) clearly interprets the phrase as Israelites (angels do not offer "young rams"), and Ps. 88:6LXX (89:6MT), while it does use the phrase υἱοῖς θεοῦ, is probably referring to human beings (ἐκκλησία ἁγίων, v. 5, and βουλῇ ἁγίων, v. 7, between which the phrase in

question is wedged, are best translated, respectively, "the congregation and the council of the *saints*"). *Auctor* thus did not have to avoid
any texts in his OT to make the point regarding angels and the designation "son." In *his* Bible angels were never called "sons."

At Qumran, on the other hand, angels are "sons of heaven" (a
circumlocution for "sons of God"?) in 1QS 4:22, 11:8, 1QH 3:22,
Gen. Apoc. II, etc., showing an almost complete disregard for the
careful distinctions drawn by *Auctor*. Until evidence to the contrary
is produced, it must be said that the Hebrew texts of (e.g.) Job. 1:6
and 38:7 would have given any Qumran recipients a weighty basis to
frustrate *Auctor*'s preoccupation with the inferior name possessed
by angels (angels are called "gods" in 4Q Deut 32:43 and 11Q Melch,
line 10,[29] quoting Ps. 82:1 – which would have provided a foil
against Heb. 1:8!).[30] As Sowers has noted, "[From] his un-Hebrew
understanding of words such as διαθήκη (9:16–17), we may conclude
that he never read a Hebrew text. It is therefore futile to think he knew
what the equivalent of his terms were and meant in any Hebrew
literature."[31]

This difficulty, coupled with the explicit indication of Heb. 2:2 that
Auctor is interested in the angels primarily in their role as mediators
of the Old Covenant, makes it unlikely that Qumran can be seen as
the background of one of the central themes of chs. 1–2.

Messianic conceptions

According to Yadin, the epistle presents Christ as priest because "this
subject is forced upon the author ... his reader's conceptions regarding
the Aaronic priestly Messiah make it impossible for them to accept
Jesus' unique authority."[32] This is the point of contact most commonly cited in discussions of Hebrews and Qumran. The readers of
Hebrews are said to have held the notion, reflected in CD and 1QS,
that a Messiah of the levitical line was expected who would overshadow the Davidic Messiah and who would resume the levitical
sacrifices in the new age. This made it difficult for the readers to accept
the supremacy of Jesus, who was not of the levitical line. *Auctor*'s
answer allegedly strives to establish three propositions: (1) Jesus is
a high priest; (2) the order of his priesthood is superior to that of
Aaron; and (3) Jesus combines in his person both offices, Davidic
Messiah-king and Levitical Messiah-priest.

Many were to be persuaded by this argument.[33] For Fensham[34]
"one is *forced* to accept that Hebrews directs polemics against the

Qumran-conceptions of the Messiah of Aaron." Others, fortunately, were more cautious.[35]

There are two points at which the theory should be questioned: (1) Was there a "two-Messiah" doctrine at Qumran? (2) Are the arguments for Jesus' priesthood in Hebrews best interpreted against such a background? Almost all of the discussion concerning Hebrews has been confined to (2), with little attention paid to (1).[36]

The "two Messiahs" of Qumran

The argument for a multiple Messiahship at Qumran has rested on at least four pillars. (1) Much attention has centered on the alleged presence of two "Messiahs" in the phrase "the *mašuaḥ* of Aaron and Israel," found four times in CD, which is said to denote two distinct Messianic characters.[37] (2) It is claimed that the Testaments of the Twelve Patriarchs contain the same idea, since in some passages (e.g., Judah 24) the priestly figure is identified with the "star" of the community − a priestly "Messiah."[38] (3) In 1QS a plural form of *mašuaḥ* is found ("until there shall come a prophet and the Messiahs of Aaron and Israel"), thus allegedly proving that what had been inferred from the CD references is correct, that two "Messiahs" were expected at Qumran.[39] (4) In 1QSa, a document of two columns which describes the Messianic banquet, it is suggested that the depiction of a priestly figure who first blesses, and then partakes of, the bread and wine, followed by the Messiah of Israel, enables one to see a domination of the political Messiah at Qumran by the Priestly Messiah.[40]

While for many this view of Qumran Messianism has had the status of dogma, not all have been convinced. Silberman,[41] tired of 1QS 9:11 "being translated and understood with capitalized and connotation laden words," suggests the translation "until the coming of a prophet and the anointed High Priest and the Davidic king." A simpler solution is the view of Higgins[42] and Fritsch,[43] who think the phrase should be rendered "the anointed ones of Aaron and Israel." Here the anointing refers to the commissioning of the traditional OT priest who serves, side by side, with the anointed king (cf. Lev. 4:3, 5 and 16 for the phrase *hacôhên hamašuaḥ*, also found at Qumran). De Jonge,[44] furthermore, questions whether the term *mašuaḥ* was used as a title until after the time of Jesus, and Smith attacks the tendency of modern scholars to read into Qumran passages a Messiah who is simply not there.

There are hints from the OT itself[45] that Higgins, Fritsch and others are correct to see at Qumran a traditional OT pairing of priest and king: (1) In Zech. 4:14 the priest Joshua and the king Zerubbabel are called "the two sons of oil," i.e., the two "anointed ones."[46] (2) In the (probably) corrupt text of Zech. 6:11–13, two crowns are placed on the head of Joshua. The most likely explanation is that the "two crowns" is original, with one to be placed on the head of Zerubbabel and the other given to Joshua.[47] (3) The same idea survived in the apocalyptic tradition, where in Rev. 11:4 the "two witnesses" are said to be both "the two olive trees" (cf. Zech. 4:3–13) and "the two sons of oil," an allusion to Zech. 4:14. That for John these descriptions still embody the normal kingly and priestly roles (although now democratized to stand for the whole martyred church) is indicated by 1:6 ("who has appointed us a kingdom, priests to his God and Father"). (4) In 1 Sam. 2:35 the rejection of the family of Eli leads to a prophecy that a new, faithful priest will be appointed, the family of whom will "serve in perpetual succession before my anointed king." In 1 Kings 2:27 this person is identified as Zadok, to whom the Qumran sect traced its heritage, and in CD 3:18–19 the Samuel oracle is seen as a prophecy of the sect. The faithful priest and the anointed one, therefore, are the historical antecedents of the two figures at Qumran who are termed "Messiahs" (although the former is distinguished in 1 Samuel from "my anointed"). The priest also "walks before," or has precedence over, the anointed king. "But in no case does the precedence of the priest make him a 'Messiah'."[48] A similar pairing of king and priest prevailed later with the rise of Simeon bar Kochba, "the Star," who issued coins with himself and "Eleazar the Priest" on opposite sides.[49]

Two final warnings should be sounded. It is doubtful that there was any unanimity in Qumran literature, any "higher synthesis," by which differences of opinion were harmonized.[50] The situation is more complex than is often appreciated. Secondly, the dating of documents and the possibility of a development of thinking about Messiahship needs to be confronted.[51] Starcky,[52] for example, has proposed four stages of development in the life of the sect. While his theory is questionable,[53] at least he has brought to the fore the undeniable fact that differences of opinion at various stages in the history of the sect make a monolithic Qumran teaching on "Messiahship" unlikely in the extreme.

The above considerations indicate that there is slender basis in the Qumran literature itself for a belief in two "Messiahs," and that the first part of Yadin's case for a link between Hebrews and Qumran in their Messianic conception has not been sustained. But what of the second piece of evidence, that of Hebrews itself?

The high priesthood of Jesus in Hebrews

Several observations with regard to Hebrews are on this point necessary. (a) Apart from the fact that *Auctor* never mentions a two-Messiah doctrine, the lack of an emphasis upon Jesus' Davidic lineage would seem odd if *Auctor* were striving to establish a union of Levitical and Davidic Messiahs in one person.[54] (b) Just as the term "Christ" in Hebrews is never linked to the famous "Branch" passages (Isa. 11:1, Jer. 23:5, 33:15) so important in the Scrolls (cf. 4QPB 2:4, 4QFl 1:7–13), nowhere does it occur with the name of Aaron. Also, "anoint" (χρίω), which one might expect if Qumran-type concepts controlled the argument of the epistle, occurs only once, in a biblical quotation (1:9). Christ's title "*high* priest," furthermore, occupies little significance at Qumran, a fact difficult to explain if this were a subject of concern.[55] (c) The suddenness with which the priestly office of Jesus is introduced into the argument of Hebrews does not sound like a polemical device against an opposing concept.[56] (d) The figure of Jesus in Hebrews is never contrasted with any other coming eschatological figures, only with the past Aaronic priests. (e) The central theme of Hebrews is not the refutation of an Aaronic Messiah, but the self-confessed inadequacy of the entire OT sacrificial order and its replacement by a better, more spiritual system.[57] It is Ps. 110 which forms the impetus for *Auctor*'s speculations rather than any alien notions of priesthood. Therefore on both counts Yadin's point (b) loses conviction.

The prophet like Moses

Those interested in Hebrews and Qumran have devoted much study to the role of the prophets in both. For Yadin "in the DSS we have one of the *clearest* formulations of matters concerning the eschatological era and an exact definition of the position of the prophet and the Messiahs respectively."[58] Thus Jesus' "superiority" to "the prophets" in Heb. 11:1 corrects a Qumranian belief, reflected in 1QS 9:11 ("until the coming of a prophet and the Messiahs from Aaron and Israel") and 4Q Testimonia (the quotation of Deut. 18:18f.) of a "Mosaic" prophet who will accompany the Messiahs and found the new covenant.[59] But will this stand up to examination? The subject needs a fresh airing on both counts.

"The prophet" at Qumran

Contra Yadin, we are forced to say that the role of "the prophet" at Qumran is anything but clear; it is one of our most vexing problems.[60] Crucial here is Yadin's identification of the three quotations from 4Q Testimonia (Deut. 5:28f., 18:18f.; Num. 24:15ff.; and Deut. 33:8–11) with the figures of 1QS 9:11 ("a prophet and the Messiahs of Aaron and Israel").[61] The one document "refer[s] clearly" to the other, claims Yadin.[62] But (1) the case for such a confident association is hardly beyond dispute, and (2) the relation of the prophet to the others (and his general place in the Qumran scheme) is not as patent as Yadin implies. Brownlee claims that "the prophet" of 1QS 9:11 should be identified with "the Messiah," whose followers will be both priests ("of Aaron") and laity ("of Israel"). The followers of the prophet were termed "anointed," says Brownlee, because the prophet is to pour out his anointing spirit on them.[63] On the other hand, J. T. Milik, attempting to make "the prophet" a figure of eschatological significance, was eventually forced to divest him of such pretensions; elsewhere in the texts he goes virtually unnoticed.[64] Hence "the prophet" is probably the Elijah *redivivus* of Mal. 3:23.[65] R. E. Brown offers a related *caveat*: it is unclear that "the prophet" here is to be a contemporary of the Messiah(s), since he is absent at the banquet and benedictions spoken of elsewhere.[66] That any of these figures may be confidently associated or identified[67] is far from clear, and Yadin's admission that the expectation of an eschatological prophet was widespread in Judaism[68] weakens his case for Hebrews and Qumran.

There is consequently little evidence for a claim that the "prophet" of 1QS 9:11 is a Mosaic figure against which *Auctor* could be polemicizing.

"The prophets" and Moses in Hebrews

According to Yadin, one of the subjects which *Auctor* "discusses"[69] is "Jesus and the prophets." But since the prophets are actually mentioned only in 1:1 can it properly be called a "discussion"? This may be the weakest point in Yadin's case: (a) His juxtaposition of the revelation brought by the prophets with that brought by Jesus is defective. Such an antithesis is forced by his premise that *Auctor* is attempting to correct a belief in the coming of an eschatological prophet. An adversative such as δέ, however, which would be required in the Greek text, is nowhere present.[70] The idea stressed by the Greek is one of continuity: the same God who sent the prophets who has now sent His son, Jesus. (b) The plural "prophets" must tell against any theory that Hebrews is combating an eschatological prophet in the singular. (c) The term προφήτης occurs only twice in Hebrews: 1:1 and 11:32 (an incidental reference). This hardly indicates the prophet(s) to be a concern of *Auctor*. (d) If, as Silberman suggests, the role of the prophet at Qumran is bound up with the restoration of anointing, it is instructive (as noted above) that the term χρίω occurs only once in Hebrews – at 1:9, within an OT quotation. (e) *Auctor*'s view of prophecy allows him, remarkably, to view the entire OT as one vast prophecy[71] which points forward to "the good things to come" (9:11); the prophetic role at Qumran, however, is more conventionally Hebraic, restricting the office to the kind of figure referred to in 1 Macc. 4:44ff. Yadin's attempt to invest the prophet of 1QS with Mosaic features must likewise overcome formidable objections before it can be seriously considered as a background for Hebrews.

Had Yadin's case for the expectation at Qumran of a Mosaic prophet who would be connected with the New Covenant been more strongly supported by the evidence, there would be more room for his proposal that in Hebrews much of the presentation of the work of Christ is in dialogue with this background. His view that the readers held certain beliefs regarding an "eschatological" Moses which *Auctor* counters in Heb. 3 and particularly in the "thrice repeated description"[72] of Jesus as μεσίτης (mediator), always in connection with the διαθήκη,[73] is attractive. Yet: (a) The Qumran community was already living in the time of the New Covenant[74] (1QS 1:16–2:22), so the connection with the coming prophet is difficult. (b) Any oblique references to Moses in the rest of the epistle (see also the possibility of Moses as the διαθέμενος of 9:16–17) are better explained as part of the overall contrast between the two covenants, in which the various entities involved in the maintaining of those covenants are mentioned. This includes tabernacle, sacrifice, priest and inaugurator. There is no hint that Moses has been specially singled out for attention. Chapter 8, which Yadin thinks is preoccupied with Moses, actually mentions him only once (v. 5, an incidental reference in connection with the tabernacle). Along the lines of the method Yadin employs, chs. 8–9 would be much more likely directed against a belief in a return of the Mosaic *tabernacle* in connection with the New Covenant![75] More attention is spent in Heb. 8–10 on the nature of the "greater and more perfect tent" (cf. 9:11) than on any eschatological figure.

Rather than indicating any Moses *redivivus* theme, Moses in Hebrews falls into the category of traditional biblical typology.[76] There is no use of Deut. 18 in Hebrews, nor is Moses anything other than a figure of the past who points forward to the "better things" of Christ. A superiority of Christ to Moses might be argued as resulting from other backgrounds (e.g., Philo, the Samaritans, Paul or John), but there is nothing in *Auctor*'s argument regarding either Moses or the prophets which requires a Qumran reference.[77]

Melchizedek

11Q Melchizedek

Yadin could not claim at the time he first wrote that the arguments in Hebrews regarding Melchizedek had any direct counterpart at Qumran because at that time not a trace of him had been produced. The situation changed dramatically, however, with the publication by van der Woude in 1965 of a fragmentary text from Cave 11.[78] Nearly one column of thirteen fragments comprising twenty-six lines with considerable lacunae, it consists of a series of biblical quotations (Lev. 25:9–10, 13; Deut. 15:2; Psalm 7:8–9; 82:1–2; Isa. 52:7; 61:1) with exposition. The theme is the eschatological deliverance of the righteous and the punishment of the wicked. Inevitably speculations relating it to Hebrews proliferated.[79] Unfortunately the text is so mutilated as to make certainty about its meaning impossible. We cannot here enter into analysis of its features or attempt to reconstruct the text. It is sufficient to note that vastly different interpretations of the scroll have been reached by, e.g., de Jonge, van der Woude and Horton, on the one hand, and Carmignac on the other. According to de Jonge and van der Woude, Melchizedek makes his entrance at line 5, and from there on, through line 14, commands stage center as the figure who saves the righteous ("men of the lot of Melchizedek"), makes atonement for "the captives", and administers judgment upon Belial and his minions. Thus Melchizedek is an angelic, heavenly redeemer, identified by van der Woude as the archangel Michael,[80] who functions both as mediator and warrior.[81]

This has been challenged by Carmignac, for whom the central figure of the text is not Melchizedek but God himself (a problem concerns the restoration and interpretation of lines 9–11), with Melchizedek a purely historical person within the Qumran sect of royal or Messianic proportions who is aptly symbolized by the biblical figure or who simply takes over his name.

Which of these diverse interpretations is correct is open to individual judgments.[82] The facts which emerge beyond dispute, however, are that Melchizedek is a mediator of atonement in the Jubilee year and the salvation predicted in the OT texts quoted (lines 3–9, 16), that he is an agent of divine eschatological retribution against Belial and his followers (lines 9–13), and that he is in company with his "inheritance" (line 5). That Melchizedek claims a prominent place amidst the angelic company (or "gods," so Fitzmyer), or that he is the Messianic herald of Isa. 52:7 is less clear, although the weight of scholarship continues to assume van der Woude's case in discussing its significance for Hebrews.

It has been claimed that this evidence[83] is crucial to a proper understanding of the argument of Hebrews. For de Jonge and van der Woude, "the most plausible inference is that he [*Auctor*] regarded Melchizedek as an angel, who appeared to Abraham long ago."[84] De Jonge, van der Woude and Fitzmyer do not follow Yadin in seeing Hebrews as a direct polemic against Qumran beliefs, but rather as a parallel reflection of common cultural concerns.[85] They do, however, view the portrayal of Christ in Hebrews as of the same general character as that of Melchizedek at Qumran.

Before the arguments for or against this position can be weighed, it is necessary to examine the use made by *Auctor* of the Melchizedek figure.

Melchizedek in Hebrews

The literature on Melchizedek in Hebrews is massive.[86] It may be said that *Auctor*'s argument at this point continues to be one of the most difficult features of the epistle to understand.

Horton has dealt with the question extensively. After dismissing such backgrounds as Qumran, Philo and the rabbis, he looks to *Auctor*'s own study of the Scriptures. This may well be the most satisfactory approach to the issue. It is an interest in Ps. 110, one of the most popular early testimonies, which seems to prompt *Auctor* to ask after the identity of the enigmatic figure mentioned in v. 4. It is only natural then to go back to Gen. 14 for the answer.[87]

Auctor's handling of these texts, however, has been much debated. Many interpreters see him subordinating Melchizedek to Jesus in a pejorative manner. Into this group fall de Jonge and van der Woude,[88] who, having admitted that ὁμοιόω can mean "compare," urge instead that it means "to make like" in the sense of to "copy," adding that "the thing or the person which is made like the other is *secondary* and *inferior* to the first."[89] This translation goes hand in glove with the assumption that in Hebrews Melchizedek is an angel, the inferior status of which as a class has been demonstrated in Heb. 1–2,[90] and that *Auctor* is polemicizing against Melchizedek.

But is this true? Whether for the addressees Melchizedek is a "divine" figure similar to van der Woude's understanding of him at Qumran continues to be the central question. Interpreters who have discussed this problem have tended to fall into two groups. (1) In addition to de Jonge and van der Woude, those who consider either the addressees or *Auctor*, or both, as viewing Melchizedek as a superhuman being have included Longenecker,[91] Thompson,[92] Fensham[93] and A. T. Hanson[94] (the last of whom equates him with the pre-existent Christ!). (2) Those who view Melchizedek in Hebrews as a "heavenly figure" in an undefined way similar to Jesus, without negating the former's humanity, include most of those who place Melchizedek and Christ into a type–antitype schema.[95] Melchizedek's priesthood is here often described as a "heavenly" priesthood without further definition.[96]

Making sense of all this is not easy. Certainly from our point of view *Auctor*'s frugality in his explanations is more than a little tragic. He never explains, for instance, how for him Melchizedek *became* a priest, or of what his "greatness" (7:4) consisted. Remaining confined to the biblical account, only portents of that greatness are explicated – the blessing of Abraham and the reception of tithes (7:1–2). Yet the most reasonable inference continues to be that for *Auctor* Melchizedek's priesthood – and greatness – lay in the quality of the life he lived.[97] This must be the central point of comparison between the two figures – the possession of an ability to stand on the "godward" side of humanity,[98] an ability located, not in any outward system of legal trappings, but in the eternal will (or purpose) of God, a will which can be done precisely because some know what that will is (Heb. 10:5ff.).

The difficulties of the "hymn"[99] of 7:3 are notorious, and continue to constitute the main problem for those who wish to see Melchizedek in Hebrews in purely human terms. How is he "without father, without mother, without genealogy"? So far there have been two common answers: (a) The literal understanding of the phrase ἀπάτωρ, ἀμήτωρ, ἀγενεαλόγητος indicates that for *Auctor* Melchizedek is a supernatural, heavenly being. And here it must be admitted that ἀπάτωρ, ἀμήτωρ are used in pagan texts for the miraculous birth of deities[100] (although it should be noted that the

Old Slavonic Book of Enoch ascribes a miraculous birth to Melchizedek without using these words).[101] Horton rightly criticizes
Moffatt for perpetuating the view of Jerome and Theodore that
ἀμήτωρ refers to Christ's pre-existence, while ἀπάτωρ refers to the
virgin birth.[102] Others who take the terms as referring to miraculous
generation are Montefiore,[103] Michel,[104] Thompson,[105] de Jonge and
van der Woude.[106] The main objection to this view, on the other
hand, remains simple: if Melchizedek was not seen by *Auctor* as
human, his arguments regarding the superiority of Melchizedek to
Abraham and Levi are altogether otiose.[107] (b) The majority of
commentators assign these words a typological significance based
upon the "silence of Scripture" principle of *quod non in Thora, non
in mundo* ("what is not in the *Thora* does not exist in the world").[108]
Into this category fall those who consider *Auctor* to be *combating*
a view (e.g., Qumranian) of Melchizedek as a supernatural being and
saviour. These scholars feel that through the use of typology *Auctor*
sees Melchizedek anticipating *symbolically* in the remarks and silences
of Scripture the actual attributes of the eternal Son.[109] There are,
however, severe objections to this view. (1) If Heb. 5–7 is a polemic
against a too exalted view of Melchizedek, it is difficult to explain
why nothing negative is said about him. The other figures from the
old order all suffer at his hands: angels lack the exalted titles; Moses
is servant, not son; Aaron and his cultus never really removed sin.
Yet nothing pejorative is ever said regarding Melchizedek. (2) As
Fensham admits, chs. 5–7 are firmly grounded in the OT rather than
any heterodox conceptions as at Qumran.[110] Several writers have
argued that there is no necessity for any such polemic in Hebrews,[111]
and until evidence from the text itself is produced to the contrary,
this must remain the *least unsatisfactory* position.

But is the "typological" approach itself an adequate solution to
Auctor's reasoning? The conventional wisdom has been that, because
Scripture omits to mention Melchizedek's generation, *Auctor*
considered him a fitting symbol for the eternal Son of God.[112]

Yet there is no hint in Hebrews that Melchizedek and Christ are
related as shadow to reality. It is not a matter of Jesus having
something "really" which Melchizedek has "figuratively." A serious
consideration of *Auctor*'s use of ὁμοιότης (7:15) implies that what
is said about the one must be taken *in the same way* to apply to the
other.[113] The difficulty lies in finding the point of comparison. This
has at least been grasped by Hanson,[114] de Jonge and van der
Woude,[115] who argue that there is a reciprocity between the two

figures. "It seems much easier to assume that the author really meant what he wrote."[116] Unfortunately, from this valid observation comes the conclusion that, since for *Auctor* Christ is a supernatural being, the same must be said of Melchizedek. For Hanson it is Christ himself, while for de Jonge and van der Woude it is an angel-saviour as at Qumran. This results from a certain understanding of the christology of Heb. 1 and 2[117] and a locating of the point of comparison at the wrong place. Here it may be helpful to recall Westcott's description of Christ's appointment as Son in Hebrews: *it is an eternal appointment which has inceptive fulfilments in time, but with no particular point in time at which it begins.*[118] Similarly, it may be said that, with regard to the figures of Melchizedek and Christ, *Auctor* argues that their priesthoods are based upon an eternal decree, and it is the power of their indestructible lives which makes that decree operative. Since their approval stems from the eternal will of God rather than from any set of human ordinances,[119] there can be said to be no "beginning of days" to their priesthood; and since both figures continue to live beyond death, there is no end to their lives. It is unlikely that ζῇ (7:8), since it is contrasted with "men who are dying," indicates a *figurative* use of the term "to live" (within the pages of Scripture), as is usually assumed. *Auctor*'s reasoning is more likely closer to that of Mark 12:26f.: because God *is* the father of Abraham, Isaac and Jacob, he is God of the living, not the dead. Likewise, because the figure of Ps. 110:4 is "like" the priest Melchizedek, it is "witnessed" that Melchizedek must "live." And because he "lives," his priesthood is perpetual. A comparison of 7:3, 8 with 7:24 suggests that the same thing is being said about both figures, a point correctly perceived by Thompson,[120] although his consequent limiting of both figures to the heavenly sphere without any contact with the sense-perceptible world is questionable.

There is therefore no need to say, as Bruce has done,[121] that Melchizedek is a priest "continually" (εἰς τὸ διηνεκές) only in the sense of the biblical narrative, while "Christ remains a priest continually without qualification." Bruce significantly uses the same English word, "continually" (used to translate the phrase εἰς τὸ διηνεκές), for *both* Christ *and* Melchizedek. Horton[122] tries to drive a wedge between *Auctor*'s use of Melchizedek and Christ by claiming that the phrase εἰς τὸ διηνεκές (of Melchizedek, 7:3) is not directly equivalent to εἰς τὸν αἰῶνα (of Christ, 7:24), maintaining that *Auctor* wished to keep a certain distance between the "type" and "antitype" through this superficial device. While admitting virtually no lexical difference, Horton maintains that in 10:1 and 10:12 εἰς τὸ διηνεκές could not be replaced by εἰς τὸν αἰῶνα. But here two points must be made: (1) Against Horton, 10:12 might just as well have read, "but this one offered one sacrifice for sins forever (εἰς τὸν αἰῶνα – cp. εἰς τὸ παντελές of 7:25, which Arndt–Gingrich, 613, render "for all time") and sat down at the right hand of God." It therefore seems that *Auctor* viewed these phrases as equivalent and interchangeable. (2) That *Auctor* could associate the phrase εἰς τὸ διηνεκές with the priesthood of Christ in 10:12 undermines Horton's point. De Jonge and van der Woude[123] agree that no difference between the two expressions should be maintained, and it is perhaps more probable that the εἰς τὸ διηνεκές of 7:3, instead of being chosen for christological considerations, as Horton thinks, looks forward to the milieu of 10:1. The point of comparison is with *Aaron*, not Christ. The priesthood of Christ *and* Melchizedek is "perpetual," while under Aaron there are many priests "perpetually."

Horton and Hay have performed a service by arguing that the burden of Heb. 7:13ff. is the question of *priesthood* rather than that of any divine qualities. This would make it easier to grapple with *Auctor*'s distinctive use of the figure of Melchizedek. The question with which he is concerned is that of the *basis* of the respective OT priesthoods. Because Aaron's was based upon an outward system of regulations, his days as priest began with the initiatory rite; it was time conditioned, limited to a beginning when the Levite reached a certain age, and terminated by death. Melchizedek's "days" as priest, on the other hand, had no such temporally bound beginning, being grounded in the antecedent will of God. With this in mind, it would be best not to take the phrases "no beginning of days" and "no end of life" as strictly parallel.[124] One is essentially backward-looking and refers to the existence of a superior priesthood within God's predestining purposes;[125] the other is forward-looking and stems from *Auctor*'s repeated theme of the afterlife. The latter *includes* the idea of perpetual priesthood, but widens in scope to include resurrection life in general.

The fact that the familiar terms ἀπάτωρ and ἀμήτωρ are combined with a word apparently coined by *Auctor*, ἀγενεαλόγητος, hints that he is using the first two words in a specialized sense, i.e., he is endeavoring to qualify the meaning of the two familiar terms with the third, as if to say, "and by that I mean ..." ἀγενεαλόγητος refers not to biology but to the lack of any genealogical credentials for priesthood.[126] Any remaining doubts are eliminated by 7:13f., where it is admitted that Jesus derived from Judah. What is true of Jesus, i.e., that he had a human genealogy, certainly cannot for *Auctor* have been untrue of his precursor Melchizedek![127] ἀγενεαλόγητος must thus have some other meaning.

The term τάξις in Ps. 110:4 has also caused enormous difficulty. Its translation as "order" implies "succession," an idea rightly to be rejected. A more suitable rendering would be "character." This is indicated by 7:15, where κατὰ τὴν ὁμοιότητα seems to paraphrase the κατά of Ps. 110:4.[128] *Auctor*'s understanding of 5:6, 6:20, etc., is probably thus best paraphrased, "You are a priest forever, according to the character of Melchizedek" (or, simply, "just as Melchizedek is"). This "character" is not rooted in any outward ordinance, but in the antecedent, eternal will of God.

Hebrews 7 and 11Q Melchizedek

We are now in a position to consider the arguments of those who either support or deny a link of Heb. 7 with Qumran. It is first necessary, however, to consider what appears to be a considerable inconsistency within these secondary treatments of Melchizedek in Heb. 7:3ff. Longenecker, e.g., states that "our author agreed with his addressees in 7:1–10 as to the nature of Melchizedek's person."[129] But Longenecker has already identified the addressees as people who have Qumran-type beliefs regarding Melchizedek as a warrior angel.[130] Is he implying that this is also *Auctor*'s view? The same writer insists that there is an "interest in Melchizedek as an *eschatological* figure in both Heb. 5–7 and 11QMelch."[131] M. Delcor says similarly that the "eschatological and celestial role" of Melchizedek becomes in Hebrews "a pivot for his argument,"[132] and Fensham actually speaks of an "eschatological expectation of Melchizedek in Hebrews."[133] Such remarks surely are the result of careless wording rather than sustained thought. Is it possible that in Hebrews there is room for an *expectation* of Melchizedek such as is found at Qumran? Most would say no. Fitzmyer, on the other hand, seems to want it both ways. In one sense he agrees with Horton that "Melchizedek is not an *angelic* figure"; but by insisting that the adjective "heavenly" is to be retained,[134] further insisting that in Hebrews Melchizedek is "an elohim, of a tradition similar to it [11QMelch],"[135] we are faced with a hollow distinction. The argument of de Jonge and van der Woude, furthermore, that the Melchizedek of Heb. 7:3 and 7:15 is an angel, is sadly ill founded. They admit that the burden of Heb. 1 and 2 is to prove "Christ's superiority over all angels,"[136] but if true it would put Christ *into conflict with* the angelic Melchizedek of 7:3, an idea to which *Auctor* would never have assented. If Christ's superiority to Melchizedek were actually anticipated in Heb. 1–2, why would the argument of ch. 7 be so framed – emphasizing the *greatness* of Melchizedek and Christ's *likeness* to him? It would seem that the polemic of Heb. 1–2 against angels is the greatest argument against seeing Melchizedek as an angel in ch. 7 (unless, of course, it is *Auctor* who is inconsistent – arguing *against* Qumran beliefs in chs. 1–2, and adopting them in ch. 7!). An argument that Melchizedek is a "heavenly" being or angel and that Christ is "like" him (7:15) would fuel the recipients' enthusiasms for angels, not dampen it.[137]

It will thus be best to confine the discussion to a comparison between the presentation of *Christ* in Hebrews and *Melchizedek* at Qumran. The similarities most noted are easily summarized:[138] (a) The Melchizedek of 11Q Melch and Jesus in Heb. 7 are both in some sense "heavenly" figures. Van der Woude and Fitzmyer think Heb. 7 should be read in the light of the Qumran document. (b) Both are "eschatological" figures. (c) Both achieve the salvation of the elect, possibly through the day of atonement. (d) Both wage a (final) conflict with the devil (Heb. 1:13, 2:14–15; 10:12–13).

The last point is certainly the weakest; *Auctor* mentions the devil only once, and the other two references are scriptural citations which do not pick up the theme of the identity of the "enemies." The differences are more numerous: (a) The presentation of Jesus in Hebrews has virtually no military features. Jesus in Hebrews is basically a mediator, while the Melchizedek of Qumran has less to do with reconciliation than with the annihilation of enemies. (b) *Auctor* focuses on Melchizedek *qua* priest, whereas Qumran does not.[139] (c) Remarkably, no clear allusion to either Gen. 14 or Ps. 110, the key texts of Heb. 7, appears in 11Q Melch.[140] Even more surprising is the complete omission of the texts quoted in 11Q Melch (Lev. 25, Deut. 15, Isa. 52, 61, Pss. 7, 82:2) in Hebrews. "There is no overlapping."[141] (d) Jesus' salvific work is accomplished in the heavenly sanctuary; the Qumran Melchizedek vanquishes Belial and his followers on earth.[142] (e) The Jesus of Hebrews is fully a human being, while the Melchizedek of 11Q Melch is, if van der Woude is correct, an angelic being. (f) Whereas the primary feature of Melchizedek at Qumran is that he vanquishes his enemies, the primary point of Heb. 7 is that Melchizedek and Jesus "abide."[143] (g) At Qumran the work of Melchizedek still lies in the future, whereas Christ's work for his people is a present reality.[144] (h) "In 11Q Melch he is directly related to levitical laws; in Hebrews stress is laid on his non-levitical status."[145]

A final question needs asking. If *Auctor* were attempting to correct such views, *would he have framed his argument as he has?* The answer is undeniably supplied if it is understood that the purpose of the theological sections of Hebrews must be gaged by the pastoral sections coming between them. The theological arguments are framed precisely because *Auctor* wants to avoid certain pastoral dangers, particularly *lapse*. But into what are the readers in danger of lapsing? Can we gage from the pastoral interludes that they are veering toward a lapse into Qumran-type doctrines? It would appear not. The problem *Auctor* confronts is "dullness of hearing" (5:11) and discouragement ("lift your drooping hands and strengthen your weak knees," 12:12). It needs to be stressed that it is almost pathetically easy to isolate the theological sections of Hebrews and not see them as part of a document which is essentially *pastoral* in its thrust. And it is precisely in the pastoral sections *where the Qumran situation does not seem to be indicated.*

There is thus little to indicate that Hebrews and Qumran may be connected in their treatment of Melchizedek. The ideas surrounding Melchizedek in 11Q Melch are based upon neither of the crucial texts of Heb. 7, Ps. 110 and Gen. 14, and the picture of him that emerges at Qumran, while using OT motifs, has little to do with the OT. 11Q Melch indicates the possibility of other traditions concerning Melchizedek circulating in the first century. In this light what is remarkable is not, as is often supposed, that *Auctor* makes so much out of so little, but that "he makes so little out of so much."[146] The superiority of Melchizedek over Aaron is never due in Hebrews to any angelic status of the former; it stems from the basis of his priesthood and the fact that Levi (in Abraham) paid him tithes. It is thus "very doubtful" that *Auctor* polemicizes against Qumran.[147] The value of Qumran is that it shows that at least one group within Judaism, roughly contemporaneous with *Auctor*, found the historical Melchizedek identical with an exalted being of some significance for salvation history. This makes the argument of Heb. 7 less "bizarre" and more intelligible than was formerly thought.[148]

The use of the Old Testament

Since *Auctor* and the Qumran community both use the OT extensively, it is not surprising that this has been seen as an area of common ground. Spicq,[149] Combrink,[150] Kistemaker[151] and Fensham[152] find an affinity in text form and interpretation.[153] According to Kistemaker, "nearly every chapter of Hebrews reveals the peculiar feature of the *midrash pesher*."[154] Comparison is here made with the Habbakuk Commentary (1QpH), which uses various devices − textual variations, conflations, plays upon words and an application of Scripture to the present.[155] Key texts which are said to conform to this pattern are Heb. 9:9, 10:15, 12:26; 2:6−9, 3:7−11 (all of which, says Spicq,[156] are given an exclusively Christian meaning *pesher*-style); Heb. 10:5−10;[157] Heb. 7:1ff.;[158] Heb. 10:37ff.;[159] and Heb. 1:5.[160] These texts, it is said, are approached always with the same question in mind: "What do these passages really mean when viewed from a *Christian* perspective?"[161] While a similarity to the *pesher* technique would not necessarily prove a relationship between Qumran and *Auctor* in their interpretation of the OT, it would at least establish ground for further discussion. Along these lines certain points must be made: (1) Against Bruce,[162] it is unlikely that *Auctor* takes the OT as "a *mashal*, a parable or mystery which awaits its explanation" in the same manner as the *raz-pesher* of Qumran. Instead, the method of *Auctor* is to inquire as to the original meaning of a passage and its relevance for Christians.[163] The difficulty (δυσερμήνευτος λέγειν) of the Melchizedek section (5:11−14) is due for him not to any intrinsically mysterious nature of the OT text, but to the slowness of the readers to grasp the plain lines of the texts which interest him, Ps. 110 and Gen. 14. This would appear to be of a different nature from the attempt of Qumran *pesher* exegetes to read *between* the lines. While Qumran and *Auctor* view the OT as "fulfilled" in their own time, "the last days," there is little sympathy in Hebrews for the notion at Qumran that the OT, shrouded in mystery, had virtually no significance for its own time.[164] (2) Thomas[165] has shown that, unlike the approach apparently adopted by Qumran and possibly by the author of Matthew's gospel,[166] *Auctor* probably did not have different OT readings of a passage before him from which he chose. The variations (see the differing quotations of Jer. 31 in chs. 8 and 10) must have resulted from other factors, such as paraphrase, quotation from memory[167] or liturgical modification.[168] (3) Dunn has noted the possibility of "pesher quotations" in the NT, in which "the actual quotation of the text embodies its interpretation within the quotation itself."[169] Although it is disputed whether documents such as 1QpH are the product of this technique or of variant Hebrew versions, J. C. McCullough has argued, convincingly in my opinion, that the quotations in Hebrews may have introduced changes to emphasize key points or to eliminate ambiguity, but that these changes never involved a tampering with what *Auctor* believed to be the sense of the passage, nor did his understanding of the sense *depend* on the changes. "He avoided the pneumatic rewriting of passages which the sectaries of Qumran considered to be part of the work of an interpreter of Scripture."[170] (4) The so-called "christological" use of the OT in Hebrews has been grossly exaggerated. The interpretations which *Auctor* gives to Heb. 1:5ff.,[171] 2:6ff.,[172] 3:7ff.[173] and 7:1ff.[174] are the result of his attempt to find the original meaning of the text. Schröger[175] has shown how many different adjectives it is possible to collect in describing the use of the OT in Hebrews. These include indirect Messianic application, direct Messianic application (both on a promise–fulfilment scheme), literal, *midrash-pesher*, and typological. Not all will agree with Schröger's placement of each text into the respective categories; it often depends on not obvious distinctions and highly subjective – almost arbitrary – judgments. Heb. 10:5–10 (Ps. 40:7–9), for example, is described by Schröger as "midrash-pesher,"[176] while Heb. 2:13 (Isa. 8:17f.) is "indirect messianic promise-fulfilment." Nairne saw no difference, viewing both as "words appropriate for the Christ to have spoken" rather than as "direct prediction."[177] Schröger[178] also feels that *Auctor* has no uniform method of interpretation. He claims to have detected in *Auctor*'s various OT quotations elements of rabbinic, Qumran–apocalyptic and late-Jewish Hellenistic synagogue style.[179] But until some consensus is reached as to which texts fall into which category (an unlikely prospect), it will be virtually impossible to conduct a comparative analysis of Hebrews with the *midrash-pesher* exegesis of Qumran which will be accepted universally.[180]

Fensham has chosen three examples which he feels demonstrate an "affinity" between the use of the OT in Hebrews and at Qumran: Isa. 45:17 (Heb 5:9 and 1QH 15:16); the combination of Ps. 2:7 and 2 Sam. 7:14 (Heb. 1:5–6 and 4QFl 1:11–12); and Deut. 32:43 (Heb. 1:6, 4Q Deut. 32:43). His first example may be quickly dismissed: it rests on the claim that the addition of τελειωθείς gives σωτηρίας αἰωνίου "a definitely eschatological colour" absent in Is. 45:17LXX, but present in 1QH 15:16. How the term in question accomplishes this, or why the "everlasting salvation" with which the Lord saves Israel in Isa. 45:17LXX is less "eschatological" than its nuance in Hebrews or Qumran, is not explained. His third example, Deut. 32:43, I have dealt with elsewhere,[181] but it should be noted that this falls more into the category of textual affinity than that of exegesis and interpretation. The second example, however, does involve interpretation, comprising as it does a collection of texts at Qumran similar to what one finds in Heb. 1, and therefore it merits some consideration here. To this should be added one more example, Hab. 2:3–4 (Heb. 10:37ff., 1QpH 8:1–3), often cited as a point of exegetical contact between Hebrews and Qumran.

4QFl and Heb. 1

4QFl[182] has been seen as significant for several reasons: (a) In view of the traditional Jewish avoidance of the title "Son of God" for the Messiah,[183] that 4QFl apparently conflates Ps. 2:7 with 2 Sam. 7:14 in referring the title "Son of God" to the Davidic Messiah[184] is seen by some as a point of convergence with *Auctor*. "This shows that the title "Son of God" *was just coming to use as* a messianic title in pre-Christian Judaism."[185] (b) The technique of collecting OT texts relating to the Messiah in 4QFl bears a certain resemblance to Heb. 1. Some have felt that this lends new life to Rendel Harris' "testimony book" hypothesis as underlying Heb. 1,[186] while others prefer to make the point of comparison the midrash of 4QFl, in which one text functions as a commentary upon another, with other texts (e.g., Ex. 15:17–18, Am. 9:11) introduced into the commentary.[187] (c) The group of texts is related to "the last days" in 4QFl,[188] which recalls Heb. 1:2a.

On the other hand, the following should be observed: (a) In 4QFl the name "son" is not taken up or given any particular significance. At Qumran the term "son" occurs almost always only in OT quotations.[189] *Auctor*, however, makes sonship a key theme, applying it not only to Christ (3:6, 5:8, etc.) but also to believers (2:10, 12:5). (b) While 4QFl stresses the Messiah *qua* descendant of David, *Auctor* remains silent regarding David in relation to "the Christ."[190] (c) Fitzmyer's observation that 4QFl consists of three main texts, 2 Sam. 7:10–14, Ps. 1:1 and 2:1, and that the other texts are introduced as a commentary on these, underlines the fact that 4QFl does not have quite the same structure as Heb. 1, in which each text functions independently and with equal weight, leading up to the key text of the section, Ps. 8:6–8, in 2:6ff. This feature, coupled with the absence of any explicit introductory formula, militates against Fitzmyer's conclusion that "the midrashic technique [in Heb. 1 and 4QFl] is basically the same."[191]

Hab. 2:3f. in 1QpH and Heb. 10:37f.[192]

Bruce calls this "probably the most striking biblical parallel" between Hebrews and Qumran, while Kistemaker,[193] Ellis[194] and Buchanan[195] refer the term *midrash pesher* to *Auctor*'s handling of the Habakkuk passage. Ellis[196] notes particularly "tendentious alterations of the Old Testament text" and the "application to present-time eschatological fulfilment." Among the "tendentious alterations" usually noted are (a) the explicit Messianic reference via the addition of the article ὁ before ἐρχόμενος, (b) the immediately preceding citation of Isa. 26:20LXX, fixing the Habakkuk passage definitely in an apocalyptic context, and (c) the reversed order of the clauses in v. 38, with ὁ δίκαιος now the subject of both.[197]

Here several observations are in order. (a) The LXX text itself, and not *Auctor*, retained the masculine αὐτός and ἐρχόμενος when coupled with the feminine ὅρασις (for masc. ḥazōn). Lindars[198] feels that this indicates "a messianic interpretation" within the LXX text itself.[199] McCullough, as noted, has argued against "tendentious" alterations in Hebrews on which *depends* the particular interpretation being given,[200] and, if the LXX had already imported into the text a Messianic nuance, *Auctor*'s emendation of ὅτι to ὁ to make this meaning more precise is in line with what McCullough has argued is *Auctor*'s method elsewhere. (b) If it is granted that a "Messianic" flavor has already been imported into the LXX text of Heb. 2:3f. *before Auctor*'s time, it can hardly be seen as a major step towards *pesher* exegesis to make the text more precisely "eschatological" by the addition of Isa. 26:20LXX. (c) The inversion of the clauses in 10:38 appears to frustrate McCullough's conclusion: here one sees a transfer of the referent of ἐὰν ὑποστείληται from the figure of v. 3 to the "faithful one" of v. 4.[201] At first blush it looks as though, because of his concern for the readers' possible apostasy,[202] *Auctor* has altered the text so that the "faithful one" now has the option of drawing back: "The reason for the inversion is not hard to determine: by this means 'my righteous one' becomes the subject of *both* parts of the verse. If he perseveres in faith he will gain his life; if he shrinks back he will prove himself reprobate."[203] Has *Auctor* "tampered" with the text? The question may only be answered affirmatively if it is held that *Auctor* read vv. 3 and 4 in the LXX of Hab. 2 as a *unit*.

The MT, significantly, does not; there is a distinct break in thought between vv. 3 and 4 ("it will not delay/behold, his soul is puffed up"). It may be that *Auctor* has preserved an exegesis of the text which is closer to the original Hebrew than has been thought, an exegesis which saw two different points being made. While it appears strange to our reading of the LXX, if v. 4 had been taken as introducing a new subject, the inversion of the clauses functions merely to clarify the subject of ὑποστέλλω. That *Auctor* is capable of atomizing an apparently continuous text into at least two separate units is evident from his treatment of Isa. 8:17b–18a in 2:13, although because 10:38 is not introduced by the phrase καὶ πάλιν, it is not quite so certain that this has occurred here.

Thus there is some ground for questioning whether 1QpH provides any helpful illumination of Heb. 10:37f. The imposition of a *pesher* label upon *Auctor*'s use of the LXX is not proven. On the other hand, it is often observed that the Qumran covenanter is not approved because of his faith in the *work* of the TR, but rather because of his faithfulness in adhering to his own work as delineated in the teaching of the TR, a fact which is then juxtaposed with *Auctor*'s emphasis on faith in Christ.[204] Hebrews, however, has often been said to be more "theocentric" than "christocentric," and the πίστις of Heb. 10:38 is probably closer to the "faithfulness" of the Qumran covenanter in terms of steadfast adherence to a goal (cf. Heb. 3:14) than has been admitted by some. This may appear to place *Auctor* closer to Qumran at this point than to, e.g., Paul, but this is illusory.[205] It does nothing, furthermore, to establish either a direct or an indirect relationship between Hebrews and Qumran, since the OT nuance of "steadfastness" is the most likely source of both.

It may be concluded that in a comparison of the use of the OT in Hebrews and Qumran there has been adduced nothing which requires (or even strongly suggests) a Qumran background for the epistle.

3 Conclusion

While a number of other points of contact[206] between Hebrews and Qumran have been proposed and discussed during the past twenty years, it has been seen in the above sections that the enthusiasm which has been attached to the suggestions of Yadin and others which relate Hebrews directly to a Qumran background is less than well founded. These suggestions involve a certain distortion of the argument of Hebrews, and in some cases the evidence of Qumran appears to have been misinterpreted. That many of the points adduced as parallel to Qumran are also parallel to Philo and other backgrounds makes it more likely that all the similarities are due to a common background – traditional exegesis of the OT. Finally, *Auctor* appears to be a "bookish" person; all the references are to Scripture. It is thus inherently improbable that what is in view is any particular situation other than the pastoral problems of the addressees.

3

OTHER NON-CHRISTIAN BACKGROUNDS

1 Pre-Christian gnosticism

With the rise of interest this century in gnosticism and its possible role in the formation of the NT, it was inevitable that a writing which had already been interpreted in terms of Philo's de-emphasis upon the material realm should be placed into a gnostic framework. Already in 1922 Scott[1] spoke of Hebrews as "gnosis," while others, without using the term, paved the way for a "gnostic" interpretation of the epistle.[2] The first thoroughgoing exposition was that of E. Käsemann in 1939.[3] While acknowledging Jewish and Alexandrian elements, Käsemann saw the main influence behind Hebrews as a pre-Christian gnosticism which, centering on a myth of the redeemed redeemer, conceived of salvation as a journey from the enslaving realm of the material to the heavenly realm of light. Käsemann thus differed from Michel, for whom Hebrews was basically apocalyptic.[4] As with Phil. 2, the Son in Hebrews was now seen to be the gnostic *anthropos* or *Urmensch*,[5] while the "enlightened" are those who advance toward the same stage of "perfection" in knowledge which the Son has already achieved. He also felt that underlying Heb. 7 was a gnostic tradition of Melchizedek as the incarnation of the *Urmensch*.[6] Käsemann relied upon Mandaean, Manichaean, rabbinic and Hermetic literature, the Testaments, the Acts of Thomas, Pistis Sophia, III Enoch and the Odes of Solomon. These texts, he felt, reflect traditions which antedate *Auctor* and Philo. *Auctor* used them critically, however, historicizing and pressing them into the service of the gospel[7] (an idea similar to what Barrett was to suggest later regarding Hebrews and Platonism).[8]

Käsemann's influence upon continental criticism was immediate. Michel[9] revised his work (however minimally) to take account of it, and Bultmann built upon it in his *Theology of the New Testament*.[10] "The Käsemann position can only gain more ground," claimed

B. Rigaux[11] in a review of recent criticism of Hebrews. If limited to continental opinion, Rigaux's judgment is supported by the appearance in the past twenty-five years of two large-scale monographs which agree in the main with Käsemann's thesis: E. Grässer's *Der Glaube im Hebräerbrief and* G.Theissen's *Untersuchungen zum Hebräerbrief*.[12] With only a few exceptions,[13] on the other hand, English-speaking criticism has not been much affected. Some have argued that the epistle *combats* a "gnostic"-like aberration similar to the "Colossian heresy,"[14] but this has not won a great deal of assent.[15] W. Manson[16] opposes Scott's view that Hebrews constitutes a "gnosis" for an intellectual elite, and admits no gnostic influences in his assessment of the epistle. While referring to Käsemann's work as "penetrating," Barrett[17] attempts to undermine the thesis that Hebrews is gnostic in its approach to the gospel. Moule,[18] reviewing Grässer, questions the parallels with gnosticism, and Grässer's entire method has been attacked (although not with particular reference to the gnostic parallels) by G. Hughes.[19]

It could be said, therefore, that the degree of sympathy which is attached to a gnostic background for Hebrews depends largely upon whether one's scholarly orientation is continental or British.[20]

The case for a gnostic background

The argument for a gnostic background for Hebrews may be treated under various headings.

Wandering, pilgrimage

Käsemann saw "the wandering people of God" as the foreground motif of Hebrews.[21] For him "men have εὐαγγέλιον on earth only as ἐπαγγελία," and "the only proper form of existence in time for those who receive revelation is pilgrimage"[22] (*die Wanderschaft*).[23] Apart from chs. 3–4, Käsemann[24] sees the gnostic pilgrimage of souls in such passages as Heb. 10:19ff., and accordingly lists verbs of movement in Hebrews.[25] Grässer likewise sees the motif of pilgrimage to the celestial city in chs. 11–12 as gnostic, and in his interpretation of faith in Hebrews he cites numerous gnostic references.[26]

Sabbath rest

Käsemann[27] connects the sabbath rest awaiting God's people in Heb. 3–4 with gnostic speculations regarding the soul's final "rest" in God. He finds little connection at this point with Philo, who identified rest as "working with absolute ease, without toil and without suffering."[28] In Hebrews it is the total cessation of activity, identified here with the state found only upon leaving this evil world. Käsemann's position was challenged by O. Hofius' *Katapausis*. Far from seeing "rest" in Hebrews against a gnostic background, Hofius argued for Jewish apocalyptic notions of the final city-state at the end of the age. Thus "rest" in Hebrews is entry into the eschatological Holy of Holies.[29] Hofius was in turn criticized by Theissen,[30] who viewed Hofius' equation of rest with entry into the inner shrine as too simple. He emphasized that, since it is linked closely with God's own rest at creation, rest is not to be interpreted entirely in apocalyptic/eschatological "local" terms.

The redeemed redeemer

Foundational to Käsemann's view of Hebrews is his belief that its christology is built on the gnostic myth of the heavenly man. He adduces late Jewish and heretical Christian parallels to show that in Hebrews a heavenly Son takes on human form, suffers and dies in order to release his followers from bondage to the evil powers and death, and then ascends once again to the world of light, where he is crowned with glory and honour. Käsemann views the motifs of the Son as creator[31] and the enthronement "on the right hand of the majesty on high" (1:2f.)[32] as gnostic. The use of Ps. 8 is also said to be pressed into a gnostic framework: the heavenly redeemer is himself redeemed, and the sons become as the Son. Käsemann claims that the application of the psalm to *both* "Son" and "sons" indicates a favorite gnostic concern.[33] Käsemann also views the high priestly motif as gnostic. By the time *Auctor* wrote, he claims, the Hasmonean Messianic high priest had developed into a fusion of this *anthropos* myth with the notion of an *Urmensch* high priest who offers himself for his people. Philo and *Auctor* both point to an early (but independent) form of this fusion.[34] "We may deny neither Philo's nor Hebrews' acquaintance with esoteric traditions of the heavenly high priest, nor find in either evidence only of a pure scriptural gnosis derived from Psalm 110."[35] This secret knowledge, which Käsemann calls the λόγος τέλειος,[36] embraced as well gnostic notions of a heavenly ἀρχηγός (Heb. 2:10 and 12:2)[37] and gnostic Melchizedek speculation. Chapter 7 of Hebrews, therefore, is said to reveal the gnostic belief that Melchizedek was one of numerous incarnations of the *Urmensch* (including also Adam, Shem, Moses, Michael and Metatron), and it is this instruction in which the recipients of Hebrews were deficient.[38]

Faith

B. W. Bacon[39] saw faith in Hebrews as "the power of penetration to the ideal. It approximates dangerously to the Buddhist–gnostic conception of 'enlightenment' or gnosis." A gnostic background for faith in Hebrews is endorsed in particular by Grässer. Building upon Käsemann,[40] Grässer views faith in the epistle as the vehicle of a gnostic journey of the soul into the heavenly realm of light. For both Philo and *Auctor* faith is seen as a pilgrimage to the heavenly world, a view arising from gnostic traditions antedating both writers. *Auctor* has accordingly "depersonalized" Paul's understanding of faith in Jesus and substituted for it an intellectual quality which is primarily interested in penetrating the unknown. The focus of faith is removed entirely from the present benefits of Christianity, including union with Christ. Any primitive Christian elements of realized eschatology are said to be replaced, under the tensions of the delayed parousia, by a focus upon the end of the wearisome pilgrimage.[41]

Dualism

For Käsemann and Grässer *Auctor* and gnosticism view this world as essentially evil and hostile, with salvation consisting essentially in an escape to the "heavenly" realm of Light and Spirit.

The case against a gnostic background

For a number of reasons these arguments may be brought into question.

Wandering, pilgrimage

Käsemann's bringing to the fore the importance of the theme of pilgrimage in Hebrews is the great contribution of his work.[42] Yet there are points at which his synthesis must be criticized. (1) In 3:7–4:13 Ps. 95 is not used to explicate the idea of "the wandering people of God," but rather the threat of apostasy.[43] Käsemann's isolation of 3:7–4:13 as the key section of *all* of Hebrews is thus dubious. (2) Käsemann's reading of 10:19ff. as a gnostic ascent of souls cannot be supported. He claims that "way" (ὁδός) is a "gnostic" technical term for such a journey, but this is doubtful (although, contra some, it probably does involve a note of forward progress);[44] in the sources cited by Käsemann (e.g., Odes Sol. 33:6f.) "way" means simply "walk" or "commandments."[45] Grässer's[46] assertion that the linking of Jesus' "flesh" with the "curtain" in

Heb. 10:20 indicates a gnostic motif in which Jesus' flesh is "demonic matter by which man is held in bondage" is an astonishing piece of eisegesis. (3) Van der Waal[47] has rightly emphasized the political dimensions of the pilgrimage in Hebrews:

> The camp that must be left behind is the camp of apostasy and sin; it is not the camp of the created world ... Jesus Christ is not the Organizer of mystical pilgrimages to heaven for individual souls ... We are not proclaiming a docetic Christ, but a Christ who gave his body to save our bodies.   (10:5, 20, 22; 13:3)

Thus, until better evidence than Käsemann's is produced, we should see pilgrimage and wandering in Hebrews *and* Philo[48] as rooted in the OT rather than in any proto-gnostic traditions.

Sabbath rest

I cannot weigh here with precision the arguments used by Hofius and Theissen. Some have been entirely convinced by Hofius;[49] others view Theissen's study as the final word.[50] Still others try to solve the problem by seeing *both* "apocalyptic" and "gnostic" notions at work in *Auctor*'s view of "rest."[51] It seems difficult to evade the point of Theissen and Vanhoye[52] that an equation of "rest" with entry into the eschatological holy of holies is too simple and lacks support in the epistle.[53] The primary problem remains simple: *Auctor* never actually defines what he means by "rest."[54] The promise of rest may be accepted today; but whether entry into that rest is accomplished now through faith, at death (12:23, "the spirits of just men *made perfect*" – i.e., "at rest"?), or at the final consummation (i.e., "rest" = "the city to come" of 13:14?) is nearly impossible to say. It probably includes all three. What is certain is that *Auctor* connects, through *gezerah shewah*, the "rest" of Ps. 95 with God's rest in Gen. 2:2, and that his understanding issues from an attempt (via Jewish hermeneutics) to deal with what the OT says about a crucial term in Ps. 95. Similarities with Philonic, gnostic *or* apocalyptic teaching at this point are probably best explained as arising from a common use of the same OT texts (although it is also possible that gnostic parallels at this point arise from a deviant use of Christian or Philonic teaching).[55]

The redeemed redeemer

The problems with Käsemann's view at this point are numerous. (1) The evidence for the existence of a pre-Christian heavenly redeemer myth has been exposed as virtually non-existent. R. Reitzenstein's[56] supposition that there flourished in the ancient world a myth of a descending heavenly *Urmensch* not only depends upon sources (e.g., Mandaean and Manichaean) too late for the NT; it depends upon sources incorrectly interpreted. Philo and Poimandres, for example, texts which were thought to speak of the *descent* of a heavenly man, actually speak of the *origin* of a heavenly man, who in all likelihood stands for humankind in general.[57] (2) The term ἀρχηγός was common in the LXX[58] and in the ancient world[59] for a head of house (e.g., Ex. 6:14LXX; cf. Heb. 2:10ff. 3:3ff.), "prince," or military leader. Käsemann's parallels with late Jewish and gnostic literature are, by comparison, irrelevant.[60] (3) The assertion that Melchizedek was ever considered an incarnation of the *Urmensch* in Jewish sources is without foundation. The few Jewish texts cited by Käsemann, following F.J. Jerome, have been apparently reworked by Christians.[61] Horton examines the relevant gnostic sources regarding Melchizedek (Kahle's Fragment 52, Pistis Sophia I–IV, and the Second Book of Ieû) and concludes that Melchizedek is a heavenly being who leads souls to the realm of light without any connection with an *Urmensch*. Melchizedek is apparently not even a human figure.[62] This differs from the Melchizedek of Hebrews.[63] (4) Bornkamm[64] points out that the high priest of Hebrews who expiates the sin of others within a historical context is unlike the heroic heavenly redeemer who breaks through the realm of darkness into the realm of light. (5) Käsemann's reading of Ps. 110:1 and Ps. 8:4–6 in Hebrews is difficult in the light of comments I make elsewhere.[65]

Faith

As noted, Grässer's analysis has been criticized severely by G. Hughes.[66] It also reflects presuppositions which I question elsewhere in this study concerning the nature of faith in Hebrews and Paul.[67] Finally, it may be said that Grässer has unsuccessfully related his gnostic parallels to the theory of a delayed parousia. In gnostic thought salvation is achieved through knowledge (communicated by a heavenly redeemer) which enables the individual soul to escape its prison in this world (the body) and ascend through various stages to the realm of light. This is accomplished primarily[68] at death (i.e., it is an individual eschatology).[69] Grässer's reading of Hebrews as an example of *Frükatholizismus*, in which salvation is postponed to the indefinite future and faith is defined as waiting during a "time of not yet" (with the "already" element jettisoned), is unlike either gnosticism or primitive Christianity, both of which emphasize aspects of salvation which occur in some sense independent of the final consummation.

Dualism

That Hebrews has a fundamentally dualistic outlook appears to run counter to the evidence. (1) Nowhere (excepting, perhaps, 2:14 – "the devil") in Hebrews is the world under evil, hostile powers. Angels are "ministering spirits sent forth to serve those who are to inherit salvation" (1:14) rather than gnostic emanations. (2) The Son (1:2b) is the one who creates "the *aions*." In the light of similarities to Col. 1:15ff.,[70] on the other hand, reference to the demiurge is hardly the only (or even most plausible) option. (3) 11:13, "strangers and exiles on the earth" (RSV, NEB) does not indicate a material/immaterial distinction, but rather the *future*-oriented idea that Abraham lived as a stranger in the country which was promised to him ("He was a *ger* in the country which had all the interest of his heart").[71] (4) The "shaking" of the earth and heavens in Heb. 12:26f. does not denote any gnostic-type material/immaterial distinction (contra, e.g., Grässer),[72] but is in line with traditional OT eschatology.[73] "The world to come" of Heb. 2:5 has nothing to do with the heavenly light-sphere of gnosticism, but is, as Michel[74] suggests, the counterpart of John's city in Rev. 21:1f. (5) The "camp" of Heb. 13:12 is, contra Thompson[75] and Johnsson,[76] not the created world, but Judaism.[77] (6) There is no negative estimate of σάρξ in Hebrews such as one finds in later gnosticism. In the OT σάρξ could mean, simply, humanity in its natural existence.[78] For Paul "in the flesh" sometimes meant "to be alive," "to exist on earth" (Phil. 1:22). Heb. 5:7, "the days of his flesh," means, similarly, "the days of his earthly existence." σάρξ in Heb. 9:10 looks fairly negative, but a few verses later, when it occurs again, it is part of an *a fortiori* argument (9:13; cf. 12:9). σάρκινος in Heb. 7:16 again means "natural" or "human." There is nothing *a priori* "gnostic" about a juxtaposition of flesh and spirit (Gen. 6:3; cp. Mat. 26:41), and in their use of such terms *Auctor* and Paul[79] appear to stay within what are essentially OT categories.[80] Taken in this light the eschatological cultus in Hebrews is not "greater and more perfect" (9:11) because it denotes the immaterial realm of the gnostic, but because its sacrifice is performed "in integrity,"[81] i.e., it is the archetype of perfect, willing obedience.

Conclusion for a gnostic background

R. McL. Wilson[82] and Batdorf[83] have noted the imprecision with which terms such as "gnosis," "gnostic," "proto-gnostic" and "pre-gnostic" are often used in these discussions. "Gnosis" should be used of "knowledge of divine mysteries reserved for an elite," "gnostic" for the full-blown Christian heresies of the second century and beyond (Valentine, Basilides, Mani, etc.); "proto-gnostic" for earlier forms of such heresies; and "pre-gnostic" for "ideas not yet lodged but usable therein once the occasion arises."[84] The main difficulty of Käsemann's approach is the lack of evidence for either a "proto-gnosticism" or "gnosticism" earlier than the second century.[85] Käsemann found it difficult to admit that these systems *arose out of Christianity*. The Mandaean literature which guides much of the thinking of Jonas and Käsemann derives from the seventh to ninth centuries A.D. Käsemann[86] claimed on methodological grounds that there is no reason to doubt that extremely late Jewish and gnostic sources had their religious-historical roots in the NT period. This amounts to a disregard for chronology which F. Filson [87] rightly describes as "amazing." Earlier writers (e.g., Scott) who spoke of "gnosis" in Hebrews were not talking about the full-blown systems envisaged by Käsemann. Some writers detect "pre-gnostic" tendencies at Qumran[88] and Philo,[89] but with regard to Hebrews the most that can be shown is a greater amount of overlapping between such backgrounds than has been previously admitted. Batdorf[90] suggests that Hebrews and Qumran lie on the same pre-gnostic "trajectory," but this also is difficult; as I have already said,[91] similarities probably result from an independent and highly different attempt to come to grips with certain OT texts and institutions. Any "gnosis" regarding Melchizedek in each is so different as to make their placing on a common trajectory unlikely.

In the face of such problems, the time may be ripe to bring to a close yet another chapter in the history of the interpretation of Hebrews. The existence of any first-century gnosticism which could have influenced *Auctor* is not established, nor do the ideas of Hebrews conform particularly well to any so-called "pre-gnostic" tendencies. With a few exceptions, the gnostic approach to Hebrews has made little impact upon responsible interpretation. In the words of Hengel,[92]

> One may hope that the "gnostic fever" ... which has already died down in the meantime will completely disappear ... [Yet]

it is remarkable how much influence it still has in popular theological literature, in theological colleges and in examination work.

2 The Samaritans

In 1927 E. A. Knox[93] published a brief study which suggested that "the Epistle to the Hebrews might have been written to Samaritan Christians,"[94] and that, as such, it would constitute "a great manifestation of the reunion of Israel and Judah in the infant church."[95] Knox isolated themes in Hebrews which he felt would have special appeal for a Samaritan audience (e.g., the idea of Christ as a new Joshua;[96] Christ as *true* priest-king (unlike Hyrcanus, "the great enemy of the Samaritans");[97] the interest in the tabernacle;[98] and the mention of Samson).[99] Knox admitted problems, particularly quotations from books which the Samaritans (who valued only the Pentateuch) would not have regarded as authoritative and the mention of "heavenly Jerusalem" in 12:22 (the Samaritans rejected Jerusalem and Zion as the true place for worship in favor of their temple on Mt. Gerizim). "But we cannot suppose," he rejoined, "that the Samaritan Christians stood out against the belief of the rest of the Church either in the matter of canonical books or of the heavenly Jerusalem as equivalent to the city of God."[100]

Except for a few passing suggestions by R. Trotter,[101] J. MacDonald[102] and S. J. Isser,[103] Knox's theory lay dormant for almost fifty years until it was revived by C. H. H. Scobie[104] in 1973. Scobie argued that Acts 7, the Fourth Gospel and Hebrews are best understood as reflecting special Samaritan concerns. He attempted to update Knox's suggestion in the light of recent studies into Samaritan history and theology.[105]

The case for a Samaritan background

Scobie's arguments, acknowledged favourably by several recent writers,[106] may be treated under the following points.

Angels
Auctor devotes considerable space to Christ's superiority to angels (1:1–2:18). Angels figure prominently in Samaritan literature.[107]

Moses

In Samaritan thought Moses is the only true prophet and the greatest of God's creations. He is almost divine. In Heb. 3 *Auctor* contrasts Christ with Moses: Christ is Son over God's house, while Moses is only a servant in God's house (3:1–6). Scobie thinks it probable that the recipients of the epistle held to "the Second-Moses concept."[108] In Samaritan literature Moses is frequently depicted as God's servant, and in *Amram Darah* and *Memar Marqah* he is the "Son of God's House" and "apostle," key terms of Heb. 3:1–6.[109] Also striking is *Memar Marqah* IV.6: "Where is there the like of Moses ... the faithful one of his House, who dwelt among the angels in the Sanctuary of the Unseen? ... He was a holy priest in two sanctuaries."[110] This links five themes of special interest to *Auctor* ("faithful one of God's house," Heb. 3:3ff.; angels, Heb. 1:4–2:16, 12:22; the "unseen," Heb. 11:1, 27; priest in heaven, Heb. 4:14, etc.; and two sanctuaries, Heb. 8:5ff.).

Joshua

In Samaritan thought Joshua is given high honor, and is occasionally identified with the Taheb.[111] Outside of the Hexateuch, Joshua is only mentioned three times in the Bible: 1 Kings 16:34, Acts 7:45 and Heb. 4:8.

David

Davidic Messianic conceptions were "anathema"[112] to the Samaritans, which could explain *Auctor*'s relative silence on this subject.

Priesthood

Samaritan life centered on the high priest, and special significance was attached to the day of atonement. This could provide the source of one of the central emphases of the epistle.[113]

Two worlds

Numerous passages in Samaritan literature reflect an interest in Platonic philosophical speculation, especially the notion of creation from "prototypes"[114] and the concept of "two worlds."[115] MacDonald[116] uses the Samaritans to illustrate "the indebtedness to Greek philosophies in the early centuries A.D. in Palestine." Scobie[117] implies – without so stating – that "the influence of Platonic thought" in *Marqah* is another point which suggests "an earlier common background"[118] between Hebrews and the Samaritans.

Melchizedek
In connection with Heb. 5−7 Scobie[119] cites a fragmentary work of probable Samaritan provenance, Pseudo-Eupolemos, which mentions Melchizedek and links him with Mount Gerizim.

The tabernacle
Auctor's interest in the tabernacle instead of the temple could be said to reflect a Samaritan concern, since the Samaritans rejected the Jerusalem temple, and some Samaritan sources linked the tabernacle to Mt. Gerizim.[120] Following a suggestion of P. Kahle, Scobie[121] thinks that the apparent placing of the altar of incense *inside* the Holy of Holies in Heb. 9:3f. reflects a reading of the Samaritan pentateuch, in which Ex. 30:1−10 (the description of the incense altar) comes *between* Ex. 26:35 and 36 − "It follows immediately upon the description of the veil which separates off the Holy of Holies."[122]

The roll-call of faith
Scobie[123] thinks that Heb. 11 indicates a Samaritan view of history, especially in its omission of Aaron and Phineas ("names redolent of controversy between Jew and Samaritan"), the concentration on the judges (especially Samson, the "last of the kings"),[124] the mention of Joseph (father of the northern tribes of Ephraim and Manasseh), and the winding down of Jewish history almost precisely (as with Acts 7) with the building of the temple.

The case against a Samaritan background

Scobie has presented in brief compass the outlines of what appears to be a respectable case for the background of Hebrews. No one, however, has subjected the theory to a systematic criticism.

Angels
I have noted elsewhere[125] that *Auctor*'s interest in angels results from (1) their presence in Ps. 8 (2:6−8) and (2) their role as mediators of the first covenant, 2:2. Ps. 8, as a non-canonical text for Samaritans, played no role in their thinking. In previous backgrounds I have explained similarities with Hebrews as arising from an independent use of the OT. But in the case of angels it is difficult even to speak

of a common use of the OT by *Auctor* and the Samaritans. Particularly damaging to this background is *Auctor*'s utilization of the tradition that angels mediated the Torah at Sinai,[126] an idea entirely alien to Samaritan thought. For the Samaritans angels were present at Sinai, but only as passive *witnesses*[127] of the events which were then taking place:

> It is noteworthy that according to most Judaist tradition relevant to the subject it was angels who actually did the writing of the Ten Words and not God himself. These traditions no doubt reflect the age-old desire to avoid anthropomorphic expressions. The whole point about the Samaritan view of the law-giving is that it was an act that took place between God and Moses. After all, Moses was the Word and he was God's man in the lower world. *With such a point of view the Samaritans could not for a moment entertain the idea that angels could intervene between God and His Apostle.* This truth ... is foundational to Samaritan thinking about God and his salvation of men.[128]

Auctor, on the other hand, says that the Mosaic revelation came *through* (διά) angels (2:2). This idea is the linchpin of the first two chapters, an argument which contrasts Christ and the angels as *mediators* of their respective revelations (δι' ἀγγέλων ... διὰ τοῦ κυρίου, 2:2f.). If no Samaritan could accept the notion that angels intervened at Sinai, is it likely that *Auctor* would have employed this argument before a Samaritan audience, whether Christian or not? With regard to the use of two citations from the prophets in Acts 7 (which he also thinks is Samaritan), Scobie[129] suggests that "possibly one 'price of admission' into the Christian church for the Samaritans was the acceptance of post-pentateuchal writings." But was part of that "price of admission" also the acceptance of angels as mediators of the Torah? This notion could be said to be peripheral to the theology of Jewish Christianity (as would not be the case of the acceptance of the canon), and it is difficult to think of it as a point on which Samaritan converts would be pressured to give way. It may be that a "Samaritan" background for Hebrews founders on this single point.[130]

Moses

According to MacDonald, "the whole [Samaritan] creed is centred on its second tenet, belief in Moses. The exaltation of Moses is not matched in Jewish faith."[131] Accordingly, in Samaritan texts Moses is equated with the pre-existent light of creation in Gen. 1.[132] *Marqah* can actually say that it was for Moses' sake that God made the world.[133] Moses' birth is thus an advent of "the Lord of the world." When God decided to send Moses earthward, he sent an angel to Amram to announce the event.[134] Here is another distance between the extant Samaritan literature and Hebrews. There is no evidence that *Auctor* is polemicizing against such a view. The view of Moses in Hebrews is generally high; anything pejorative said about him probably concerns his role as representative of an obsolete covenant (3:1–6, 8:5) rather than as a super-being who poses a threat to Christ. Most significantly, when *Auctor* treats Moses' birth (11:23) there is no hint of anything other than a straight reading of the OT narrative (Ex. 2:1f.LXX), no awareness of a belief of his readers in an "incarnation" of the pre-existent light of Gen. 1. Nor can it be said that *Auctor* has taken over the Samaritan view of Moses in his presentation of the pre-existent and incarnate Christ, since this language is better explained from other sources.[135] "Son of God's house" and "apostle" in the third- and fourth-century Samaritan texts *Marqah* and *Amram Darah* may well reflect the influence of *Auctor* upon Samaritan sources rather than *vice versa*.[136] A contrast of Christ with Moses, furthermore, is hardly unique to a Samaritan background, since it could equally issue from contact with Philonism,[137] Pauline theology (see 2 Cor. 3:7ff.), or Johannine theology (see John 1:16, 6:32, etc.). There is nothing in *Auctor*'s portrait of Moses which is *better* answered by a Samaritan background than any of these backgrounds.

Joshua

The reference to Joshua in Heb. 4:8 is an incidental allusion in connection with "rest"; it issues from *Auctor*'s treatment of Ps. 95, another text not recognized by Samaritans. There is no evidence of preconceptions on the part of the readers concerning the figure of Joshua which affects the argument.

David

The omission of David in Hebrews probably results, as with Acts 7,[138] from David's undesirable associations with earthly security and power, a clinging to which *Auctor* discourages. There is no reason to introduce notions of Samaritan antipathy to David resulting from the Jerusalem–Gerizim dispute.

Priesthood

Auctor's interest in Christ *qua* priest is best understood as resulting from his attempt to understand the fourth verse of one of the most popular early Christian testimonies, Ps. 110. To explain it as issuing as well from a concern with the Samaritan priesthood multiplies hypotheses.

Two worlds

While MacDonald has argued convincingly for an influence of Platonic speculation on Samaritan sources, the evidence for Platonism in Hebrews is weaker than was once thought.[139]

Melchizedek

The point made above applies here as well. *Auctor*, furthermore, gives no hint of an interest in linking Melchizedek to any particular *place*, whether Gerizim or Zion. His interest is in the basis and the durability of the priesthood of the figure mentioned in Ps. 110:4.

The tabernacle

Auctor's concern with the tabernacle issues from his attempt to interpret from a Christian viewpoint various OT institutions which he found in his LXX. His main interest is a comparison of the two covenants, and this leads him to those sections of the LXX which describe the institution of the first covenant. It is therefore natural that the tabernacle, and not the temple, is the focus of his remarks. His fascination with this period of Jewish history may also result, as W. Manson[140] suggests, from an interest in the OT theme of sojourning and pilgrimage, which he possibly inherited from the Stephen tradition. This notion is antithetical to the stationary temple. It is worth noting that the Samaritans were not opposed to the temple *on principle* – its proper location was Gerizim, not Jerusalem.[141] To say that *Auctor* polemicizes against such a view would again be a multiplication of hypotheses. His remarks are adequately explained from OT statements.

The roll call of faith

In ch. 11 *Auctor* is attempting to trace the history of faith in his LXX. In this light it is hardly remarkable that Joseph and the judges should be mentioned. *Auctor* clearly states that his reason for breaking off when he does is lack of time (11:32; cf. 13:22).[142] *Pace* Knox, Samson is only one judge mentioned among several, with no hint of any special interest in him.

To these observations should be added the following: (a) The portrait of Christ in Hebrews is unlike what was probably the earliest Samaritan concept of the Taheb − a "restorer" and "revealer" (cf. John 4:25), and no more.[143] Contrary to the view of Christ in Hebrews, God did not delegate his authority to the Taheb. Nor is there any evidence that the picture of Christ in Hebrews is intended as a *polemic* against the Samaritan view of the Taheb.[144] Christ as God's appointed ruler in Hebrews is drawn primarily from the exegesis of two psalms (8 and 110) which had already been adopted by Christians as relevant for Christ. There is no need for any "Samaritan" influences.[145] (b) Perhaps because they were not considered to be true Jews by those at Jerusalem, the Samaritans were relatively Gentile-conscious. On the Samaritan day of vengeance, it is notable that the Gentiles are the chief objects of retribution. Thus the coming day constitutes "a field day for Israel," and things go badly for Gentiles. "An evil smell comes from their graves and they emerge tattered ... they are ready for the burning of the fire, where they will be speedily consumed ..."[146] Here is one more divergence from the atmosphere of Hebrews. *Auctor shows no Gentile consciousness.* Those who suffer God's burning judgment are depicted in a context of *Jewish* disobedience, and in 10:30 God's vengeance is upon his people, not the Gentiles. (c) The dating of Samaritan literature is another problem. Our earliest sources (e.g., *Memar Marqah*) are assigned to the late third or early fourth centuries, and MacDonald repeatedly stresses that they may reflect Christian influence.[147] The homogeneity of the material is also questionable. Bowman[148] is skeptical of "the unity of Samaritan eschatological doctrine even before Abisha." Scobie[149] claims that in some texts the Taheb is linked with Joshua, while in others he is Moses *Redivivus*.[150] But with what confidence can we claim to reconstruct "a Samaritan theology" for the first century A.D. with which to compare Hebrews, when that reconstruction may be based upon late, Christian-influenced, and ultimately irreconcilable sources? (d) If Hebrews were written to Samaritan converts, the mention of the city to come as "Mount Zion" and "heavenly Jerusalem" (12:22) seems unnecessarily provocative. Scobie[151] says that *Auctor* avoided Aaron and Phineas in Heb. 11 because "they are names redolent of controversy between Jew and Samaritan"; but it is not clear why the same principle would not apply to "Mount Zion" and "heavenly Jerusalem" (or, for that matter, to angels as mediators of the Torah). (e) It may be that acceptance of post-pentateuchal writings was a "price of admission" for Samaritans into the church. But that *Auctor* builds virtually his entire argument[152] (all five of his main texts fall outside the Pentateuch − Ps. 8, 110, 95, 40 and Jer. 31) upon OT passages which the projected readers had not, in their pre-conversion days, accepted as authoritative seems at least insensitive to peculiar Samaritan inclinations and biases.

Conclusion for a Samaritan background

In the light of the above, it seems difficult not to conclude that, while at first blush a Samaritan background may contain certain perspectives for an understanding of the epistle, in the end it brings one no closer in our search than did Philo, Qumran or pre-Christian gnosticism, and at at least one point − the angels of Heb. 2:2 − a Samaritan background actually seems to be ruled out.

3 Merkabah mysticism

The year 1976 saw yet another background suggested for Hebrews. Several years earlier H.-M. Schenke[153] had suggested that *Auctor* was influenced by an early form of Jewish *Merkabah* mysticism. R. Williamson,[154] who had earlier dealt with the Philonic background of Hebrews, took up this suggestion and developed it. The same year Hofius,[155] questioning why *Auctor* is so concerned with the angels, came out strongly in favor of *Merkabah* mysticism as the answer.

The case for *Merkabah* mysticism

Of the three writers Williamson has provided the most comprehensive statement of this hypothesis. His case is essentially cumulative, and may be represented as follows.

"For the *Merkabah* mystic 'God's pre-existing throne ... is at once the goal and theme of his mystical vision.' "[156] *Auctor* shows an interest in God's throne (1:3, 6; 4:16; 8:1; 12:2).

The *Merkabah* mystic emphasizes God's majesty, holiness and transcendent glory. "The work of Christ, a priestly mediator between earth and heaven, is described as the bringing of many sons 'to glory' (2:10)."[157]

In *Merkabah* mysticism God is frequently connected with the image of *fire* (see, e.g., Ḥagigah 14b).

As noted, *angels* play an important role in *Merkabah* mysticism. These angels consist of those who form the heavenly chariot, the "ministering angels" around the heavenly throne, Metatron and Sandalfon. *Auctor* likewise dwells much on angels (1:4–14) who are "ministering spirits" (1:14).

The *Merkabah* mystic placed much emphasis on a journey through the heavens, with the heavenly curtain and the throne of God as the goal. The curtain was the symbol of "the last secrets of heaven and earth which are kept with God, hidden ever from the angels."[158] According to Williamson, Christ is superior in Hebrews in that "he alone can conduct the worshipper through the heavens and the curtain into the presence of God."

In Hebrews "the athletic ascent"[159] or "athletic pilgrimage"[160] to the city of God is led by a πρόδρομος or "forerunner" (6:20). This would be of special concern for someone from a background of *Merkabah* mysticism.

The "numinous hymns" of the *Merkabah* mystic enabled him to participate in the angelic liturgy.[161] In Hebrews, Christians participate "through him" in Christ's priestly functions, offer the sacrifices of 13:15ff., and share in the heavenly altar of 13:10. For Williamson, 3:14 ("we share in Christ") means "a relationship between Christian 'high priests' and their one great High Priest similar to that between the *Merkabah* mystic and his angelic guide through the heavens."[162]

In *Numbers Rabbah* Metatron offers the souls of the righteous on the heavenly altar to atone for Israel's sins. Williamson sees a "close similarity" between this picture and that of Christians in Hebrews.'[163]

"The language of praise" is the native language of the *Merkabah* mystic, and in 10:25 Christians are to meet in order to offer up sacrifices of praise.

In *Merkabah* mysticism little emphasis is placed upon the *love* of God, and the same may be said of *Auctor*.

The case against *Merkabah* mysticism

There is a basic attractiveness to this particular collection of parallels. It would certainly provide some rationale for *Auctor*'s talk of a heavenly cultus. Williamson, on the other hand, admits what is certainly the most damaging objection to his case. All of his similarities may be explained "simply on the basis of a common indebtedness to the Old Testament."[164] He adds, unfortunately, that "the large number of terms, themes and ideas common to Hebrews and the Merkabah literature ... makes a direct relationship between them *likely*."[165] The latter assertion will be difficult for many to accept. Nowhere are the OT texts which one normally associates with the later phenomenon of *Merkabah* mysticism (e.g., Dan. 7,[166] Isa. 6, Ps. 97,[167] Ezek. 1) quoted or even alluded to by *Auctor*. Williamson[168] admits that *Auctor*'s idea of Christ's sacrifice offered in heaven "probably entered the thought-world of Hebrews from another direction" than *Merkabah* mysticism. I would wish to extend this to the larger argument: most of the same themes are found in the psalms (with which we know *Auctor* was familiar) or the apocalyptic tradition. The psalms in which *Auctor* was interested contain many of the terms and ideas which also occur in the *Merkabah* literature (e.g., Ps. 110:1, "throne"; Ps. 8, "angels"; Ps. 8, "glory"; Ps. 95, pilgrimage; Ps. 40, spiritual sacrifice), but these psalms do not expand or dwell upon such terms in the same way or to the same extent as the later mystics. A clear allusion to one of the *"Merkabah"* oriented passages of the OT, or the production of a feature within the argument of Hebrews which could not be answered by either the OT or the apocalyptic tradition, would have strengthened Williamson's case considerably. Unfortunately he provides neither.

Conclusion for *Merkabah* mysticism

Williamson is aware that most of the literature he uses for his parallels with Hebrews is later than the NT, and in his search for first-century antecedents he appeals, e.g., to Talmudic literature, Qumran, the Therapeutae and Paul.[169] One is thus confronted with a similar problem to that raised by the gnostic background: Was there in the first century an entity which may confidently be labeled as *"Merkabah* mysticism,"* with which Hebrews may be compared in the same way it is compared with Philo, Qumran, Paul, Acts 7, etc.? As Scholem[170] has observed, in the Second Temple period there existed among the rabbis an esoteric doctrine which focused upon the mysteries of Gen. 1 and Ezek. 1; but, as with the mystery religions, the fact that these interests were kept secret means that we know virtually nothing about them today. Scholem[171] suggests a direct line between "the old apocalyptics," "the Merkabah speculation of the Mishnaic teachers," and the later post-Talmudic *Merkabah* mysticism, arguing that such a progression proves that "all the productive religious energies of early apocalyptic" were not absorbed exclusively by Christianity. Such a reconstruction would mean that some of the early evidence used by Williamson to suggest a first-century form of *"Merkabah* mysticism" could with equal legitimacy be understood as one element within the larger phenomenon of early Jewish apocalyptic. In this case it may be better, recalling the above distinctions with reference to gnosticism, to speak of "pre-*Merkabah*" tendencies *within* Jewish apocalyptic which may then have gone on to influence *Auctor*.

PART 2

CHRISTIAN BACKGROUNDS

4

THE STEPHEN TRADITION

1 History of discussion

The speech of Acts 7 is one of the peculiarities of the New Testament. Many think that it stands unique among the speeches of Acts, and attempts to explain its purpose, background and idiosyncrasies have occupied more studies than any other Lucan discourse.[1] The interest which this "manifesto"[2] of early Christianity has engendered among modern biblical interpreters has led inevitably to a comparison of Acts 7 and Hebrews. Yet, since no consensus regarding the background and significance of the speech seems likely, it is not surprising that there is little agreement regarding a possible relationship to Hebrews.[3]

The best-known argument for Acts 7 and Hebrews remains William Manson's Baird Lecture for 1949. According to Manson, it was Stephen who first *"grasped and asserted the more-than-Jewish-Messianic sense in which the office and significance of Jesus in Religious history were to be understood."*[4] The "universalist" stance of Stephen and the "Hellenists," moreover, is to be distinguished from that of the "Hebrew" (Galilean) Christians of Jerusalem, who, still bound to the static temple and law, were waiting for the Kingdom to be restored to Israel.[5] Stephen's speech, a historically reliable report of the "Hellenist" teaching,[6] thus reflects a primitive breach within Christianity; Stephen's dying vision discloses him as an eschatologist who "saw that the Messiah was on the throne of the universe."[7] This meant it was time to recall the people of God to their pilgrim origins, and, like Abraham, to "go out" in order to *"anticipate the Son of Man's coming by proclaiming Him to every nation and people ... now included in His dominion."*[8] Such an emphasis on advance explains Stephen's stress on the wilderness period (with its mobile sanctuary) and his hostility to the static temple and the earthly security it invites.[9]

It is in this tradition, claims Manson, that *Auctor* stands. Ideas "uncoloured by Paulinism ... had come, through Stephen, as a direct heritage from the church at Jerusalem."[10] They form the "matrix within which the theological ideas elaborated in Hebrews first took shape."[11] In attempting to reconstruct the specific situation addressed by *Auctor*, Manson formed the important corollary that, wherever it existed, Jewish Christianity tended to separate into two parties corresponding to the primitive division reflected in the early chapters of Acts.[12] It was a minority within the church at Rome which, "asserting principles and counter-claims akin to those of the original 'Hebrew' section in the Jerusalem Church,"[13] produced the need for Hebrews. By returning to the example of the wilderness generation, says Manson,[14] *Auctor* warns these Jewish converts of the dangers of "living in the past" and of "holding on to old securities."[15]

Manson has assembled what seems to be an impressive list of correspondences between Acts 7 and Hebrews.[16] Some, however, are convinced that his argument is circular – that he has read Stephen in the light of Hebrews, and that some of the parallels are trivial and accidental.[17] Others, accepting the basic premise, demur at points of detail.[18] A careful examination of this important thesis is still wanting.

2 Acts 7 in Lucan redaction

An attempt to examine Manson's hypothesis will first need to ascertain what Luke is doing with the speech in Acts 7. It has been argued[19] that Luke is using a source (although whether that source can be linked with a wing of the early church known as "Hellenists" is less commonly agreed upon).[20] This at least seems foundational to Manson's thesis. If one is dealing in Acts 7 only with Luke, then any correspondences would have to be traced between Hebrews and Luke rather than between Hebrews and any one Jew, or group of Jews, within or on the fringes of the early Jerusalem church. This would alter Manson's case to the point of making it unrecognizable. I cannot treat here the complexities involved in proving that a source lies behind Acts 7, or that Acts 7 goes back to the historical Stephen or the group known as "Hellenists";[21] I will, however, maintain that even if the source hypothesis is granted, it should also be stressed that Luke has redacted this source into his general purpose so that it is saying what he wants it to say. Our position, consequently, will be a more modest form of Manson's hypothesis, namely that the use of certain Old Testament traditions in Acts 7 comes at points rather close to the same emphases one finds in Hebrews.

The point at which one should begin, as G. N. Stanton[22] has demonstrated, is a recognition that in Acts 7 the normal picture which is drawn – that the chapter stands unique in Acts in depicting a hostility to both law and temple – is surely wrong. Stanton rejects the usual disconnection of the speech from its context in chapter 6, stressing that, apart from certain anomalies, the speech reflects Lucan style and theology.[23] He relates the charges brought against Stephen in 6:13f. to similar charges made against Jesus and Paul in Luke–Acts, noting that in the case of Jesus and Paul Luke goes out of his way to show the charges to be false (cp. especially Acts 6:13 with Acts 21:28). The charges brought against Stephen then, from a redactional perspective, are *ipso facto* capable of the same interpretation, and this is precisely what is borne out by a careful study of Acts 7. Here I shall attempt to expose what the speech actually says about the primary institutions of Israel.

The view of the law in Acts 7

Contrary to many,[24] the persecution of Stephen and the church[25] (Acts 8:1) cannot have been intended by Luke to have arisen from the view of the law itself reflected in Acts 7. The law there is held high: it was of divine origin (v. 53) and valid (v. 38).[26] The charge of 6:14b has been explained by the future tense: the implication of Jesus' teaching *will* inevitably affect any future approach to the law.[27] However, such an idea is hardly explicit. This is one reason why it is difficult to connect the speech with the picture drawn of the Hellenists by Manson and others. On the other hand, since it is possible that the Hellenistic synagogues were *stricter* in their law observance than were the "Hebrew" synagogues of Jerusalem[28] (and since Stephen was said to have been facing a charge of antinomianism), one purpose of the speech in Luke's scheme may have been to show Stephen's accord with his colleagues, i.e., that the charge against him is patently false. It is unlikely that this question will ever be resolved so as to fit completely the usual picture of any "progressive" wing in Acts such as is assumed by Manson. Schmithals observes that if one takes the speech seriously as a document of the "Hellenists," the split can "hardly have lain in the greater or lesser extent to which the law *was observed*."[29] Thus, even if Luke wishes his readers to see the difference between "Hebrew" and "Hellenist" Christians as one of attitude, to make the point of departure the speech's attitude toward the law is clearly impossible. As is seen in Philo,[30] a radical spiritualizing of the law, while at the same time urging that it be kept entirely as a token of the truths to which it pointed, is quite admissible in Judaism.

The view of the temple in Acts 7

This is also a source of enormous debate. Many detect in vv. 47–50 a hostility to the temple itself. Gaston[31] and others see Stephen as representing "the climax of a growing opposition to the Temple among certain groups within Judaism," while Moule thinks Isa. 66:1–4 indicates a form of "Quaker Judaism," "opposed to the temple cultus on principle," which existed even in OT times.[32] My question, however, is this: Does Acts 7 stand in a thoroughly *well-precedented* prophetic tradition, or does it stand as a radical new element in Judaism which transcends anything going before?[33] It has been argued that χειροποίητος in v. 48 sees the temple as an act of idolatry, since in the LXX (e.g., Lev. 26:1, Isa. 46:6) and Philo (*De vit. M.* I.303, II.165ff.) the term is connected with idolatry.[34] Simon, noting Acts 7:41, views the speech as putting the construction of the temple on the same level as making the calf.[35] (1) That χειροποίητος always denotes idolatry is not true. Philo (*De vit. M.* II.88) calls the temple a ἱερὸν χειροποίητον.[36] *Auctor*, closer to Acts 7 at this point than is Philo, also calls the tabernacle χειροποίητος (Heb. 9:11, 24), and few argue that *Auctor* saw the building of the tabernacle as idolatrous.[37] (2) As Manson[38] and Stanton[39] rightly observe, the point of vv. 47ff. is not condemnation of the temple *per se*, but a reaffirmation that the temple was never intended, "any more than the Tabernacle, to become a *permanent* institution halting the advance of the divine plan for the people of God."[40] Contra Simon, the inferiority of the temple lay not in its being "made by hands," whereas the latter was not (Acts 7 is certainly in line with the view of *Auctor* that the tabernacle was also "made by hands"), or in God's living in one and not in the other, but in the fact that, by its very nature, the wilderness tent pointed *away* from a static quality of earthly life. Its function was as the tent of witness (v. 44), and its comparatively modest nature testified that God cannot be confined to any earthly place or institution.[41] The problem of a stone house is that, while in itself it may be good,[42] it tempts one in the opposite direction. This is why Solomon is never actually condemned. His own warning is quoted (1 Kings 8:27). Stanton has thus rightly argued that Acts 7:44–50 is not an attack on the temple – "There is no indication that in building the temple Solomon was disobedient."[43]

An appreciation of Luke's redactional purpose is at this point crucial. Luke's problem is the belief that *only at Jerusalem* can true worship be offered. "No centre of worship has priority over others."[44] In the Lucan scheme, then, the destruction of the temple is not ultimately disastrous, "since from the beginning God has never shared Israel's excessive veneration for it."[45] Elsewhere in Acts Paul's "defilement of this holy place" is recorded (Acts 21:2), but clearly this is a *false* charge.[46] Paul never brought a Gentile into the court of the Israelites. In Acts 7:49, furthermore, God asks "where is the place of my rest?" (quoting Isa. 66:1), implying that there is none; but the idea is not that God does not rest, but that his rest cannot be limited *to any one place on earth*. In Acts chapter 7 it is the building of a stationary house which, leading one to ignore this divine quality, forms the gravamen of the complaint. Had the temple been viewed as a *provisional* place where God's "name" was (which, if removed, would mean nothing decisive for true worship), there would have been no case. It was the elevation of the temple to an exclusive and indispensable dwelling which led to the subject of the murder of the prophets.[47]

Thus Acts 7 constitutes "an attack on the fundamental position of the Temple in the Judaism *of that time*."[48] But, as Dunn[49] suggests, since "so much of the Temple is bound up with the sacrificial system," any devaluation of it "was bound to lead sooner or later to a questioning of the law as a whole." This may well be the correct way forward. Acts 7 cannot *itself* be said to disparage the law, but its various emphases (particularly those of exodus, forward progress and an interest in the spiritual nature of God and his demands) might lead to the movement which the Hellenists are represented by Luke as undertaking.

The view of mission in Acts 7

As in the case of the law, the supposition that Stephen or the Hellenists had a different attitude to mission cannot be proven from Acts 7. There is no indication of its views about Gentiles.[50] On the other hand, the emphasis on Israel outside of the land accords well with

"Diaspora Judaism," which had more contact with proselytes and God-fearers. Certainly Luke, whose main redactional concern in Acts is to depict the progress of the gospel, regards the speech, from the amount of space he devotes to it (one-twentieth of Acts, according to Stanton) as a major advance. His relating of the first mention of Paul's name to it is a clear redactional alignment of the speech with the Pauline and not the Petrine thrust of early Christianity.[51] It may be concluded, therefore, that while a Gentile concern *per se* cannot be argued for the speech, elements which could have catalyzed a Gentile mission can be found.[52] Thus Luke has skilfully redacted it into his overall purpose − that of the gospel penetrating beyond the bounds of recalcitrant Judaism.

3 Points of contact

It remains now to examine points of contact between the distinctive use of OT traditions in Acts 7 and those in Hebrews. Manson[53] has listed eight places where he feels the emphases of Acts 7 recur in Hebrews:

(1) the attitude of Stephen to the Cultus and Law of Judaism;
(2) his declaration that Jesus means to change and supersede these things;
(3) his sense of the divine call to the people of God being a call to "Go out";
(4) his stress on the ever-shifting scene in Israel's life, and on the ever-renewed homelessness of the faithful;
(5) his thought of God's word as "living";
(6) his incidental allusion to Joshua in connection with the promise of God's "Rest";
(7) his idea of the "angels" being the ordainers of God's Law;
(8) his directing of his eyes to Heaven and to Jesus;

This list may be slightly altered, and to it may be added one other:

(9) the citation of Ex. 25:40.

The approach I will take to Manson's parallels in this study may be clearly stated. Although there is little specifically Christian in the speech of Acts 7,[54] it does contain distinctive uses of the OT which are also characteristic of Hebrews. One way to support this claim would be to take Manson's argument point by point, although great care needs to be taken along the way.

The attitude to the cult and law

Here Manson made no distinction between the Mosaic law and temple. They must, however, be treated separately.

The law

The view of the law in Acts 7 *and* Hebrews is that it was of divine origin and valid for its time. In Acts 7 the law is "living oracles" (v. 38). For Hebrews it is "valid" and "just" (2:2). While *Auctor* dwells more on the sacrificial aspects of law than Stephen, both would agree on the central fact that, for one reason or another, the law did not reach its goal. Acts 7 nowhere claims that "the blood of bulls and goats could never remove sin" (Heb. 10:4) or that the law dealt only with outward regulations "imposed until the time of reformation" (Heb. 9:10), but it would not be difficult to see how one influenced by the viewpoint reflected in Acts 7 would argue for an inability of the law to deal with the central problem facing mankind, hardness of heart. There is no need to contrast Acts 7 and Hebrews, as does Scharlemann,[55] by claiming that, unlike Hebrews, Acts 7 depicts that law as *never* having been kept by the Jews. Stephen's use of the second person plural ἐλάβετε (v. 53) is probably not intended to indicate Jews as a whole throughout their history — the usual assumption.[56] It is a form of retrojection which, resulting from the idea of corporate guilt, indicates a *part* of Judaism — those Jews who, by their murder of Jesus, had implicated themselves in the sins of other past reprobates (hence "sons of the murderers of the prophets"). Luke 11:47–50 provides an illuminating redactional clue: there, as in Acts 7:51–53, the hearers are called sons of the murderers of the prophets, and a similar succession of ideas occurs. In both passages the phrase "your fathers" occurs, even though Acts 7 begins with the phrase "our father" (v. 2) in referring to Abraham.[57] Perhaps even more impressive is Matthew's version of the same Q pericope (Mat. 23:29–36), which also employs the second person plural for a remote past event ("Zechariah son of Barachiah, whom *you* murdered"; cp. Acts 7:53 — "*you* who received the law"). Is it likely that Matthew saw the law throughout its history as never having been kept? Surely the viewpoint of Mat. 5:18–20 or 13:52 would rule that out. Matthew thus shows that it was possible to speak in this way *without* rejecting all Jews, and the view is strengthened that Jesus and Stephen are represented by Luke as viewing the guilt of only *part* of Judaism, i.e., past rebels, as coming upon the heads of the A.D. 30 generation. By their attitude and actions, they show themselves to be one with those who (a) killed righteous men from Abel to Zechariah, and (b) violated the law in the wilderness. These past acts may thus be attributed to them.[58] This would make Acts 7:5ff. not a blanket rejection of the Jewish people throughout their history, but an alignment of one generation with another, equally unworthy, generation. Stanton[59] notes the alignment in the speech of Stephen with Moses, who, like the prophets, Jesus and later Paul, is rejected by a *remnant* of Israel. This would indicate that in Luke's purpose Stephen was killed not so much for the way he summarized Jewish history (including *any* attitude to law and/or temple), but for the pedigree he attributed to his hearers (sons of notorious past renegades).[60] Stephen, Moses, the prophets, Jesus and Paul all share the same fate at the hands of a segment of Israel in Luke's scheme.

This appears to come close to Hebrews, where one finds repetitive *patterns* of Jewish disobedience (ὑποδείγματι τῆς ἀπειθείας, 4:11) which may be imitated by later generations.[61] *Auctor*'s stern warning to avoid implication in the sins of the past is not identical to Acts 7, however, since for the readers of Hebrews the point of no return had not yet been reached (as it had for Stephen's audience).

Moffatt,[62] on the other hand, suggests a cleavage between Acts 7 and Hebrews in that nowhere are the Jews as a people condemned: "Stephen, again, argues that believers in Jesus are the true heirs of the Old Testament spiritual revelation, not the Jews; while in πρὸς Ἑβραίους the continuity of the people is assumed, and Christians are regarded as *ipso facto* the People of God, without any allusion to the Jews having forfeited their privileges." But this rests on two misconceptions. (1) Once it is admitted that Stephen did not preach a wholesale rejection of Judaism, Moffatt's distinction between "believers in Jesus" and "the Jews" collapses. Just as the speech nowhere mentions Gentiles, neither does it say that the Jews as a nation had "forfeited their privileges." (2) As represented by Luke, probably writing after A.D. 70,[63] Acts 7 is set in Jerusalem, and the disobedience of the contemporary Jews is no doubt intended as part of his apologia for the destruction of the temple. If Hebrews was written to diaspora Jews *before* A.D. 70, however, such an emphasis would play no part in his purpose.[64] As in the case of Paul, *Auctor* could have viewed himself and his readers as among the righteous remnant, with hope still held out for Israel as a whole (cp. Rom. 10:1ff.).[65] But a failure to mention ethnic categories would not be surprising in an author who had been influenced by some form of the tradition preserved in Acts 7, which, for one reason or another, also shows no concern for this issue. Both could be said to be interested primarily in the role of Israel in God's purposes for human history.

The temple

Attempts to distinguish Acts 7 and Hebrews in their view of the Jewish temple have been based upon two unprovable assumptions. (a) Stephen condemns the temple outright, while *Auctor* does not.[66] But if the speech is seen as in line with Hebrew prophetic tradition, a tradition which rejected the elevation of the temple to an exclusive confine of God's presence, this point collapses. It is because Simon sees Acts 7 as radically antipathetic to the temple *itself*, and not to an excessive veneration of it, that the absence of this antipathy in Hebrews looms so large in his comparison of the two.[67] Here, again, the respective purpose of each would explain the difference: Stephen takes the view of the Jerusalem temple by Jews in that city as his example of a disobedient clinging to an institution which, although valid in the terms in which it was originally given, was never designed to be ultimate; *Auctor*, probably writing to people who had little contact with the temple, focuses on the biblical tabernacle. Both, however, are concerned with the same problem: *treating as final and ultimate what God intended to be earthly and provisional.*[68] For Stephen *and Auctor*, once the eschatological era has dawned, the days of the old center of worship are ended.[69] The principle is the same.[70] (b) Stephen shows no concern with a *new* temple, whereas *Auctor* does. This point has a certain force. While some have suggested that both Stephen[71] and *Auctor*[72] see the new temple as the church invisible, such a view cannot be sustained. There is nothing in Acts 7 to indicate the predication of a new temple.[73] Yet there is an appeal in both Acts 7 and Hebrews to Ex. 25:40.[74] Whereas the negative use of the text in Hebrews (to show the inferiority of the tabernacle to what was to come) is not seen in Acts 7, it remains that for both the tabernacle, which serves as the basis of the argument, points to *some* kind of transcendent reality. While it cannot be proved that for Stephen the τύπος points toward a heavenly tent, neither can it be disproved.[75]

Jesus' claim to supersede the cult and law

"A declaration that Jesus means to change and supersede the cultus and Law of Judaism" is hardly obvious in Acts 7, and seems to be drawn instead from the "false" charge of 6:14. As Cullmann[76] observes, the speech does not connect its emphases very much to the work of Christ because, as Luke depicts it, it is a speech for the defense designed to answer charges concerning law and temple. This must be viewed as one of Manson's weaker points.

Israel in motion

Manson's points (3) and (4) should be treated jointly. According to Manson, *Auctor* inherited his theme of the transient nature of the Christian life on earth from Stephen's emphasis upon the "homelessness" and "ever-shifting" quality of Israel's life. The readers of Hebrews were not in danger of falling away: they were in danger of not going forward. Acts 7 focuses on OT examples which illustrate that God's revelation is independent of any one place. God appears to Abraham in Mesopotamia (v. 2), he prepares Moses in Egypt (vv. 21f.), land in Arabia is called "holy" (v. 33), God announces his removal of his people "beyond Babylon" (v. 43), and the tabernacle is constantly in motion.[77] While admittedly these can all be found in the OT,[78] it is the particular selection and balance of the speech which is striking. The emphasis of Heb. 11:10, 14–16, 23–31 and 13:12–14 upon the independence of true faith from any earthly place, including even the earthly Jerusalem itself, while not demonstrably derived from Acts 7, is so much like it as to make Manson's case credible. The depiction of the wandering Israelites as "the church in the wilderness" inevitably calls to mind Heb. 3:7–4:11 and 13:11–13.[79] "The author, following Stephen's general approach, calls on them to march on the promised land of *spiritual* inheritance and not to go back into *material* Judaism which is just about to be destroyed."[80] For Moule[81] all of the heroes of Acts 7 reject the static life for the forward call of God. The people of God must be ready to "pull up their tent-stakes," says Bruce.[82] Munck urges that the speech, with its emphasis upon "fugitive Israel serving God in a strange land," occupies for Luke the transition from the Jerusalem church to the world-wide mission of Acts 1:8.[83] Davies[84] similarly sees Acts 7 as raising "the question of [the relationship of] the gospel to non-palestinian Jews, if not to Gentiles", and he expresses indebtedness to Manson at this point.

Such a view has been strongly attacked by Simon and Scharlemann, whose arguments may be summarized thus: (a) Stephen appears to approve of the settlement into the land. In 7:5 the entry into the land is promised to Abraham's posterity, and in v. 45 entry into the land is accompanied by their dispossessing "the nations." "Stephen describes the patriarchs and their descendants as people on the move. The story, however, comes to rest in Canaan with the conquest of Israel's enemies .. Stephen's discourse contains no hint of moving out of the land where his hearers lived."[85] So too for Stanton, who mentions that in Acts 7 "there is no attempt to hide the fact that God's promise to Abraham that his people would possess the land was fulfilled – indeed fulfilment of the promise is stressed."[86] For Simon the promise "implies at least some amount of 'fixture,' although it certainly does not legitimize the building of the temple."[87] Acts 7, therefore, is interested in movement toward a goal, but that goal was achieved by entry into the land: no further seeking after a "heavenly goal" is enjoined.[88] (b) In Acts 7 the repeated sin of the Jews cannot have been a resisting of the "ever-onward call" or "supra-historical purpose of God," since "Israel's sin and apostasy had begun long before the Hebrews became sedentary, at the very time when they were marching out of Egypt ... the sin of the Jews consisted much more ... in opposing and disobeying the saviours sent by God and, consequently, in becoming idolators, first when they worshipped the calf and later when they built the temple."[89] (c) Hebrews itself is not as interested in the motifs of pilgrimage and homelessness as is often assumed. Scharlemann[90] attacks Käsemann[91] for including in a list of verbs denoting "movement" in Hebrews the term προσέρχομαι (10:22, 11:6, 12:18, 22), which, he argues, refers to the cultic notion of access into God's presence and not to any idea of "forward progress." Moses (11:27) and the prophets (11:38) were forced into movement, furthermore, not by any sense of homelessness, but by threat of persecution.[92] The concern of ch. 4 is not with movement *per se*, but with failing to obey God's voice.[93] Hebrews is interested in its readers remaining firm in the Christian tradition, not in any idea of "going out."[94]

These points are impressive and must be given some weight. They do not, however, necessarily constitute the end of Manson's case. The emphasis of the promise to Abraham (v. 7) seems to be shifted in Acts 7: the idea is now not the inheriting of the land but deliverance from enemies and the opportunity for unhindered worship (cf. Luke 1:73f.[95]).[96] The use of Deut. 2:5 to underscore absolutely that Abraham owned no land is significant.[97] Abraham purchases burial ground not at Hebron but at Shechem (Samaria). Israel's punishment for her disobedience is not said to be temporary exclusion from the land, but being handed over to worship the host of heaven (v. 42). The settlement into the land in v. 45, furthermore, is brought into the discussion not as an end in itself, but only as something which leads to the gravamen of the complaint, the temple and its veneration.[98] Thus, Moffatt is forced to conclude, in Acts 7 the possession of the land was not "final." This certainly would seem to be the correct interpretation. The change in v. 43 of "beyond Damascus" to "beyond Babylon" points decisively to the diaspora. Acts 7:5 is generally agreed to be a quotation of the promise of Gen. 17:8, but the subtle elimination of permanence (implied by the Hebrew *olam* and the LXX αἰώνιος in the Genesis text) does not escape notice. An equally subtle injection of a temporal dimension into the Jews' possession of the land may be suggested by the addition of νῦν to κατοικεῖτε in Acts 7:4 ("*now* dwell"), which could point to past and future dispersions. Also, in terms of proportion, the speech *does* depict the history of Israel as one of movement; it begins winding down precisely at the point of entry into the land. The repetition of verbs of movement is striking,[99] showing the idea to be as prominent in Acts 7 as in Hebrews, which has its own impressive collection of such terms.[100] Finally,[101] Scharlemann's argument that in Hebrews the Old Testament heroes "went out" because of threat of persecution rather than any inherent attitude is misleading. It is because they had *already* decided to make their stand against the *status quo* (cf. Moses) that the threat of persecution had arisen in the first place.

The case of Manson, Moule, Munck and Davies therefore may not be lightly dismissed. Despite minor differences between Acts 7 and Hebrews, evidence exists for Manson's idea that they agree sufficiently in their picture of the people of God as pilgrims, habitually jettisoning earthly fixtures and following God's lead, to make a case for some kind of relationship reasonable.

God's "living" word

The unusual depiction of God's word as "living" in Acts 7:38 seems to be repeated in Heb. 4:12.[102] Scharlemann inadvertently underscores the uniqueness of this parallel by adducing texts from

Samaritan literature which he thinks are closest to Acts, but which are, in fact, irrelevant.[103] More to the point is Deut. 32:47LXX: "For this is no vain word (λόγος κενός) to you; it is your life (ζωή), and because of this word you shall live long upon the land ..." The juxtaposition of a "vain" word with one which "lives" (or "operates") is seen, e.g., in Sophocles, *Oed. Rex* 481f., where ζῶντα is used with μαντεῖα to mean "living auguries" (those which come true, as opposed to those which have no substance).[104] This is probably the usage of the term in Acts 7; the words delivered by Moses were not vain or inoperative,[105] but accomplished what they indicated. This, therefore, made the Jews' rebellion against them all the more serious (see also 7:53). There are good reasons for seeing Deut. 32:47 as the background of Stephen's statement. It comes at the end of Moses' song in Deut. 32, which is largely concerned with Israel's disobedience in the face of the deliverance of the law (see, e.g., v. 17: "They sacrificed to foreign demons, Gods who were strangers to them"; cp. Acts 7:42f.), and is prefaced by Moses' deliverance of the completed law "as a witness *against* you." Deut. 31:24 – 32:43 is saturated with the notion of present and future rebellion against "the way I have told you to follow" (v. 20), and closes with Moses' *final* warning (v. 47) before his death: these words are not vain, they are life. This comes very close to the context into which Luke puts the phrase ("and he received living oracles to give to us. Our fathers refused to *obey* him, but *thrust him aside* ..." vv. 38b – 39). It also resembles Hebrews at several points. (a) At Heb. 2:2, "the word (λόγος) spoken through angels (again, cf. Acts 7:53) was certain" (βέβαιος)[106] is a statement likewise set in a context of Jewish disobedience. (b) The "living word" of Heb. 4:12 similarly occurs in the context of the rebellion of the generation which received the law (3:7 – 4:11) and is immediately preceded by a specific warning against repeating their "pattern of disobedience." (c) Elsewhere *Auctor* quotes Deut. 32:43 (1:6), showing it to be a context with which he is familiar. Scharlemann[107] objects that Acts 7 differs from Hebrews in that the former refers to "something apart from God," but he does not argue the point. Simon's[108] assertion that the idea of "living words" belongs to "the commonstock of diaspora Judaism" is likewise difficult to consider, since he provides no evidence whatever for his claim.

There is a certain similarity of Acts 7 and Hebrews at this point to I Pet. 1:23[109] ("born anew ... through the living and abiding word of God") and John 6:63, 68[110] ("words ... are spirit and life," "words of eternal life"). John is closer than 1 Peter to Acts and Hebrews, since the "words of life" likewise are connected with the wilderness generation and the problem of disobedience. But the episode there is plainly the provision of manna, not the giving of the law, and in John the ῥήματα of Jesus seem to be *distinguished from* those of Moses (cf. 1:17; also, the claim of 6:68 that Jesus *only* has "living words" would run counter to the climate of Acts 7 and Hebrews). Thus the idea that God's word "lives," *human disobedience notwithstanding*, is peculiar to Acts 7 and Hebrews.

God's "rest"

The collocation of Joshua's entry into the land (7:45) with a reference to God's rest (7:49) is, as Manson points out, striking.[111] That in Acts the two ideas occur within a space of four verses, however, is not the most arresting aspect of this convergence. Since one of the emphases of the speech is that possession of the land was never final,[112] the conclusion is not far off that, as with the temple, the Jews could never really claim it to offer lasting security,[113] a point very close to Heb. 4:8.[114] The "rest" of God in Acts 7:49 is, fittingly, something entirely independent of any earthly fixture or particularity, an idea perhaps closer to the general argument of Hebrews than anything else in the Christian tradition. The point of *both* documents might be paraphrased: the habitation of any land, whether Mesopotamia (Acts 7:2), Haran (Acts 7:4), Egypt (Acts 7:21ff.), Midian (Acts 7:31ff.) or Canaan (Acts 7:43d, 45; Heb. 4:8, 11:8, etc.), with the earthly security it invites, was never guaranteed by God to be final to those who heed his voice (Heb. 3:7, 15, etc.; Acts 7:3, 6, 31ff.), for he himself transcends any created fixture (Acts 7:49f.; Heb. 1:10–12, 12:27). It might be further noted that Acts 7 and Hebrews closely juxtapose the same four themes: (a) "rest"; (b) hearing; (c) defect of heart; and (d) the Holy Spirit ("*rest*," Acts 7:49; "*uncircumcised in heart and ears*, you always resist *the Holy Spirit*," Acts 7:51; cp. "Therefore, as the *Holy Spirit* says, 'today, when you *hear his voice*, do not *harden your hearts* as in the rebellion ... they shall never enter my *rest*,'" Heb. 4:7–11). A further similarity is the depiction in Hebrews and Acts 7 of God as master builder, occurring in both cases in a context of God's "rest" (cp. Acts 7:49 – "what house will you *build* for me ... did not *my* hand make *all* these *things*?" with Heb. 3:4 – "for every house is *built* by some one, but the builder of *all things* is God").[115] Such coincidence, unique to Acts 7 and Hebrews, enhance Manson's idea of a relationship between the two writings.

The law and angels

While to some it is "striking,"[116] to others the mediation of the law in Acts 7:53 and Heb. 2:2 is a dubious parallel, since it is also reflected in Gal. 3:19, Josephus (*Ant.* XV.136), Jub. 1:29 and the rabbis.[117] It should be observed, however, that within the Christian tradition at least, Acts 7 and Hebrews stand *against* Paul in that they do not put the idea to a negative use.[118] Paul uses it to demonstrate the inferiority of a mediated promise – the law – to an unmediated promise – that to Abraham. Scharlemann objects rather pedantically that Hebrews "makes a distinction between this angelic word and the apostolic word as spoken by the Lord. Stephen makes no such comparison,"[119] claiming further that Stephen "mentions angelic mediation, but he does so to exalt the law and so to stress the seriousness of Israel's disobedience," whereas Hebrews "sets the word spoken by the Lord *over against* words spoken through angels."[120] But surely the point is that in Stephen *and* Hebrews the angelic mediation is set in the context of the seriousness of disobedience. The "betrayal and murder of the Righteous One" in Acts 7:52 as the *consummate* act of rebellion corresponds to the final seriousness of rebelling against God's Son in Heb. 2:2. Heb. 2:2, furthermore, does not set "the word spoken by the Lord" *over against* that spoken through angels; the argument is *a fortiori*. Above all it should be noted that *only in Acts 7 and Hebrews is this notion set in the context of disobedience*. Again, this seems to suggest that Manson has put us on the right track.

"Looking to Jesus"

Manson's connection of the dying Stephen's gazing at Jesus with Heb. 12:2 is not very convincing, and takes one into the historical question of whether the particular source used by Luke for Stephen's trial speech may be automatically linked to the martyrdom narrative.[121] The most I am suggesting is that Hebrews appears to bear some similarities to the thought embodied in the *speech* of Acts 7. To argue that *Auctor* was also familiar with the details of Stephen's martyrdom as described by Luke would take us beyond our brief, and, since it is based solely on the phrase "looking to Jesus"[122] in Heb. 12:2

(which, incidentally, could be said to encapsulate the entire New Testament theme of *imitatio Christi*), this point should be abandoned.[123]

Exodus 25:40

As noted above, the citation of Ex. 25:40 by Stephen and *Auctor* is unique to these two writers in the New Testament. While there is no evidence that Stephen connects the τύπος of that passage with a *heavenly* tent, this should not be allowed to obscure that fact that in the New Testament these two writers alone evince an interest in the text. What is striking is the way that both writers have taken the text and developed it in a context of the spiritual nature of God and his consequent demands.

4 Lingering doubts

So far Manson's basic premise of a special relationship between Hebrews and Acts 7 appears to have stood up fairly well. There are, however, points which are not as friendly to his thesis. (1) Stephen shows no interest in the priesthood. Aaron is mentioned only in connection with the golden calf.[124] Manson anticipates this and claims that Christ's priesthood is "consonant enough with his [Stephen's] reaction away from the older cultus," adding that the early church had probably founded a christology upon Ps. 110:4[125] long before *Auctor* wrote. This unprovable supposition does little to enhance a case for Stephen and Hebrews, and Higgins[126] is correct to criticize Manson for underestimating *Auctor*'s originality at this point. C. P. M. Jones tries to link Christ's priestly role of intercession with Stephen's "intercessory posture of standing" in Acts 7:55f., but this is not the only way to explain the vision.[127] Manson's case is not served by attempting to read *all* of the elements of Hebrews into Acts 7; one should rather credit *Auctor* with his own creative additions to (and emendations of) traditions preserved in Acts 7 as perhaps they came to him. But this then raises the (perhaps unanswerable) question of which came first, Hebrews or the sources lying behind Acts 7. (2) Simon[128] contrasts Acts 7 and Hebrews in their use of the Old Testament, describing Stephen's exegesis as "historical and critical."[129] Yet his classification of Hebrews with Paul in a use of "allegorical exegesis" is now somewhat question-begging. A better approach would be to say that Acts 7 exhibits a *limited* typology, in which case one can see, in the careers of Joseph[130] and Moses, a subtle preaching of Jesus. It is this "restrained" typology which also occurs in Hebrews.[131] (3) Manson's idea that "the Son of Man" standing at God's right hand in Acts 7 indicates a "more-than-Jewish" significance for the gospel is tenuous. While (unlike others)[132] he does not see in Jesus's *stance* an indication that the gospel is about to be preached world-wide, he extrapolates the same idea from the "Son of Man" title. For Manson this sole occurrence outside of the gospels demonstrates that "the call to the church of Jesus was to leave the Temple and all that went with it behind, and to go forward..."[133] According to Manson, this is the fulfilment of Dan. 7:13f. that "all peoples, nations and languages" should serve the Son of Man.

The problems with this, however, are serious. The "Son of Man" of Dan. 7:13f is not a universalistic figure as Manson suggests. He represents the triumph of God's people over pagan enemies.[134] Moule[135] actually says that "Son of Man" is "as much implicated with kingship, nationalism, [and] vindication" as was "Messiah," while Simon[136] cites Acts 2:32, 36 as indicating the same idea.[137] And, as Moule also points out, if Manson is correct, it is difficult to explain the disappearance of the term in the Paulines.[138] It would thus be best to view with detachment Manson's emphasis upon the completely original or isolated nature of Stephen's "eschatology" vis-à-vis that of his contemporaries, together with attempts to read into the speech prematurely a viewpoint which may not be there.

5 Conclusion

We have now seen that once certain adjustments are made to Manson's thesis, a case exists for seeing some form of contact between the viewpoint preserved in Acts 7 and that of *Auctor*. Acts 7 (1) appears to depict Stephen as one who has a high view of the law but sees the land and temple as dispensable, and (2) thinks of the contemporary Jews as sons of the murderers of the prophets. If Luke is using a source, and not simply inventing the speech on his own,[139] it *could* be said that we have here a relatively early collection of OT traditions which supplied a starting point for special emphases one finds in Hebrews, especially the inferiority of the earthly cultus and the dangers of repeating past patterns of disobedience. Manson produced eight parallels between Acts 7 and Hebrews. These were examined, and, of the original eight, two (2 and 8) were found to be weak. But five (3 and 4 were combined) stood up reasonably well. To these was added one other (9). Consequently at least *six* points of contact could be cautiously adduced. While the matter is open to discussion, it might be said that when dealing with such a small piece of writing as Acts 7, the parallels are impressive and numerous enough to suggest that some form of Manson's case is plausible. The insistence of Scharlemann (and to a lesser degree Simon) that Acts 7 and *Auctor* must exhibit "air-tight" agreement in every detail (an "all or nothing" approach) should be abandoned.[140] The differences militate against any literary dependence of *Auctor* upon a source Luke might be using. But this does not mean that *Auctor* could not have been exposed to an independent form of the same use of OT traditions which also turn up in Acts 7.[141]

The weight of the evidence considered thus indicates that, despite some defects in his case, Manson has directed scholarly attention in a helpful direction in the attempt to uncover one of the streams of thought which may underlie Hebrews. At six different points Hebrews and Acts 7 utilize a similar interpretation of OT traditions. The significance of such a connection, yet far from exact, should constitute a point of future discussion.

5

PAULINE THEOLOGY

1 History of discussion

The introduction last century of the "Alexandrian" interpretation of Hebrews soon made it fashionable to see little if any connection between Hebrews and Paul. Ménégoz began the movement when, in concert with his idea that Hebrews had been written by a convinced Philonian, he declared that "it is no less certain that he had not been his [Paul's] disciple."[1] The subsequent addition of other backgrounds has strengthened this idea. W. Manson,[2] for instance, viewed Hebrews and the Pauline mission as having little or no contact. For him they run on separate but parallel tracks. Accordingly, he summarized three points which he felt precluded serious contact; (1) For Paul the gospel is juxtaposed with the old order as legal code; for *Auctor* it is as the cultic "apparatus of grace." (2) For Paul the cross, following the old covenant, stands as a shocking paradox; for *Auctor* it is neither shocking nor new, since it was already contained in shadow form in the old covenant. (3) Paul emphasizes the resolution of conflict within the present soul of the believer and stresses union with Christ; for *Auctor* "the Christian life is a tense and unending conflict which finds resolution and rest only at the End." In addition to these there have been noted other differences: (1) *Auctor* nowhere mentions either the Gentiles or the question of circumcision. (2) In Hebrews characteristic Pauline terms are missing ("Christ Jesus," "the gospel," "mystery," "to fulfil," "to build up" and "to justify"). (3) *Auctor* may have an anti-eucharistic bias.[3] (4) *Auctor* only once mentions the resurrection (13:20) and justification by faith (11:7). (5) For *Auctor* the angels who mediated the law are "ministering spirits sent forth to serve those who are inherit salvation" (1:14); for Paul they are the principalities and powers who killed Christ. (6) Paul makes a different use of Hab. 2:3f. than *Auctor*.[4]

Others, however, do not rule out Pauline influence entirely. Windisch[5] lists fifteen impressive convergences: (1) A similar view of the incarnation, including Christ's previous glory and his role in creating and sustaining the cosmos (Heb. 1:2, 3, 6; Col. 1:15–17; 1 Cor. 8:6; 2 Cor. 4:4); (2) his humiliation (Heb. 2:14–17; Rom. 8:3; Gal. 4:4; Phil. 2:7); (3) his obedience (Heb. 5:8; Rom. 5:19; Phil. 2:8); (4) his offering for us (Heb. 9:28; 1 Cor. 5:7; Eph. 5:2; Gal. 2:20); (5) Christ as an ἀπολύτρωσις for sin (Heb. 9:15; Rom. 3:24; 1 Cor. 1:30); (6) his intercession for us (Heb. 7:25; Rom. 8:34); (7) the superiority of the new covenant (Heb. 8:6ff.; 2 Cor. 3:9ff.); (8) the inheritance of an exalted name (Heb. 1:4, 5:10; Phil. 2:9–11); (9) a reference to signs and wonders performed (Heb. 2:4, 2 Cor. 12:12) and gifts distributed by the Holy Spirit (Heb. 2:4; 1 Cor. 12:11); (10) the depiction of Christ as our brother (Heb. 2:11; Rom. 8:29); (11) the use of Abraham's faith as an example (Heb. 11:11, 17–19; Rom. 4:17–20); (12) the deterrent example of the wilderness generation (Heb. 3:7ff.; 1 Cor. 10:1ff.); (13) the Christian life as a race (Heb. 12:1; 1 Cor. 9:24ff.); (14) conversion as enlightenment (Heb. 6:4, 10:32; 2 Cor. 4:4); (15) the use of the same OT passages (Ps. 8 in Heb. 2:6–9 and 1 Cor. 15:27; Deut. 32:35 in Heb. 10:30 and Rom. 12:19; Hab. 2:4 in Heb. 10:38, Rom. 1:17, and Gal. 3:11). To Windisch's list may be added others: (16) a view of Christ's death as the defeat of evil powers (Col. 2:15, Heb. 2:14); (17) Christ's death as an expiation (ἱλάσκομαι, Heb. 2:17; ἱλαστήριον, Rom. 3:25) for sin; (18) a "waiting" for Christ's return (ἀπεκδέχομαι, Heb. 9:28, Rom. 8:19, 23, 25; 1 Cor. 1:7, etc.); (19) a "Pauline" style ending (Heb. 13:18–25, which displays a number of distinctive Pauline terms and interests ending with a reference to Timothy, v.24);[6] (20) "righteousness by faith" (Heb. 11:7; Rom. 4:13ff.);[7] (21) the description of Christians as "the descendants of Abraham" (Heb. 2:16; Rom. 9:7ff., Gal. 3:7); (22) Paul's mention of the gospel being "preached beforehand" to Abraham (Gal. 3:8) and *Auctor*'s point that Abraham and others "saw and greeted" the promise "from afar"; (23) a rebuke of the readers as fit for milk, not meat (Heb. 5:12ff.; 1 Cor. 3:2); (24) a link of the last point to the term τέλειος; (25) Christian teaching as a θεμέλιος (Heb. 6:1; 1 Cor. 3:10f.); (26) the nature of stewards as πιστός (Heb. 3:2ff.; 1 Cor. 4.1ff.).

Windisch's arguments cannot be treated here, but at least it can be said that he has shown a large amount of common ground to exist between Paul and Hebrews. His conclusion is that either *Auctor* was a Pauline disciple or they depended upon a large amount of common

Christian tradition.[8] Forty years later Montefiore[9] was so impressed by the number and nature of the parallels with 1 Corinthians alone that he argued "that Paul had read the Epistle to the Hebrews when he wrote I Corinthians, or that he wrote from a similar background of thought." Lohmeyer, Hofius[10] and Barnett[11] all argue as well for a literary relationship, only in their view it is *Auctor* who is dependent on Paul.

I suggest that, as in his treatment of Philo and Hebrews, Ménégoz demonstrated imbalanced judgment. Lohmeyer, Hofius and Barnett, on the other hand, have been too extreme in the other direction. It needs to be recalled that, despite the many questions which have surrounded it almost from the beginning, the epistle was regarded by Greek-speaking authorities such as Clement of Alexandria and Origen as Pauline either in authorship or thought-form, and they were hardly stupid. A more moderate – and sensible – position would be to maintain that Paul and Hebrews come at points very close, yet without any direct literary connection. Yet this position carries problems of its own if one is attempting to determine the exact relationship between Hebrews and Paul, since it is extremely difficult to distinguish those places where *Auctor* has drawn upon a tradition which antedates both writers from a tradition Paul may have helped to frame. Dodd[12] asked who was responsible for "the pool of tradition" regarding the use of the OT, and his answer was Jesus. But if the tradition is not to be explained *in toto* in terms of Jesus, including also the efforts of Christian thinkers, it would be difficult not to include Paul in this process. The idea of "pre-Pauline" tradition thus becomes extremely elusive.[13] One criterion will be whether the tradition is attested more widely than these two.

We might assume, furthermore, that the reference to Timothy in 13:23 would indicate that *Auctor* was a member of the Pauline circle. It may be, on the other hand, that the doubt which has been cast upon chapter 13 as part of the original epistle[14] has subtracted from the weight this verse might normally have in consideration of Paul and Hebrews. I shall assume in this section that there are no compelling reasons for rejecting chapter 13 as the original conclusion of the epistle,[15] and shall go further in saying that *Auctor* appears to have had some exposure to the same ideas that are developed in Paul, albeit they are worked out rather differently.

2 Points of contact

It is not possible here to analyze all possible points of contact. I shall consequently choose three representative samples of themes developed by both writers, in the hope that the reader will be able to draw from them conclusions which may be applicable to the larger question. These sample themes are: (a) the destiny of humankind (Heb. 2:6–9; 1 Cor. 15:22ff.); (b) Christ's humbling as a human being, including his obedience and subsequent exaltation (Heb. 1:2–2:17, Phil. 2:5–11); and (c) the role of faith in the Christian life.

The destiny of humankind

In dealing with this topic, Paul and *Auctor* both make much use of Ps. 8. Their treatments are similar and diverse enough to require an extended examination.

Psalm 8 in Hebrews

From the amount of time devoted to it in ch. 2, Ps. 8 is clearly *Auctor*'s first main scriptural support. Following the quotation of the psalm, he comments that "in subjecting all things to him he left nothing that is not subject," adding furthermore that

> we do not yet see all things subject to him. But we see Jesus, who for a little while was made lower than the angels, now crowned with glory and honour because of the suffering of death, so that, by God's gracious will, he might taste of death for every man.

This requires comment. In its original setting Ps. 8 concerned the glory and destiny of man. It was not "Messianic" in the LXX or rabbinic Judaism.[16] Thus one would normally take Jesus in 2:8 as proleptically fulfilling what is as yet unfulfilled for humankind – he represents the ideal state for which Adam was created ("glory").[17] Some, however, have taken the passage to mean Jesus Christ uniquely.[18] Rather than referring αὐτῷ to what immediately precedes, "man" (and its periphrasis, "Son of Man"), Jesus is said to be the only one in view. "Son of Man" may even be a christological title for *Auctor*.[19] I have dealt elsewhere[20] with these arguments, but here it may be said in summary that the recent interpretation which sees Jesus as the only one in view falls short at a number of points. (1) There is no evidence that *Auctor* takes "Son of Man" in 2:6 in any other sense than as a periphrasis for "man." Had he taken it as a "christological title" he would certainly have explicated it elsewhere. (2) The conjunction of Ps. 8 with Ps. 110:1 in Hebrews, as in the rest of the NT, involves Jesus' enthronement as the representative of glorified humanity. *Auctor* shows little or no interest in developing his understanding of the "enemies," but they are probably the enemies of humankind in general, "spiritual enemies" (Lindars),[21] or "dämonischen Mächten" (Michel).[22] There is little to support Sowers'[23] view that in Heb. 1:13 Ps. 110:1 means the subjection of *humanity*. (3) That the fulfilment of the psalm is said to be ὑπὲρ παντός (2:9) indicates that Christ's role is as the representative of all humanity. (4) The plan of God to which the psalm is taken as witness is defined as πολλοὺς υἱοὺς εἰς δόξαν ἀγαγόντα, indicating that δόξαν picks up δόξῃ καὶ τιμῇ ἐστεφάνωσας αὐτόν of 2:7.[24] (5) The angels mentioned in the psalm, to whom God subjected the present age and under whose authority Jesus himself lived "for a little while,"[25] are defined in 1:14 as "ministering spirits sent out to serve on behalf of those who were to inherit salvation." This indicates that the reversal of conditions in the future age will result in the supremacy over these angels by redeemed humanity rather than exclusively by a single individual.

Psalm 8 in Paul

In Paul's undisputed writings Ps. 8 is either quoted or alluded to in 1 Cor. 15:22ff.,[26] Rom. 8:20 and Phil. 2:10 and 3:21. It is the lengthy treatment of 1 Corinthians which invites comparison with the treatment of Hebrews. The coupling of Ps. 110:1 with Ps. 8:6 occurs in the midst of Paul's "second Adam" theme (vv. 21ff.), indicating that he is developing Ps. 8 not in terms of the unique dignities of an individual but in terms of one who represents and leads humankind to its appointed destiny. He views Jesus, in other words, as fulfilling the psalm representatively and inclusively. Just before the quotation of the two psalms, Christ is presented as the "firstfruits" (ἀπαρχή) of the appointed order (τάγμα), v. 23. In this schema Christ's present reign is not as a single individual or as an end in itself. For Paul the reign of Christ[27] spoken of in Ps. 110:1 is limited, an *ad hoc* appointment for the purpose of eradicating the enemies of God (and hence of humankind). He is a "divine plenipotentiary holding absolute sway for a limited period."[28] The reign is then handed over (παραδίδωμι) to God, followed by the subjection of Christ to the One who subjected all things to him, "so that God may be all in all."[29] For Paul the saints will judge the world and possibly "reign" (1 Cor. 4:8),[30] and, according to Rom. 8:21, the freeing of the creation from its bondage to mortality is bound up with its entering into the "glory of the children of God," probably an echo of Ps. 8 and Paul's democratic version of 2 Sam. 7:14 (2 Cor. 6:18). This would seem to be the point of the handing over of the kingdom,[31] for although the unchallenged reign of God alone may be implied,[32] the central point of the passage is the predestined role of humankind as the mirror reflection, in the new creation, of God's universal rule.[33] Paul thus uses Ps. 8:6 to postpone the complete subjection of "all things" to the future.[34] Ps. 8 is thus not for Paul "narrowly christological," a conclusion made certain by the close of the argument in vv. 46–49. There the entire discussion is brought to a climax when Christ becomes the second, last or heavenly Adam at his resurrection, having first borne the image of the χοϊκός. Christians, likewise, who bear the image of the χοϊκός, are destined to bear the image of the ἐπουράνιος. This means that in 1 Cor. 15 the reference to Ps. 8 comes not after (v. 22f.), but firmly in the middle of, an entire, continuous exposition of Christ as the representative of humankind which now culminates in v. 49. In other words, just where Ps. 8 is thought to be most detached from its original meaning (1 Cor. 15:27), in fact it is not.[35]

A comparison of Hebrews and 1 Cor. 15

Paul and *Auctor* have been contrasted because of their "christological" and "anthropological" interpretations of Ps. 8, respectively.[36] As we have now seen, this is to be rejected. There are, to be sure, differences between the two writers' handling of the psalm. Note, e.g., the following: (1) Paul's reference occurs in the middle of his discussion of the resurrection, a theme not developed by *Auctor*. (2) Paul refers to Adam (v. 21). (3) Paul identifies the enemies (left unsaid in Hebrews) as the principalities and powers (v. 24). (4) Paul includes "death" among the enemies (v. 26). (5) Paul adds the word πάντας (absent in Heb. 1:13) to the phrase τοὺς ἐχθρούς (Ps. 110:1, v. 25, apparently as a result of conflation with Ps. 8:6).[37] (6) Paul qualifies τὰ πάντα by the exemption of God (v. 27b), and mentions the subjection of Christ to God. None of these differences can be viewed as theologically significant, although they would seem to preclude literary dependence.

On the other side of the ledger, apart from the obvious point that both see Jesus as fulfilling the psalm representatively and inclusively,[38] several impressive theological convergences occur:

(1) God's subjecting *in the aorist*; (2) man's inability to fulfil the subjection; (3) Christ's subsequent fulfilment of it; (4) the conquest of death (v. 26, cf. Heb. 2:14b); (5) the relation of God to all things (v. 28, Heb. 2:10); (6) the adding of the definite article to the "all" of the psalm (τὰ πάντα, vv. 27ff.; cp. Heb. 2:8); and (7) the post-ponement of the salvation of Ps. 8:6 to the future.[39]

Of these convergences, (7) is without doubt the most striking. It could be argued that points (1) through (6) result from an entirely independent Christian exegesis of the psalm. But the apparent reading of the psalm by both writers as indicating *two successive stages of human history* is not something which could have been expected by even a *Christian* exegesis of Ps. 8 in the LXX. *Auctor*'s depiction of the ἀρχηγός (2:10, 12:2) who takes the lead in fulfilling Ps. 8 is similar to Paul, who "places the firstfruits in the 'front rank' of the human harvest"[40] (see also the forerunner penetrating the veil in Heb. 6:20). *Auctor* and Paul, in other words, produce an exegesis of the psalm unlike anything in the rabbis or surviving Alexandrian Jewish literature.

Outside of Hebrews and the Pauline corpus, Ps. 8 is briefly alluded to in Mat. 21:16 and 1 Pet. 3:22.[41] It is, in other words, virtually unexploited in the rest of the NT, and *Auctor* and the Pauline circle thus stand alone not only in their similar understanding of the psalm but in their view of its importance. This would seem to indicate that Hebrews and Paul are coming out of the same kind of intellectual ferment.

Christ's obedience, humbling as a human being and subsequent exaltation

The argument of Heb. 1 and 2

Although it is a phrase seldom discussed or explained, the "pre-existence" of Christ is almost always assumed to be the exegetical star-ting point of the first two chapters of Hebrews.[42] But does this greedy concept really consume as much of this section as is usually assumed? Robinson,[43] Caird,[44] Dunn[45] and I[46] have questioned that this is the case, and have hinted strongly that the Jesus of Heb. 1 and 2 is essentially a human figure who is *raised to* an exalted status. Such studies collectively point out that the epistle opens with a reference to the historical Jesus (God's speaking "in these latter days" can hardly be a reference to the pre-existent Christ), and that the same figure is said to be *appointed* (τίθημι, v. 2b) "heir of all things," to have *become* (γίνομαι, v. 4) "greater than the angels," and to have *inherited* (κληρονομέω, v. 4) "a name more excellent than theirs." The opening paragraph then closes with a reference again to the work of the historical Jesus ("purification for sins," v. 3c). Thus, even if it is maintained that the writer made no *mental* distinction between the heavenly Son and the human Son, there is *prima facie* a case for saying that if one reads the chapter *from the beginning*, the figure in view is essentially a human one. "Nowhere, in fact," says Robinson,[47] "in the New Testament more than in Hebrews do we find such a wealth of expressions that would support what looks like an adoptionist christology – of a Jesus who *becomes* the Christ."

Along these lines I have argued[48] that the passages in Heb. 1 (1:2b–3, 8 and 10–12) usually associated with personal pre-existence in fact draw upon concepts surrounding the pre-existent Wisdom who is embodied in the ideal Hebrew king. The only way it can be sustained, furthermore, that personal pre-existence *controls* the argument of ch. 1 is by claiming that *Auctor* disregards the contexts of his Scripture passages, an idea powerfully refuted by Caird[49] and Kistemaker.[50] A case thus exists that the king who embodies the nation in ch. 1 paves the way for the larger concept of one who fulfils God's will for humankind in ch. 2. To what extent notions of a pre-cosmic figure are also present must remain a delicate matter of scholarly judgment. Heb. 1:2b–3 and 1:10–12 certainly provide the starting points for a christological process which will end at Chalcedon. But it is equally evident that the *emphasis* of the chapter is not placed upon a divine being who "trails clouds of glory from his pre-existent home"; it is upon a human being *who attains to* a status greater than that of the angels.

The argument of Phil. 2:5–11
Even more than in the case of Heb. 1 and 2, Phil. 2:5–11 remains a magnet of controversy.[51] Recent discussion has centred on its alleged "hymnic" structure, whether the hymn is "pre-Pauline," what ancient myth or figure served as its basis, and whether the passage refers to a pre-existent being who "empties himself" and "becomes" man, or thinks from start to finish of the action of a human being, Jesus. Recent studies[52] have suggested that the human Jesus is the subject of the self-emptying, and that personal pre-existence was far from Paul's mind. In this view the passage indicates a straight parallel between the two Adams, one aspiring to be like God, the other

renouncing such claims. While collectively the arguments of these studies have been attractive and powerful, they have also been vigorously criticized.[53] Some critics have suggested that the internal evidence of Philippians strongly favors the classic interpretation of Lightfoot and others, namely that in Phil. 2 Jesus, who is personally pre-existent, renounces his claim of equality with God, empties himself, and becomes man. Since at present the above-mentioned critiques of the "thoroughly anthropological" interpretation have not yet been answered, I shall maintain that the "pre-existent" understanding − the contours of which have been well explored by Martin[54] − must remain the starting point of any comparison of Hebrews and Paul at this point.

Hebrews and Phil. 2:5−11 compared

Hebrews and Phil. 2 are frequently said to enshrine the same viewpoint. Hengel, e.g., has spoken of Hebrews as "a large-scale development of the christological theme which is already present in the Philippians hymn."[55] In this he follows Lohmeyer, who, according to Hengel,

> is quite right in stressing in his interpretation of Heb. 1:1ff.
> that the essential point here is that the christological outline
> of Phil. 2:6−11 is being made more precise. Here the "notion
> of equality with God is defined (more exactly); the meta-
> physical determination "Son" frees it from the indefiniteness
> which the phrase "being in the form of God" still carries
> with it.[56]

Thus for Hengel Hebrews goes *beyond* Phil. 2 in attributing to the pre-existent Christ a more precise "metaphysical substantiality." Käsemann,[57] Michel,[58] J. T. Sanders[59] and Spicq[60] see the writings as in such close proximity in terms of their central thrust that a literary relationship might seem much the easiest explanation. Spicq denies that *Auctor*'s christology is a "servile transcription" of Paul's in Phil. 2, but in claiming that the expression "although being Son" of Heb. 5:8 is the exact parallel of the proposition "who being in the form of God" of Phil. 2:6, and in suggesting that at this point *Auctor*'s "christology is in direct dependence upon Paul," he seems to make a case for literary dependence plausible.

The treatment of O. Hofius[61] deserves special consideration. According to Hofius, Phil. 2 and Hebrews not only agree in beginning the "journey of Jesus" (*Weg Jesu*) with pre-existence; they agree in their ordering and depiction *of every stage* of the journey. The proto-logical statements of Heb. 1:2−3 establish why Christ, who is heir to the universe because he is the pre-existent one, is raised to the heights of 1:3−4. According to Hofius, in Hebrews the Son, as the risen one, becomes what he already was, the pre-existent one.[62] His enthrone-ment over the angels in 1:4ff. corresponds to his enthronement over them before he humbled himself to become man. The apparent ten-sion between pre-existent and exaltation christologies in Hebrews is resolved when it is recognized that by becoming at the exaltation what he already was from all eternity − Lord of all − Christ reproduces the "high-voltage tension" of the OT in its statements about God, who *both* rules from eternity and is enthroned as king when the times are fulfilled.[63] Hofius, following Bornkamm,[64] asserts that Heb. 1:3−4 enshrines a hymn to the pre-existent Christ, reflected in several sur-viving Hebrew sources, which in structure and content is indebted to the hymn of Phil. 2. In Hebrews, however, only fragments of the hymn survive, which are then intertwined with *Auctor*'s own state-ments. In Philippians the hymn is quoted intact.

Except for minor variations of detail, Hofius does not substantially differ from Spicq and others, for whom the christology of Hebrews is in one way or another directly dependent upon the hymn enshrined in Phil. 2. Numerous points of contact have been noted:

Philippians 2	Hebrews	
6. who, *existing* in the form of God ... to be equal to God	5:8	Although *being* Son
	1:3	*being* the effulgence of his glory and the very stamp of his being
7. taking the form of a slave	2:11	he is not ashamed to call them "brothers"
he emptied himself	2:7	You made him for a while lower than the angels
... in the *likeness* of men	2:14	he partook of the same nature
8. being found in fashion as man	2:17	in all things made *like* his brethren
he made himself lowly and became *obedient* to death	5:8	He learned *obedience* by the things he suffered
9. He gave him a *name* above every name	1:4	he has inherited a *name* more excellent than theirs

These convergences are impressive, but care needs to be exercised in how they are interpreted. At this point we might begin by noting the differences: (1) In Philippians the similarities are hymnically concentrated, whereas in Hebrews they are not. (2) Against those who take the "anthropological" interpretation, the central theme of Phil. 2 appears to be that of a pre-existent being who becomes man, whereas in Hebrews it is an act of God which appoints a human being to an exalted status. Accordingly, "Son" in Hebrews is not a "metaphysical determination" referring to pre-existence (contra Lohmeyer, Hengel, and Hofius) which expands upon "the form of God" of the Philippians hymn; it is a royal title taken from certain psalms which denotes an exalted status of humanity which Jesus is said to "inherit" (1:4). (3) Unlike Philippians, there is no kenosis *per se* in Hebrews which involves the giving up of one status for another.[65] The Christ of Hebrews shares humankind's lowly estate *while being Son*. Being "Son" and becoming "like" the brethren are not incompatible states in Hebrews, as are, in Phil. 2, "being in the form of God" and "taking the form of a slave." The closest one comes in Hebrews to a tension between the two states is 5:8, "*though* he was Son, he learned obedience by the things which he suffered," but it could be said that in Hebrews the essence of sonship *is* obedience, whereas in Philippians Christ's existing "in the form of God" denotes an ontological (or, one might say, "metaphysical") status quite independent of any conditions of behaviour. *Logically* speaking, Hebrews is still a long way from the exchange of forms clearly implied by Phil. 2. It appears that the Christ of Hebrews does not *start* from a superior position. There his position is *achieved* (1:4). Hebrews certainly stresses the last two of the three stages of Hofius' *Weg Jesu*, but the first is not so evident. (4) The statements in Hebrews (except for 10:5) which could imply pre-existence relate him to *creation*, a motif not mentioned in the Philippians passage. At this point the christology of Hebrews is closer to that of Col. 1:15ff. than to Phil. 2. (5) Because of the LXX wording of Ps. 8:5a, *Auctor* dwells explicitly upon Christ's being made lower than the *angels*; no such idea is developed or even mentioned in Philippians except for the tacit implication of the δοῦλος parallel with Gal. 4:3f. Because of the generally acknowledged Semitic features of the Philippians passage, on the other hand, a reference to the LXX version of Ps. 8:5 (as in Hebrews) is not proven. (6) *Auctor* nowhere picks up the important term δοῦλος. (7) The name bestowed upon Christ at the conclusion of the Philippians hymn (v. 9) appears to be his alone, whereas in Hebrews the name "Son" is shared with others (2:10). They cannot, therefore, be equated.[66]

At these points there seems to be a somewhat different working out of the themes common to the two passages. Yet the points of similarity are such that they should not be ignored either: (1) In both writings there is great stress laid upon the humility and obedience of Christ. In Phil. 2 the assumption of the form of a servant and the self-humbling to the point of death parallel Christ's unwillingness to shrink from calling men "his brothers" (Heb. 2:11), his refusal to exalt himself (Heb. 5:8) and his willingness to endure the cross, "despising the shame" (Heb. 12:2). (2) In Phil. 2 Christ's coming to be "in the likeness of men" is hauntingly like Christ's being made "like his brethren in all respects" (Heb. 2:17), and his "taking on the form of a servant" in Phil. 2 has a distinct resemblance to the plan of God in Hebrews which calls for the Son to be made subject to all the constraining hardships of human experience, including bondage to fear of death (2:16; note the reference to Christ's fear of death in 5:7). (3) In Phil. 2 and Heb. 1 Christ acquires an exalted name, and in both cases this name is linked to a superiority over spiritual beings (Phil. 2:9, Heb. 1:4).

We have thus examined a Pauline passage which has traditionally been associated with the pre-existence of Christ.[67] That stance has been challenged recently, but the view that the Philippians passage has as its central theme a human Jesus has yet to be established. The degree to which the case for a thoroughly human figure in Philippians is not strong makes the case for a direct literary relationship with Hebrews that much weaker. The most that can be said is that Hebrews appears to have similarities with Phil. 2 at a much earlier stage, *before the latter was written down* and before it had reached a certain point in Paul's thinking. One cannot imagine that *Auctor* had read the "hymn" of Phil. 2, digested it and taken it to mean what it appears to mean, and then produced the christology of Hebrews as an offprint of that. Put into traditional terminology, the christology of Hebrews is not as "high" as that of Phil. 2.

The view of Hofius that Hebrews and Phil. 2 agree at every stage of the *Weg Jesu* is thus to be rejected, as is his claim that in both Phil. 2 and Hebrews Christ, as the exalted one, "becomes what he already was as the pre-existent one." In Phil. 2 Christ becomes man, but is then exalted *as* man. This may be implied at times in Hebrews, but it is never actually said that he "became" man (except for *possibly* 10:5).[68] The emphases of Hebrews place it at a logically (but not chronologically)[69] earlier stage than Philippians. This, together with other differences noted above, rules out the argument of Lohmeyer and others for a literary relationship between the two. The convergences, on the other hand, again demonstrate a similar intellectual ferment regarding the person of Christ.

Faith

How does one relate *Auctor* and Paul on the topic of faith?[70] Here we must face a topic which has suffered considerably at the hands of twentieth-century interpreters. The belief begun last century that *Auctor*'s view of faith is Philonic[71] has resulted in little attempt being made to detect points of contact between the two writers on this point. Indeed, at present it is quite "unfashionable." The differences, of course, cannot be denied. For Paul faith is primarily the vehicle of justification, while for *Auctor* it is the ground of hope and the means of access; for Paul it is often directed to the person and work of Christ, while for *Auctor* it is primarily in the promises of God and the reality of the unseen.

If Williamson[72] is correct, on the other hand, to suggest that the view of faith in Hebrews can no longer be viewed as strictly "Philonic," one might be permitted to raise afresh the question of its relationship to the "Pauline" view. This topic is treatable under five headings.

Faith in Christ

According to this seemingly tireless viewpoint, "in the epistle faith is never christologically focused."[73] Put another way, "Jesus is not the object of faith, but the supreme model of it."[74] Paul speaks commonly of πίστις ’Ιησοῦ (see Rom. 3:26, Gal. 3:22, etc.), and it is true that such explicit formulations are not found in Hebrews. It must be said, on the other hand, that *Auctor* does focus on Christ's high priestly work as the basis of the Christian's confidence. It is that which provides boldness (παρρησία, 3:6, 4:16, 10:19, 10:35) and steadfastness (ὑπομονή, 10:36, 12:1), two terms bound up for him with his notion of faith. In 6:1 the elementary doctrines are ὁ τῆς ἀρχῆς τοῦ χριστοῦ λογός, and in 13:8 Jesus is "the same yesterday, today and forever." The latter statement significantly follows a plea to imitate the faith of their (dead?) leaders. Most feel that there is a connection between vv. 7 and 8.[75] But what is it? Some have suggested a contrast between their dead leader's absence and Christ's perpetual availability.[76] Yet such an idea does not give enough weight to the preceding plea, "imitate their *faith.*" The more probable link between the two verses is that the latter is an amplification of the nature of the leader's faith, a faith which was in Christ and his work; since he is the same "today" as he was then, they may with confidence imitate such faith.

It is, in essence, faith in Christ.[77] Cullmann,[78] interpreting 12:2, feels it also implies such faith: it means "both that Jesus himself believed and that he brought men to faith in his work." Thus, while faith in Christ hardly receives the emphasis it does in Paul, it cannot be said that the epistle is devoid of it.

Faith as hope in God's promises

It has been alleged that in Hebrews "what is most distinctive is that when faith and hope are related to each other, it is faith that is subordinated to hope as a means to an end."[79] Such statements represent one of this century's most common approaches to the question of Paul and *Auctor* on faith – the elevation of faith *qua hope* in Hebrews is a point of divergence from Paul, for whom faith is primarily a means of "mystical" union with Christ in the present.[80] Yet words such as "faith" and "hope" cannot be put into rigid categories in any thinking person's vocabulary; in different contexts the nuances of one will spill over into the other. Thus, as Bultmann[81] shows, in Paul (1 Thes. 1:3, 1 Cor. 13:3; cp. 1 Pet. 1:21) faith and hope are at times *distinguished*, while at other times, "in so far as trust in God is faith in his promise, it is *at the same time hope*":[82] Hope in the future fulfilment of God's promises is a thoroughly Jewish – not Hellenistic – idea,[83] and the judgment of Leonard[84] that Heb. 11 "is more Jewish and more full of the future and the unseen than any correspondingly long piece" in Paul turns the question on its head. It is primarily a preoccupation with the "definition" of faith in Heb. 11:1 and its alleged "Hellenistic" coloring which has drawn attention away from the fact that the rest of the chapter is thoroughly Jewish in its emphasis on promise and fulfilment. The emphasis on faith in Hebrews as "insight into the heavenly world" has consequently been blown out of proportion.

As noted, there is a close connection in Paul between faith and hope, and at times the two become almost interchangeable. Thus "by hope we were saved" (Rom. 8:24), hope is the Christian's "helmet" (1 Thes. 5:8); and the Thessalonians are praised for their "*hope* in our Lord Jesus Christ" (1 Thess. 1:3). Rom. 4:17ff. is of special interest for Hebrews, as Windisch[85] noted. There are points at which it looks as if some relationship exists: (a) Rom. 4 and Heb. 11 both connect Abraham's faith with a figurative use of the resurrection of the dead (Rom. 4:17; cp. Heb. 11:19). In Paul it is Abraham's body which, as it were, is "raised" by being given power to conceive; in Hebrews it is the restoration of Isaac. What is significant is the interpretation in both writers of an episode from the life of Abraham which combines his faith with a symbolic resurrection. This points at least toward a similar mind at work. (b) Both Paul and *Auctor* connect the idea of faith with the notion of creation *ex nihilo* (Rom. 4:17d, "who ... calls into being the things that do not exist"; Heb. 11:3, "what is seen was made out of things which do not appear").[86] That the idea is worded differently in the two writers should not obscure the fact that in both faith is that faculty which focuses upon God's ability to call into being visible realities out of the non-existent. (c) According to Rom. 4:20, Abraham was "fully convinced that what God had *promised* he was able to perform." Here is a very important text in Paul which firmly states that for Abraham "faith" is hope that God *keeps his promises*. Of all passages within and without the NT which deal with faith, Rom. 4:20 perhaps comes nearest to Heb. 11, a chapter which constantly emphasizes faith as hope in God's promises (e.g., "all these died in faith, not having received the promise," 11:39). The statement that "in hope" Abraham believed (ἐπίστευσεν) "against hope" (Rom. 4:18) also provides an illuminating parallel to Heb. 11:1. (d) Both writers (Rom. 4:19, Heb. 11:12) attach the unusual participle νενεκρωμένος[87] to Abraham's faith in his power to conceive. (e) Apart from Rom. 4, hope is linked to the seen/unseen dichotomy in a way very similar to Hebrews in Rom. 8:24f.

Faith and sight

As noted above, Williamson, Käsemann and others have argued that the entire thrust of faith in Heb. 11 is that of hope in the future. This must be seen as the correct approach. *Both* halves of 11:1 signify that faculty which trusts in God's ability to act as he has promised. The "things not seen" of 11:1b are "the things not *yet* seen" of 11:7. If faith also involves things already present, it is because all things exist invisibly in God – not because they constitute any noumenal realm of the "philosopher." There is no evidence that Heb. 11:1 fuses a "Hebrew" and "Greek" view.[88] Trust in God who is invisible (11:6, 27) is inevitably linked to trusting in God's promises for the future.[89]

Moses "sees the invisible" but also "looked to" the future reward. This element of promise–fulfilment in *Auctor*'s view of faith is extraordinarily close to what one finds in Paul. In 2 Cor. 4:17ff. (the comparison of present affliction with the eternal "weight of glory"), the opposite of the present affliction is the *future* resurrection body. Visible and invisible, in other words, are worked out in terms of *present and future*. "Our eyes are fixed, not on things that are seen, but on the things that are unseen: for what is seen passes away, what is unseen is eternal." Here the "unseen" (μὴ βλεπόμενα; cp. Heb. 11:1, οὐ βλεπομένων) and "eternal" is the resurrection body to come (5:1ff.).[90] *Auctor*, of course, has little place in his argument for the resurrection body. But should this obscure the fact that in both writers the seen/unseen dichotomy is worked out, not in spatial terms, but in terms of present/future? That in 2 Cor. 5:7 and 1 Cor. 13:12 faith seems *opposed to* (complete) sight is not ultimately significant; since the most this can be said to show is the fluidity of these ideas when used in different contexts. There appears to be nothing in either text with which *Auctor* would have disagreed.[91]

Faith as "steadfastness"

Faith as that faculty which focuses upon the fulfilment of God's promises is also closely linked by both writers with "steadfastness," "obedience," "boldness," "holding on," "perseverence" and "faithfulness." It is disputable whether or not Paul and *Auctor* take Hab. 2:3f. in the same way (Paul may have tailored the passage to meet his own specific requirements in Rom. 1),[92] but what has been ignored is that, in different words, Paul makes quite the same point as *Auctor* by emphasizing (Rom. 4:20), in a context of faith in God's promises, that such faith is "steadfast" or "not wavering." Part of the problem has been the assumption that *Auctor*'s discussion of "faith" begins at 11:1; in fact it begins at 10:34 ("since you knew that you yourselves have a better and lasting possession"). The readers similarly are enjoined not to throw away their "boldness" (v. 35 – in *Auctor*'s vocabulary a synonym for faith – which has a "great reward" – μισθαποδοσία, cp. Heb. 11:26). The ὑπομονή of v.36 (and its opposite ὑποστολή, v. 38f.) has its Pauline counterpart in Abraham's refusal to waver in unbelief (τῇ ἀπιστίᾳ) concerning God's promise (Rom. 4:20): "For he grew strong in his faith (τῇ πίστει) ... being fully convinced that what he (God) has promised he was able to do." Despite the distinctive nuance which Paul might give to Hab. 2:3f., that both writers relate this passage clearly to an argument for faith (subsequently defined by Paul in terms of Abraham's refusal to waver – cp. "draw back," Heb. 10:39) in the face of God's promises puts them at this point so close as to make *Auctor's* membership in the Pauline circle quite the simplest explanation.

Faith as *obedience* is a central theme of Hebrews. In Heb. 4:6f. the Israelites' lack of faith (ἀπείθεια) is equivalent to disobedience; in 12:2 Christ is the pioneer and perfector of faith, while in 5:8 his office as redeemer is grounded in his *obedience*; and in 11:8 it is by faith that Abraham *obeyed* when called to go out. Paul similarly links faith closely to obedience. His mission is εἰς ὑπακοὴν πίστεως (Rom. 1:5, cf. 6:17, 10:16, 15:18, 16:19), and God's vengeance is upon those who do not *obey* the gospel (2 Thes. 1:8). It is inevitable that in any situation where there is danger of retreat from the gospel, faith – or hope – will show up as obedience, "holding," "faithfulness," "patience" or "boldness" (the opposite of "shrinking"). In 2 Thes. 1:4 Paul speaks of "your steadfastness and faith in all the afflictions which you are enduring" (cp. 1 Thes. 1:3, the "endurance of your hope," ὑπομονῆς τῆς ἐλπίδος). To hope for what is not seen (Rom. 8:25; cp. Heb. 2:8b – "we do not yet see …") is "to wait for it with patience" (ὑπομονή; cp. Heb. 10:36, where ὑπομονή is identically linked with delay and waiting, vv. 37f., and things not seen, 11:1). In 2 Cor. 1:7 hope is βέβαιος, while for *Auctor* ὑπόστασις – here 'confidence," a synonym for "faith," "boldness," etc. – must be made βέβαιος, 3:14).

Faith as trust in God

Trust in God is the dominant meaning of faith in the teaching of Jesus (Mark 2:5, 5:34, 36, etc.), and for Paul (1 Cor. 13:2) trust in his power to act is the greatest example of faith. It has been claimed that in Hebrews "faith even in God is barely mentioned – 6:1, 11:6,"[93] and that *Auctor* has "depersonalized" Paul's understanding of faith, substituting for it an academic, noetic quality.[94] It should be noted, however, that in Hebrews the word of God, preached and obeyed, is the object of faith (2:3f., 4:2), and Christ, representing humankind, shows his solidarity with it by saying "I will put my trust in him" (2:13f., Isa. 8:17f.)[95] (this is the same Jesus who, incidentally, at the end of the catalogue of faith-heroes is the "pioneer and finisher of faith"). Faith in God's ability to fulfil his promises, found throughout ch. 11, is essentially faith in him (cp. again Rom. 4, where Abraham's trusting God – hardly distinguishable from having "faith" *in* him[96] – is belief in God's promise – v. 17ff.). Faith in God's ability to move mountains (1 Cor. 13:2) is not unlike faith in God's power to create things out of nothing (Heb. 11:3).

In both Paul and Hebrews there seems to be a similar intermingling of terms and ideas connected with the notion of faith. A certain overlapping may be found in other NT writers. But at least Hebrews and Paul are closer at this point than has been generally acknowledged. Many have attempted to "pin down" Paul and *Auctor* to one particular idea of faith and then contrast them. Such a method ignores that any given situation will inevitably bring to the fore certain nuances of an idea, nuances which, when given the same situation in Paul's letters, appear there as well. Nowhere in the two writers' treatment of faith does there appear to be enough closeness to indicate literary borrowing; but at least it can be said that the two writers reflect a similar, if not the same, intellectual milieu.

3 Conclusion

In the three motifs considered there is evidence that in Hebrews one finds a similar development of some central themes of Pauline theology. In some cases this is seen in the same ideas being expressed by a different deployment of the same terms; in others these ideas are expressed in different language and imagery. Such unity and diversity are what one would expect if both writers are engaging in a deep interaction with the same traditions. Whether this points to the common pool of Christian tradition or to a form of pre-literary contact with Paul himself must remain an exercise of subtle scholarly judgment. What cannot be evaded is that Hebrews appears to relate to Paul in a way quite unlike Qumran, Philo, gnosticism or the other non-Christian backgrounds discussed thus far. This evidence leads us to draw the following three conclusions: (1) The differences rule out Hebrews as "deutero-Pauline" in the sense of literary borrowing by a Pauline disciple. (2) The similarities indicate an interaction with the same ideas normally identified with Paul himself, and rule out the view of Ménégoz and others that *Auctor* could *not* at some point have been a disciple of Paul. (3) If it is recognized that there is a sense in which the apostolic tradition grew in a way in which Paul and his associates may have had a significant part, there may be a basis for claiming Pauline influence in the epistle without recourse to the literary solution. Taken in this highly qualified sense, then, the phrase "deutero-Pauline" might be suitable for Hebrews.

6

FIRST PETER

1 History of discussion

An early Christian document which some have felt may constitute a background of Hebrews is 1 Peter. Grässer, who notes the numerous other NT writings with which Hebrews has been compared, says that "this comparison has nowhere been as justified as in the case of 1 Peter."[1] The resemblances seen by many have been used to argue variously that: (1) Hebrews was written at about the same time, to the same recipients, as 1 Peter; (2) Hebrews was written by a disciple of both Peter and Paul, and (in keeping with the Tübingen hypothesis), was intended to serve as an olive branch between the Pauline circle and the circle of Peter and James; (3) Hebrews was written by the author of 1 Peter.[2] T. E. Ferris,[3] in a special study of the two documents, attempted to prove that 1 Peter is "the paramount influence in Hebrews," that Hebrews displays extensive literary borrowing from 1 Peter, and that 1 Peter's place as "the foundation" of Hebrews is a conclusion that cannot "be evaded." Even Selwyn, who was more aware of the parallels between 1 Peter and other NT writings than most, was sufficiently impressed by the parallels with Hebrews in general, and those concentrated in Heb. 13:20f. in particular, to suggest either that "the author of Hebrews may have read 1 Peter and been haunted − as who would not be? − by its language," or that "among 'those from Italy' (Heb. 13:24) who were beside him [Auctor] as he wrote there was one who had been the close associate of St. Paul in writing to Thessalonica and of St. Peter in his first Epistle" (not unlike the Tübingen solution mentioned above). This, Selwyn concludes, serves well to account for "the intimate links ... which seem to bind Hebrews and 1 Peter together."[4]

2 Points of contact

If one is to evaluate whether the evidence supports such assessments, it is necessary to list the parallels most frequently noted. The following conflates lists from Ayles, Grässer,[5] Spicq,[6] Selwyn, Moffatt,[7] Ferris,[8] Wand[9] and Masterman:[10] (1) for 1 Pet. 1:1 and 2:11, "strangers and aliens," cp. Heb. 11:13; (2) for 1 Pet. 1:2, "the sprinkling of Christ's blood" cp. Heb. 12:24; (3) for 1 Pet. 1:4, "inheritance," cp. Heb. 9:15 (cf. 1:1,2,4 — in both writings the inheritance is retained in heaven — 1 Pet. 1:3f.,21; 3:18,21); (4) for 1 Pet. 1:4, "undefiled," cp. Heb. 7:26, 13:4; (5) for 1 Pet. 1:6ff., testing through suffering, cp. Heb. 2:9–18 (in both writings the suffering of Christ is the great example to the suffering congregation); (6) for 1 Pet. 1:10f., prophets who foresaw and foretold Christ's suffering (serving not themselves but Christians), cp. Heb. 1:1,2; (7) for 1 Pet. 1:12, angels who desire to look into these things (as if into something greater), cp. Heb. 1:4ff.; (8) for 1 Pet. 1:13, "gird up the loins of your mind" (as if for a race), cp. Heb. 12:1; (9) for 1 Pet. 1:13, "set your hope fully on the grace that is coming to you at the revelation of Jesus Christ" (cf. 1:21, 3:15), cp. Heb. 11:1ff. (in both writings faith is primarily hope that God's promises will soon be fulfilled); (10) for 1 Pet. 1:14 and 2:25, God's people as "ignorant and erring," cp. Heb. 5:2, 9:7; (11) for 1 Pet. 1:17, "invoke as father ... who judges ... conduct with fear throughout your time of exile," cp. Heb. 4:1, 10:30, 12:7–9; (12) for 1 Pet. 1:18, "ransom," cp. 9:12; (13) for 1 Pet. 1:19, the link of blood with "spotless," cp. Heb. 9:14; (14) for 1 Pet. 1:20, Christ "destined before the foundation of the world, but manifest at the end of time," cp. Heb. 9:26 (same linking of καταβόλη κόσμου with πεφανέρωται) and Heb. 1:2 ("at the end of the days"); (15) for 1 Pet. 1:22, 4:9, brotherly love and kindness to strangers, cp. Heb. 13:1–2; (16) for 1 Pet. 1:23, the "living" word of God, cp. Heb. 4:12; (17) for 1 Pet. 2:2,3, "babes ... milk of the word ... tasted," cp. Heb. 5:12–6:6; (18) for 1 Pet. 2:5, "house" (οἶκος) for the Christian community, cp. Heb. 3:6; (19) for 1 Pet. 2:5, "bear up sacrifices to God through Jesus Christ," cp. Heb. 13:5; (20) for 1 Pet. 2:5,9, Christians as "a holy and royal priesthood" who offer up "spiritual sacrifices," cp. Heb. 7:1ff. and 7:26 (Jesus as a royal priest after the order of Melchizedek); (21) for 1 Pet. 2:19f. and 4:12ff., the sharing of Christ's sufferings as a sign of grace, cp. Heb. 11:26 and 13:13; (22) for 1 Pet. 2:24, the redemptive nature of Christ's "body," cp. Heb. 10:10; (23) for 1 Pet. 2:24, "bearing sins," cp. Heb. 9:28; (24) for 1 Pet. 3:9, "inherit a blessing," cp. Heb. 12:17 (Esau); (25) for 1 Pet. 3:11, the pursuit of peace, cp. Heb. 12:14; (26) for 1 Pet. 3:18, "once for all" (ἅπαξ), cp. Heb. 7:27, 9:7, 26ff.; (28) for 1 Pet. 3:21, ἀντίτυπος, cp. Heb. 9:24; (29) for 1 Pet. 3:22, "at the right hand of God, with angels, authorities, and powers subject to him," cp. Heb. 1:3, 13, etc.; (30) for 1 Pet. 5:2, the warning of presbyters against "filthy lucre," cp. Heb. 13:5 (warning against "covetousness"); (31) for 1 Pet. 5:5, "you that are younger, be subject to the elders," cp. Heb. 13:17; (32) for 1 Pet. 5:9, suffering among the brotherhood, cp. Heb. 13:3.

To this list may be added Selwyn's[11] detection of a special relationship between Heb. 13:20f. and 1 Peter: (33) for "God ... who brought from the dead," cp. 1 Pet. 1:21; (34) for "the great shepherd of the sheep," cp. 1 Pet. 2:25 and 5:4; (35) for "through the blood of the eternal covenant," cp. 1 Pet. 1:2 and 1:19; (36) for "equip you with every good thing," cp. 1 Pet. 4:19 and 5:10; (37) for "the doing of his will," cp. 1 Pet. 4:2; (38) for "to whom be the glory forever and ever," cp. 1 Pet. 4:11.

Such compilations are, *prima facie*, impressive. The parallels, however, as was seen in the case of Hebrews and Paul,[12] are susceptible of various explanations. Spicq thinks that the verbal resemblances are neither more numerous nor of a different nature than those between Hebrews and other NT writings.[13] Spicq,[14] Lindars[15] and Montefiore[16] assign the resemblances to the common stock of (Hellenistic) tradition. Ayles[17] thinks that the parallels consist of things central to Hebrews, but merely peripheral to 1 Peter, which means that the latter may simply have "got them from a friend." The latter judgment is reminiscent of the relationship which some have felt to exist between Paul and 1 Peter.[18]

Any one explanation for the resemblances, however, is probably too simple. At least four different factors may account for them: (a) common Greek idiom; (b) an independent use of the OT; (c) common Christian tradition; and (d) Pauline influence (whether direct or through Christian tradition at points affected by Paul) upon *Auctor* and 1 Peter. Each of these options may be adduced at various stages to account for the parallels. Within the scope of this study not all of the parallels may be classified, but examples of each may be chosen (with, of course, some overlapping):

Common Greek idiom

(14), "the foundation of the world," is a common idiom in the NT (cf. Mat. 13:35, 25:34, Luke 11:50, John 17:24, Eph. 1:4, Rev. 13:8, 17:8), and since it frequently refers to God's purposes which are "hidden" from human beings (see especially Mat. 13:35), its coupling with the notion of manifestation in history is not particularly remarkable.[19] (17), "to taste," is stock metaphor for "to experience" in biblical language and is not peculiar to *Auctor* and 1 Peter (see, e.g., Ps. 34:8, "taste and see").

Independent use of the OT

This is particularly applicable in the use of cultic imagery – (2), (13), (19), (20) and (23). (2), the "sprinkling" of Christ's blood in 1 Pet. 1:2 and Heb. 9:13ff., 10:22 and 12:24 alludes to rites connected with the inauguration of the covenant (Lev. 8:10f., 23f.) and the day of atonement (Ex. 29:1 and Lev. 16). But while in Hebrews this is developed at some length and given a theological rationale, in 1 Peter it is simply one of numerous undeveloped allusions to OT events and institutions. The same may be said of the nature of the sacrifice as "spotless" (13), except that here the two authors appear to refer to different OT contexts. In Hebrews (9:14) it relates to Ex. 29, Lev. 8 and 16; in 1 Pet. 1:19 it apparently refers to the paschal lamb of Ex. 12,[20] mentioned in Hebrews, but not in connection with Christ's work.

(18), "house" (οἶκος) as a term for the Christian community, while unique to the two writers, is used differently. In 1 Pet. 2:5 it is an alternate term for "temple,"[21] a usage frequent in the LXX (Ps. 69:9, Isa. 56:7, etc.), while in Heb. 3:6 it comes from the quotation of Num. 12:7 and is *not* an alternate for "temple." (19), "bear up sacrifices to God," may be drawing upon OT cultic imagery, or it may be "simply making use of the vocabulary of the earliest preaching and worship."[22] (20), the "holy and royal priesthood," is in 1 Pet. the priestly *nation* of Ex. 19, whereas the "royal priesthood" of Hebrews is drawn from Gen. 14 and Ps. 110:4, and refers to an individual figure.[23] (23), "bearing sins," undoubtedly refers in Hebrews to the day of atonement ritual, whereas in 1 Pet. the allusion is probably to Isa. 53:4f.[24] (34), the leader of God's people as a "shepherd," is familiar in the OT (Ps. 23:1, Isa. 40:11, 44:28, etc.). *Auctor* appears to have in mind one specific text, Isa. 63:11 (referring to Moses).

Common Christian tradition

(6), Christ's suffering as foretold through OT prophetic activity, is more akin to Luke 24:27 or John 5:39 than Heb. 1:1. (11), God as the father who judges and is to be feared, may be drawn by both writers from such sayings as Mat. 6:15, 7:2, 10:28, etc. (29) 1 Pet. 3:22 contains allusions to Ps. 110:1 and Ps. 8:5f. Ps. 110:1 is one of the most widely cited passages in the NT; there is no evidence that in his use of it *Auctor* depends upon 1 Peter.[25] The allusion to Ps. 8 in 1 Pet. 3:22 may result simply from previous Christian use of the psalm as a *testimonium*,[26] or it may result from the influence of Pauline theology, either direct (less likely) or indirect (more likely). The coupling of Ps. 110:1 with Ps. 8 in Paul, Hebrews and 1 Peter does not *a priori* point to a link between the three writers. The coupling may go back to tradition antedating all three. "Principalities and powers" in 1 Pet. 3:22 looks Pauline,[27] but this may simply indicate a Pauline phrase let loose in Christian tradition. It would be difficult to draw from the phrase in 1 Peter a doctrine of principalities and powers.[28] (16), the "living" word of God, is found also in Acts 7:38 and John 6:63ff. In Acts 7 and Hebrews it may go back to Deut. 32:43.[29]

Pauline influence

(3), the Christian's lot as an "inheritance," and (24), the inheritance of a blessing, are central themes in Paul[30] (cf. especially Rom. 4); (6) prophets who are serving not themselves but Christians, is closer to 1 Cor. 10:11 ("they were written down for our instruction") than to anything in Hebrews. (9), faith as hope, is found in Rom. 4:18ff.[31] For (14), the designation of the present era as "the end of time," cf. 1 Cor. 10:11 ("upon whom the end of the ages has come"). For (17), "babes ... milk," cf. 1 Cor. 3:1ff. For (22), the redemptive nature of Christ's "body," cf. Col. 1:22. For (25), the pursuit of peace, cf. Rom. 14:19, 1 Cor. 7:15, Col. 3:15 and 2 Tim. 2:22. For (26), the notion of "once for all" attached to Christ's death, cf. Rom. 6:10. For (32), suffering among the brotherhood, cf., e.g., 2 Cor. 1:6f. In addition to these may be cited Goppelt's[32] suggestion that (28), ἀντίτυπος, in 1 Pet. results from Paul's usage of τύπος (Rom. 5:14, 1 Cor. 10:6). (33), (36) and (37), as noted by Selwyn,[33] are equally reminiscent of 1 Thes. 1:10, 2 Thes. 2:17 and 1 Thes. 4:3, 5:18 as they are of anything in 1 Peter.

Further observations may be made which make it unlikely that either of the writers has depended upon the other: (1), "strangers and aliens," is used differently in the two writings. In Hebrews the context of the phrase is OT saints (e.g., Abraham) who, because of their heavenly goal, lived as strangers upon the earth. In 1 Peter the idea is that of isolation from the surrounding Gentile culture (cf. 2:12, "among the Gentiles"). The usage in 1 Peter is closer to James 1:1 than it is to Hebrews.[34] (10), "ignorant and erring," appears in Hebrews in a cultic context (cf., e.g., Num. 15:28),[35] whereas in 1 Peter the two terms are not found together, nor is the context cultic (cf. 2:25, where "wandering" combines quite naturally with "sheep"). Brotherly love (15) is a frequently enjoined virtue in Christian tradition (cf. 1 Thes. 4:9f., 1 John 3:16f.), while "kindness to strangers" was commonly ranked high as a virtue in antiquity.[36]

There are, of course, points at which the two writers do seem quite close; note, e.g., the necessity in both writers of Jesus' sufferings for bringing about his entire perfection (Heb. 2:14, 4:15; 1 Pet. 4:1)[37] and as an example of testing for the community – 1 Pet. 2:21ff., Heb. 12:2ff.).[38] But on the whole the parallels consist mainly of verbal or formal similarities[39] scattered throughout both epistles in a somewhat random fashion, with little substantial development in 1 Peter of major ideas as were noted above in the case of Hebrews and Paul.[40]

3 Conclusion

The most that can be said is that 1 Peter and Hebrews belong to the same general type of early Christian literature which was written to bolster faith in the face of persecution.[41] No form of literary dependence of *Auctor* upon 1 Peter can possibly be sustained. 1 Peter is valuable in the discussion of the sources underlying Hebrews, however, in that it provides another early Christian document which bears similarities to the Pauline letters, yet allows those similarities to be explained as either (1) direct borrowing from Paul, (2) a common use of the same traditions, or (3) the use of a tradition already influenced by Paul. Except for the fact that, following Selwyn, the similarities between 1 Peter and Paul appear to be superficial as compared with the deeper similarities noted above between Hebrews and Paul, 1 Peter *and* Hebrews may be termed "deutero-Pauline" in a non-literary use of the phrase.

CONCLUSION

Our analysis of possible backgrounds of Hebrews has yielded negative and positive results. On the negative side, attempts to locate *Auctor*'s center of gravity in Philo, Qumran, gnosticism, the Samaritans or *Merkabah* mysticism presented difficulties which outweighed any advantages. At one or two points (e.g., a "spiritualized" heavenly cultus) some form of modified Philonic influence could be said to be a possibility. But those emphases could equally be explained by influences within the apocalyptic tradition, and other indications suggest that this is the direction that future study should take in the effort to uncover first-century parallels for Hebrews.

On the positive side, surprisingly productive insights may be gained if William Manson's theory for Acts 7 and Hebrews is applied with sympathy and a bit of caution. A similar use of several of the same OT traditions, often clustered very closely in both writings, seems to point to some kind of contact between the two traditions. The exact form of that contact should constitute a focus of future study. The speech of Stephen, on the other hand, cannot be said to constitute the whole answer to the question of from where the author derived his use of OT traditions. Pauline theology must be considered somewhere in the process. When *Auctor* and Paul were compared on certain crucial themes, some major agreement was discovered, but with individualized features and divergences which one would expect from either a form of pre-literary contact between Hebrews and the Pauline circle or a similar thoughtful use of Christian traditions. The notion of faith, the comparison of the two covenants, the juxtaposition of "heavenly" and "earthly," Christ as "the heavenly man" and Christ as mediator and sustainer of the creation are only a few ideas of Hebrews which, previously explained by recourse to a Platonic-type philosophical background, could be explained from the same thought-world in which Paul moved.

The numerous backgrounds proposed this century for Hebrews

cannot all be correct. What is probable is that they are all *partially* correct, i.e., they indirectly testify to the same or a similar attempt to apply to changing circumstances the teaching of the OT. R. McL. Wilson draws our attention to what may be a modern example of the same phenomenon. Wilson, who had seen an earlier version of this study before it reached print, says "I have read Dr Hurst's work ... but do not have a copy at hand for reference and can no longer remember the detail." He then adds somewhat wryly:

> Any parallels are therefore due not to borrowing or to influence but to independent work on the same material. Something of the sort may be true of parallels between Hebrews and the others [intellectual backgrounds] mentioned above.[1]

Quite so. *Auctor*, Philo, Qumran, the Samaritans and *Merkabah* mysticism appear to represent a development of the OT which does not point to any real interdependence. They happened to be working on the same material at the same time.[2] Something of a slightly different nature, on the other hand, may be operating in the case of Hebrews, Stephen and Paul.

In *Auctor*'s case, a partially satisfactory explanation of the data is supplied if we proceed along the following route. After his conversion to Christianity, *Auctor*, a "bookish" Christian, studiously searched the LXX for its proper meaning in the light of the recent climactic events of Christ's life, death and resurrection. In particular, he was drawn to the psalms, with their emphasis upon the will and disposition of the worshiper over the necessity of literal sacrifice (Ps. 40) and the dangers of treating lightly the laws which operate in the sphere of God's dealings with humankind (Ps. 95). The Christian coupling of Pss. 8 and 110 led him further to reflect upon the nature and destiny of humankind in relation to Christ. At some point he came under the influence of certain uses of the same OT traditions which also appear in Acts 7. This may well have been some form of the same source used by Luke.

Affecting his thinking at several points, particularly in the area of the necessity of advance in the light of the spiritual nature of God and his demands, this in turn pushed him further to delineate those lines of thought which he found corroborated in his OT and in the form of Christian teaching which had been entrusted to him. An additional factor entered the pictures via an exposure to teaching which also surfaces in Paul. This crystallized his thinking regarding the relation of the two covenants and the meaning of Christ for the OT. These three factors – the impact of certain sections of the LXX, the same use of the OT preserved in Acts 7, and an exposure to a "Paul-like" theology – were mingled with a fourth, an exposure to strands of Jewish apocalyptic similar to that which also appears in 4 Ezra and 1 Enoch 90. These four influences could cautiously be isolated as those which produced the distinctive and potent brew which we call the Epistle to the Hebrews. The evidence considered in this study indicates that, taken individually, the case for each of these factors has certain attractions. The question which remains now is how many features of the epistle may *not* be accounted for by this fourfold hypothesis. The answer, of course, must be determined largely by the subjective judgments of individual scholars. But the number of features which the hypothesis does answer makes the question valid.

The apocalyptic tradition, in particular, supplies at several points a cogent Jewish alternative for ideas which were previously considered Platonic or gnostic. The entry by Christ into the heavenly sanctuary and its cleansing with blood could be explained against such a background. A main feature of the epistle, on the other hand, which might be said to remain unanswered by these various factors is Christ's depiction as heavenly high priest. How *Auctor* proceeded from Christ as the "priest like Melchizedek" of Ps. 110:4 to a *high* priest who operates within a Levitical-type framework remains a riddle. Whether he made this jump himself or whether the jump had already been made by some external influence which acted upon him may be difficult to determine. It was once felt that Philo's *logos* doctrine supplied the answer to this question, but now that any direct influence of Philo upon *Auctor* may be said to have been seriously undermined, the search for another answer must go on.

NOTES

Introduction

1 For other surveys of the question, cf., e.g., Buchanan, "Present State"; McCullough, "Recent Developments"; and Wilson, *Hebrews*, 18ff.
2 Cf., e.g., C. P. M. Jones's well-known study of Hebrews and Luke.
3 *Beginnings*, 51.
4 This, of course, goes against the consensus of opinion on Heb. 8:5 and 9:23f; but see below, pp. 13–19.
5 Here the distribution and frequency of references is telling. Thompson's index contains six columns of references to the Old and New Testament writers put together, and one and a half columns given to the apocalyptic writers. Philo, on the other hand, alone receives eight columns, while Plato and other classical writers, including Plotinus, receive over three columns.

1 Philo, Alexandria and Platonism

1 The first writer to suggest Philonic influence appears to have been Grotius in 1646. For a brief list of others with similar ideas before the twentieth century, see Burtness, 54.
2 197–219.
3 Among the many writers who could be cited are Blackman, 88 ("If there is any one of the NT writers on whom the mantle of Philo might be said to have fallen, it would be the author of Hebrews"); Burtness, 54, for whom *Auctor*'s dependence upon Philo "is so obvious that there is not the smallest room for doubt in the matter"; Chadwick, 290 ("The analogies are so near as to make a relationship of direct dependence much the simplest and most probable hypothesis"); Cody, 3, who warns against "forcing Hebrews to speak in terminology and categories quite foreign to its own brand of Platonism"; Eager, 263–87; Filson, "Hebrews", 23; Gilbert, 521–32; Grant, 54–56; Howard, *Fourth Gospel*, 115; Kennedy, *Theology*, 193; Kuss, 18; McNeile, 222 ("Its basis is the Platonic theory of ideas"); Moffatt, *Hebrews*, xxxi ("The philosophical element in his view of the world and God is fundamentally Platonic"); Montefiore, 6ff. ("It is almost impossible to deny the

validity of Ménégoz's conclusion ..."); Moule, "Commentaries on Hebrews", 228f.; T. H. Robinson, xvff. ("There can be little doubt that the author was brought up in the school of Egyptian Judaism"; see also 108); Rust, 174f.; Schaeffer, 362; Taylor, 148f.; and Windisch, *Hebräerbrief*, passim. See also the full-length studies of Thompson and Dey.

4 *Hébreux*, especially vol. I, 39–91, and "Le Philonisme."
5 A suggestion quoted with approval by, e.g., Chadwick, 287f., and Montefiore, 8.
6 *Hermeneutics*.
7 *Ibid.*, 66.
8 Cf. Spicq, "Hébreux, Apollos," 365–90, especially 388.
9 "Eschatology."
10 *Allegory and Event*, 83–86.
11 *Ibid.*, 94–96.
12 *Verfasser*, 301–307.
13 *Philo and Hebrews*. See also his earlier article on "Platonism."
14 *Philo and Hebrews*, 524. Bultmann and Lührmann, 2, cite Heb. 11:3 as "the only NT instance of the dualistic distinction between the visible on earth and the invisible." For the same distinction in Paul, however, see below, pp. 119–24.
15 "Purpose," 215.
16 "Greek Element," 528.
17 In *Praep. evang.* XII, Eusebius, in commenting on Heb. 8:5, refers to Plato's *Republic*.
18 Cf. Sowers, 104, n. 38.
19 *NT Teaching*, 257.
20 Cf. Spicq, *Hébreux*, I, 52f. (although this should be contrasted with "Le Philonism," 48, n. 6) and Chadwick, "Paul and Philo," 297.
21 Gilbert, 527.
22 Cf., e.g. Westcott, *Hebrews*, 242; Spicq, *Hébreux*, I, 72–76; Moffatt, *Hebrews*, xxxiff., 107ff.; W. Manson, 124–26; McNeile, *NT Teaching*, 222; Cody, 155; Taylor, *Atonement*, 101f.; Rawlinson, *NT Doctrine of Christ*, 177; Barclay (DSB), 94f.; Howard, "Hebrews," 89; Kennedy, *Theology*, 190f.; Héring, *Hebrews*, xii; Dunn, *Unity and Diversity*, 89f. and *Christology*, 52f.; Dodd, *Companion to the Bible*, 410; T. H. Robinson, *Hebrews*, 108; Scott, *Hebrews*, 115f.; and McKelvey, 206.
23 *Beginnings of Christian Philosophy*. See also above, pp. 3–4.
24 *La Naissance du christianisme* (1946), 373, cited in Grässer, "Hebräerbrief 1938–63," 224.
25 "Eschatologie ou Hellénisme."
26 *Hebrews*, xxxii, xxxiv, and liv ("The category of the Highpriesthood ... could not be fitted in with his eschatology any more than the idea of the two worlds could be").
27 Cf., e.g., *Hebrews*, 109, 115. See also Héring, "Eschatologie biblique et idéal Platonicien," 453.
28 Barrett, "Eschatology," 393.
29 *Katapausis*, passim.

30 *Hebräer*, passim.
31 "Eschatologie ou Hellénisme," 94.
32 "Der Glaube an Jesus," cited in Grässer, "Hebräerbrief 1938–63," 225, n. 1.
33 *Christ and Time*, 54f.
34 "Hebräerbrief 1938–63," 226f., and *Glaube*, 171, 174ff.
35 *Die Eschatologie*, 11–13, 21, etc.
36 "Heavenly Temple and Eschatology", 191.
37 Rowland, *Open Heaven*, 23ff.
38 For a much fuller treatment of (3), cf. Hurst, "Eschatology and 'Platonism.'"
39 See above, p. 8.
40 Cf. the apparent allusion to Wis. 7:26 in 1:3. Bruce, *Hebrews*, 5, thinks that *Auctor* "may well have been acquainted" with Wisdom, while T. H. Robinson, 3, in discussing the same passage, views verbal independence as "practically impossible." Farrar, 56, records the verdict of some scholars of his day that Hebrews and Wisdom were written by the same author! For verbal parallels, cf. Milligan, 45, n. 1, and Vanhoye, *Situation*, 351f.
41 Cf. e.g., Stacey, 32–35, and Davies, *Paul*, 116.
42 In addition to 8:19f. and 11:17, see 1:7, 7:24 and 8:1 (the notion of a world-soul) and 9:15 (the notion of the human body as a mere weight and clog to the soul).
43 Stacey asserts that 8:19f. is not the highly developed belief of the philosophers (98), and (32f.) quotes Goodrick in speaking of "eclectic Stoicism," yet "without ... any deep knowledge of Greek philosophy." For a full discussion, see Reese, 41ff.
44 For a full discussion, see Pfeiffer, 197ff.
45 For the apparent influence of Hellenism on the rabbism, see, e.g., Bonsirven, 522–24; Daube, "Rabbinic Methods" and "Alexandrian Methods"; and G. Hughes, 157, n. 4. Davies, *Paul*, 303, notes such ideas as the immortality of the soul in Josephus' description of the Essenes and in apocalyptic (cf. Jub. 3.4).
46 We know virtually nothing of the kind of literature which diaspora Jews of Rome or Tarsus would have produced, but there is no *a priori* reason why an attempt to amalgamate Judaism with Greek philosophy such as one tends to associate with Philo could not have occurred there as well. Marshall, 274, following the landmark work of Hengel (*Judaism and Hellenism*), correctly states that "it is no longer possible to use the mere presence or absence of Hellenistic ideas as a criterion for establishing the area of origin of the literature or concepts in question. A *geographical* use of the terms 'Palestinian' and 'Hellenistic' becomes impossible" (my italics).
47 For a more extensive treatment of pp. 13–19 below, cf. my article "How 'Platonic.'" I am gratified to learn from Professor Metzger that based upon my arguments the New Revised Standard Version has substituted "sketch" for its original rendering "copy" in Heb. 8:5 and 9:23.

48 This is only partially Williamson's fault; he was following the vocabulary list of Spicq.
49 *Allegory and Event*, 92.
50 "Plato, Philo," 58.
51 See also McKelvey, 145, who includes ὑπόδειγμα among terms by which "the author reveals his indebtedness to Greek thought."
52 *Timaeus* 29b.
53 See Mayer, who lists no fewer than 83 occurrences of παράδειγμα in Philo.
54 Cf. Lee, 167–69.
55 *Ibid.*, 168 (my italics).
56 Theophilus, *Ad Autol.* 2:14–16, cited in Grant, 125.
57 Contra Sowers, 110, who refers to ὑπόδειγμα as "the technical allegorical term found in Philo."
58 See e.g., *Tim.* 48e–49a.
59 E.g., *ibid.*, 29b.
60 Cf. Williamson, *Hebrews*, 75: "The way in which the thought of 8:5 has been expressed has perhaps been influenced, and thereby for us obscured, by philosophical ideas and language which came ultimately from the great Greek philosopher, Plato ... The distinction in 8:5 between 'that which is a copy and shadow' and 'the heavenly things' is remarkably similar to the way in which Plato was accustomed to speak of 'Ideas' and their earthly 'copies' or 'shadows'" (see also 91). That this characterization of *Auctor*'s argument stubbornly persists is shown by three of the more important recent works to be published on Hebrews, those of G. Hughes (1979), D. Peterson (1982), and R. McL. Wilson (1987). Although he recognizes the essentially "horizontal" nature of *Auctor*'s eschatology, for Hughes the notion of promise and fulfilment is worked out "throughout the epistle" in terms of what is "copied" and what is "eternal and archetypal" (45). Peterson, who quotes Williamson approvingly, finds in ὑπόδειγμα and σκιά "certain linguistic parallels between 8:5 and Philonic Platonism" (131), as does Wilson, for whom the "copy and shadow" of 8:5 indicates that *Auctor* "could have known the language of Alexandrian Jewish philosophy as represented by Philo, even perhaps have read some of Philo's writings" (135).
61 Wycliffe (1380) chose "saumpler"; Tyndale (1534) and Cranmer (1539), "ensample"; Geneva (1557), "patrone"; Rheims (1582), "exampler"; Authorized (1611), "example."
62 Cf. Lee, 168.
63 *Ibid.*, 168.
64 Barclay (DSB), 95 (my italics). He does not, however, allow this to prevent him from Platonizing 8:5 ("God had shown Moses the real and eternal pattern of which all earthly worship is the ghost-like copy").
65 Schlier, 33.
66 Cf. Eusebius, *Praep. evang.* XII.19.
67 It should also be noted that in the Ezekiel account an angel plays

an important role in communicating the instructions for the new temple to the prophet, an idea which undoubtedly would have caught the attention of *Auctor*, for whom angels as mediators of revelation are very important (cf. Heb. 1:4–2:2).

68 "Heavenly Temple," 385–402, 530–46.
69 Cf. 2 Baruch 4:3–6, as discussed in Fritsch, "TO 'ANTITYΠOV," 104.
70 For another opinion that Ezek. 40–48 provides the proper background against which to read Hebrews 8–10, see Muilenburg, 585.
71 It is of particular interest that the rabbis chose a Hebraized form of δεῖγμα (used in the papyri for "plan" or "outline") to represent the "pattern" or "blueprint" from which God, the divine architect, made the world. In B.T. Sanhedrin 98b it is used for a sample, in this world, of the world to come. Cf. Knox, "Pharisaism and Hellenism," 75.
72 This meaning is suggested by Spicq, *Hébreux*, I, 75, for σκιά, but he does not apply it to ὑπόδειγμα.
73 Torrance, 20f.
74 Cf. Fritsch, "TO 'ANTITYΠOV," 102; Macrae, *passim*; Cambier, 62–96; Klappert, 50; and Johnsson, "Pilgrimage Motif," 247f. Barrett, "Eschatology," 386, n.1, claiming that σκιά in 10:1 is a "*fore*shadowing" (his italics), adds that "this meaning is not absent from viii.5." The latter assertion, however, is not developed.
75 As with most commentators, Williamson (*Hebrews*, 95), sees the sacrificial system in 10:1 as "but a dim foreshadowing ... an imperfect approximation." It is difficult to escape the impression that the virtually universal acceptance of the rendering of ὑπόδειγμα in 8:5 as "copy" has prevented writers from using the same language to describe the import of that passage as well.
76 Cf. Bruce, *Hebrews*, 166: "There is indeed some affinity with Platonic idealism here, but it is our author's language, and not his essential thought, that exhibits such affinity."
77 For a complete history of the term, see Schulz, 394ff.
78 See McKelvey, 38f.
79 See, e.g., Job 8:9, 14:2; Ps. 101:2, 108:23; Eccl. 7:1, etc.
80 *Hebrews*, 105.
81 Contra R.P.C. Hanson, 81f., who claims that it is not used in Philo.
82 Cf. Goppelt, "τύπος, κτλ," 248.
83 *Ibid.*, 248.
84 *Typologie*, 110f. See also the discussion in R.P.C. Hanson, 67f., and Reicke, *Disobedient Spirits*, 144ff.
85 See Sowers, 90, n.3, who claims that "it is not certain" whether ἀντίτυπος in I Pet. 3:21 "has a different meaning than in Heb. 9:24 or not." He does not, however, elaborate.
86 Goppelt, "τύπος, κτλ.," 258.
87 See the apparent allusion to Wis. 7:26 in 1:3.
88 This is normally taken to refer to a heavenly tent and its earthly copy (see, e.g., Moffatt, *Hebrews*, 106, for whom the prior

tent is "the eternal archetype"; Macrae, 182ff.; and Kennedy, *Theology of Epistles*, 191).

89 Selwyn, *I Peter*, 298.

90 For a much fuller development of this idea, cf. Hurst, "How 'Platonic,'" 167f.

91 Cf. below, pp. 23–24.

92 The use of τύπος for a mould is found in a number of ancient writers, including Plato and Paul. See the useful discussion of Lee, 169f.

93 Cf. the above comment of Schlier regarding ὑπόδειγμα in John 13.

94 Williamson, "Platonism," 420, by his apparent acceptance of ἀντίτυπος in 9:24 as "copy," finds himself forced to say (against his general thesis) that "it seems impossible to deny the presence here of thoughts which have been influenced, at least in the way they are expressed, by the doctrine of Plato that the phenomenal world is simply a *copy* of the world of ideas" (my italics). The evidence, however, seems to suggest that such a denial *is* possible.

95 Moffatt, *Hebrews*, 135.

96 Cf. below, pp. 33–37.

97 Cody, 153f., defines εἰκών in 10:1 as "the very substance of reality, in as far as it is given to men."

98 *Tim.* 29b is particularly noteworthy. There the "copy" is termed εἰκών and the original παράδειγμα. *Tim.* 48e preserves the same usage, except that μίμημα is substituted for εἰκών. Since παράδειγμα is related to ὑπόδειγμα via the root δεῖγμα, it would appear that *Auctor* has completely reversed the Platonic usage – the δεῖγμα term, rather than representing the non-earthly, represents the earthly, while the εἰκών, instead of pointing toward the earthly, represents the heavenly. Stewart, 287, is therefore correct to note that in Hebrews ὑπόδειγμα is now "the precise opposite" of παραδεῖγμα, but his assumption that because of this ὑπόδειγμα now corresponds to "the Platonic image" does not follow. *Auctor* differs from Plato by making the δεῖγμα term represent the earthly, but he agrees with him that the term represents that which comes first.

99 See Sowers, 104f., n. 42.

100 Bruce, *Hebrews*, 226f., who cites 2 Cor. 4:4 and Col. 1:15 as closer to *Auctor* than Plato/Philo at this point.

101 Cf. Arndt–Gingrich, 703f.

102 *Hermeneutics*, 107.

103 See "ἀληθινός," 250.

104 On the ambiguity of this term, see below, pp. 33–37.

105 Caird, *Paul's Letters*, 134, and *Language and Imagery*, 93.

106 Lewis, *Studies in Words*, 19.

107 "Purpose," 215.

108 "Eschatology," 389.

109 See Cullmann, *Christ and Time, passim*, who draws a hard distinction between the "Greek" and "Hebrew" views. In Hebrews,

he says, the "Greek" view does not show up: the invisible is not thought of in terms of space, but in terms of time (54).

110 Minear, 23ff. (see below, p. 22).

111 See, e.g., Moffatt, *Hebrews*, 106; Fritsch, "TO 'ANTITYΠOV," 102, n. 3; and McKelvey, 25.

112 As does, e.g., Cody, 15, 24, and Knox, "Pharisaism and Hellenism," 72ff.

113 "Cosmology," 35.

114 That *Auctor* can use the present tense to stand for events which are past is well known. Westcott, 219, commenting on the fact that in Heb. 8:5 Moses *is* warned, says "the direction of God is still present in Scripture." See also Nairne, *Hebrews*, cxlviif. ("often a present is due to the author's habit of referring to what stands written in books or pictured in history"); Milligan, 41f.; and Thomas, "OT Citations," 311.

115 See, e.g., Barth, 269, n. 28: "In Heb. 8:5 'type' means archetype; the antitype mentioned in 9:24 corresponds to it."

116 Cf. Gray, 533: "Neither Ezekiel nor Moses is represented in the Old Testament as having seen a temple in heaven."

117 Cf. Michaelis, "σκηνή, κτλ.," 375: "The fact that the heavenly σκηνή pre-dated the tabernacle as its τύπος is used in Heb. as evidence of the high antiquity and indeed the pre-existence of the heavenly σκηνή before all times."

118 It is, however, going too far to say with Strathmann, 531, that because Abraham "looked for a city with foundations" [11:10], "the patriarchs already knew of the heavenly Jerusalem."

119 Philo interprets Ex. 25:40 as the giving to Moses of a mystic vision of the whole realm of incorporeal ideas (*De vit. M.* II.74, *Qu. in Exod.* II.90; *Leg. all.* III.96–103; *De somn.* I.206; *De plant.* 27). What is also interesting is that for Philo Moses' obedience to the command produced what were in themselves the "archetypes" (*Leg. all.* III.102). Bezalel then produced *copies* (μίμημα) from, as it were, a shadow (σκιά). At this point the distance of *Auctor* from Philo is not merely linguistic: it is strikingly conceptual.

120 "When the Jew wished to designate something as pre-destined, he spoke of it as already existing in heaven" (Selwyn, *I Peter*, 124). "The notion of blessings kept in reserve in heaven (Mt. xxv.34), to be brought out at the decisive moment, was thoroughly Jewish, being familiar both in apocalyptic (1 En. xlvii.7; lviii.5; Asc. Is. viii.25f.) and to the rabbis (SB. III, 762; IV, 1146f.; 1156f.)" (Kennedy, 51f.).

121 See Barrett, "Eschatology," 381, and Howard, *Hebrews*, 82 ("The eternal realities are in heaven in the mind of God").

122 See Cody, 18, who, assuming that the "holy tent" of Wis. 9:8 is "the whole cosmos," claims that "Wis. 9:8 affords the best background for an understanding of the notion of the heavenly sanctuary in Hebrews."

123 Cf. below, pp. 28–29.

124 Swetnam, "Imagery and Significance" and "'Greater and More Perfect Tent.'"
125 Vanhoye, "'Par la tent plus grand.'"
126 E.g., Westcott, 260.
127 *Hebrews*, 145.
128 *Hebräer*, 113.
129 "Eschatology," 383ff.
130 *Hebräer*, 285ff. and *passim*.
131 On the notion of the new temple in the OT, apocrypha and pseudepigrapha, see McKelvey, 9ff.; on the existence of a temple *in heaven* in the pseudepigrapha, rabbis and Qumran, see McKelvey, 28ff.
132 "There were thus opposing tendencies in the Judaism of Jesus' time: the spiritualizing of the cultus, and the belief in a restored or new cultus, with the latter acting as a kind of brake on the former" (McKelvey, 56f.).
133 See Westcott, 258ff., for whom "it is obvious that all images of local circumscription must be laid aside ... the spiritual Tabernacle must not be defined by the limitations which belong to 'this creation' ... we must look for some spiritual antitype to the local sanctuary." Westcott subsequently defines this "spiritual antitype" as the body of Christ in heaven, in which "the redeemed and perfected hosts [are] made one in Christ as His body." This, of course, is a Paulinizing of *Auctor*'s argument; it imports Pauline notions of the church as the body of Christ and the use of "tent" in 2 Cor. 5:1ff. Wickham likewise rejects an actual sanctuary in heaven; for him it must be a "correspondence of the idea embodied, not of the form of their embodiment. All types are the shadowing forth of something that cannot be grasped" (167).
134 Schrenk, 241.
135 Josephus (*Ant.* III.181) focuses on the three parts of the tabernacle constructed by Moses: the first two are the earth and sea, accessible to human beings; the third is reserved "for God alone."
136 "Heavenly Temple," 538.
137 "Purpose," 216.
138 *Hebrews*, 136f.
139 *Hermeneutics*, 106 (see also 94f.).
140 "Heavenly Temple," 189.
141 Montefiore, 137.
142 "σκηνή, κτλ.," 376.
143 For this interpretation, see Cody, 158ff. and the articles of Swetnam. Michaelis, 377, Héring, *Hebrews*, 77, n. 21, Williamson, "Eucharist," 305, and Peterson, 142f., argue against this view.
144 See, e.g., F. F. Bruce, *Hebrews*, 199f., 219, and "Kerygma," 10. Bruce connects the "tent" of 9:11 with the "house" of 3:3ff., noting that the consciences of the people of the house and the true tent are both connected with the term καθαρίζω (cp. 9:14, 10:2 with 9:22f.).
145 For the local interpretation of διά in 9:11, cf. Héring, "Eschatologie biblique," 176, and Macrae, 187.

146 Using Cody's well-publicized distinction.

147 Macrae, 185.

148 See, e.g., Michaelis, "σκηνή, κτλ.," 376ff. Michaelis carries the correspondence between the two tents to the point of denying that God is actually "present" in the heavenly holy of holies, since it does not contain his throne (377). This, of course, is an error, since in Judaism God's throne is always symbolically present in the sanctuary.

149 *Ibid.*, 377.

150 Westcott, 258, and Montefiore, 151f.

151 Just as, in 1:1f., God speaks *by means of* (instrumental), not *in* (local) his Son.

152 Montefiore, 160.

153 *Hebrews*, 166f., n. 32. Gray, on the other hand, uses Rev. 4–7 as evidence (against Philo and Hebrews) for a temple *in* heaven.

154 "Eschatology," 386.

155 See Gray, 396, n. 2, who, in interpreting the Code of Hammurabi, points out that the phrase *šu-ba-at ša-ma-i* may mean either "dwelling *in* heaven" or "dwelling place which *is* heaven."

156 The phenomenon of synechdoche or "enlarged reference" is a common occurrence in the NT (Caird, *Language and Imagery*, 135f.).

157 Williamson, "Eucharist," 36, seems to admit this possibility as well ("The greater and more perfect tent which is [in?] heaven itself"). See also Traub and von Rad, 528, for whom it "does not clearly say whether one enters God's presence in the heaven or whether this heaven is in some sense identical with God's presence."

158 "Cultus," 107.

159 *Hebrews*, 143 (my italics).

160 See 2:14, 7:5, and 13:15 (accus.–accus.); 9:11 and 11:16 (gen.–gen.).

161 Westcott, 322.

162 The phrase is that of W. Manson (67).

163 "Himmlisches," 206ff.

164 See, e.g., McKelvey, 149, 154, 205, and Floor, 74–78.

165 Floor, 74f.

166 McKelvey, 9ff., 40f.

167 Michel, "ναός," 889, n. 36.

168 See, e.g., Charles, *Apocrypha and Pseudepigrapha* II, 307.

169 Contra Sowers, 108, who implies that, according to Wis. 9:8, the Jerusalem temple is a copy of Moses' tent. But Wis. 9:8 is usually taken to refer to a heavenly tent (Moffatt, *Hebrews*, 106 – it is "the eternal archetype"; Macrae, 182f.; and Kennedy, *Theology*, 191).

170 Fohrer and Lohse, 326.

171 Charles' translation.

172 Fritsch, "TO 'ANTITYΠOV," 104.

173 Hurst, "How 'Platonic,'" 161f.

174 But cf. Charles, *Apocalypse of Baruch*, 7, who is uncertain whether this "paradise" is a pre-existent heavenly paradise or the earthly paradise into which Adam is put.

175 McKelvey, 33, n. 1.
176 "Heavenly Temple," 184.
177 *New Temple*, 27. Yet McKelvey's supposition that 'the NT writers were influenced" by Platonic ideas is prompted largely by his unnecessary, quasi-Platonic reading of Hebrews (see especially 206, where he rejects Barrett's arguments for the role of apocalyptic influences in Hebrews in favour of Platonism).
178 "Σιών," 326.
179 *Ibid.*, 326.
180 McKelvey, 30, states that the Jerusalem of 1 En. 90 appears to be the heavenly Jerusalem come to earth, although he admits that this is not completely certain.
181 Strack–Billerbeck, III, 701, 848–52, etc.
182 *Ibid.*, III, 796.
183 *New Temple*, 35.
184 "Eschatology," 375.
185 Bruce, "Kerygma," 9f.
186 In addition to the comments of Westcott and Wickham above, see Milligan, 175 ("the idea of *locality* is to be removed as far as possible from the epithet 'heaven.'").
187 McKelvey, 39.
188 "Cosmology." Traub and von Rad, 528, helpfully note that in Hebrews "God is high above the heavens, and yet He is in the heavens."
189 Caird, *Language and Imagery*, 149ff.
190 Barrett, "Eschatology," 383, n. 2.
191 "The future Jerusalem without a temple is an impossible thought for the ancient Synagogue" (Michel, "ναός," 889); see also Cody, 22f.; Barrett, "Eschatology," 374.
192 "Eschatology," 384 (my italics).
193 *Ibid.*, 389.
194 *Ibid.*, 384. See also Bruce, *Hebrews*, 374, who claims that the new Jerusalem which comes down out of God in Rev. 21:2 has "existed eternally in heaven," without any clarification of what he means.
195 "Eschatology," 385.
196 *Ibid.*, 393.
197 *Ibid.*, 393.
198 *Ibid.*, 393.
199 This extends also to the attribution to *Auctor* of Platonic-sounding Greek terms which he does not employ. I find it extraordinary that Cody, 20f., in comparing Hebrews with Wis. 9:8, can speak of "*their* views of μίμημα and παράδειγμα" (my italics).
200 It is not clear whether πνεύματος αἰωνίου in Heb. 9:14 refers to the Holy Spirit (see RSV) or the spiritual nature of the sacrifice (see NEB).
201 Contra Michaelis, "σκηνή, κτλ.," 375f. He admits that the tent is not called αἰώνιος or αἰώνια, but "it is called ἀληθινή (8:2) and fundamentally this can only mean that it is eternal in character." But on ἀληθινός, see above, pp. 20f.

202 "Eschatology," 393.

203 "Platonism," 423.

204 "Eschatology," 385 (my italics).

205 *Ibid.*, 424.

206 *Philo and Hebrews*, 159 (my italics).

207 LSJ and Lampe and Woolcombe, *Lexicon*, q.v.

208 According to the *Oxford Shorter Dictionary*, 93, "archetype" may be used of "a coin of standard weight," or, in comparative anatomy, "an assumed ideal pattern of each division of organized beings." In neither case is "prototype" synonymous.

209 *Hist. eccl.* 10.4.55 (cf. Lampe's lexicon for ἀρχέτυπος).

210 Arndt–Gingrich, 111f.

211 See also Barrett, "Eschatology," 384.

212 *Hermeneutics*, 111.

213 Williamson, *Philo and Hebrews*, 142ff.

214 I owe some of these rabbinic references to Cody, 24.

215 Although this might be classed with (a), since Philo's world of archetypes was created first as the blueprint.

216 Implied rather than stated: "Six things preceded the creation of the world; some of them were actually created, while the creation of others was contemplated." The temple is among those things only contemplated.

217 If ἀπ' ἀρχῆς is taken to mean "from creation."

218 "At the time when the Holy One, blessed be He, commanded Israel to set up the tent His words also included a command to the ministering angels that they should set up a tent on high" (cf. Strack–Billerbeck, III, 701f.; Michaelis, "σκηνή, κτλ.," 375, n. 38).

219 *Hebrews*, 132.

220 *Hebrews*, 160.

221 *Hebrews*, 338.

222 Cf., e.g., Héring, *Hebrews*, 82.

223 Moffatt, *Hebrews*, 132.

224 Montefiore, 160; Bruce, *Hebrews*, 219.

225 See Lünemann, 344, who argues that καθαρίζειν "is an idea which entirely subordinates itself to the idea of the ἐγκαινίζειν, v. 18."

226 See also III.206: "He purified (ἐθαράπευε) the tabernacle."

227 See P. E. Hughes, 380.

228 Cody, 183ff., who argues that 9:24–38 is a new section.

229 See Kennedy, *Theology*, 200, n. 2, 211f.

230 "Gospel," 204ff.

231 "ΤΟΥΤ' ΕΣΤΙΝ."

232 Williamson, "Platonism," 420f., notes another interesting facet of this text, the relation of the two cleansings in 9:23 as "earthly" and "heavenly" without the use of the "vertical" scheme. The earthly cleansing comes *first*; the heavenly comes *second*. This is a further indication that when *Auctor* thinks in terms of "heaven" and "earth" he is not thinking as a Platonist.

233 See Horton, 164, n. 1, who observes that "in Heb. ix the earthly

tent, the antitype, is also the 'first' tent (ix.2) whereas the true tent is the 'second' tent.''
234 "ὑπόστασις,'' 586, n. 139 (my italics).
235 See also Heb. 12:25, where it is said that the old covenant was ratified on earth (ἐπὶ γῆς) and the other from heaven (ἀπ' οὐρανῶν). Commenting on this, G. Hughes, 45, says that ''the one stands to the other as anticipation to achievement and therefore in horizontal or historical relationship.'' Hughes' point is well taken, although he might have strengthened it by a reference to the very similar language in 1 Cor. 15:47.
236 The viewpoint reflected in 1 Enoch 90:29 (discussed above, pp. 31–32) could also help to explain the enigmatic argument of Heb. 9:8: ''The way into the holy place had not yet been made manifest while the first tent was standing.'' According to 1 Enoch 90:28f., ''before the new temple of the eschatological age is erected, the existing temple will have to be broken up and taken away'' (cf. McKelvey, 23).
237 "Eschatology,'' 389; see also 386 (my italics).
238 *Ibid.*, 375ff. (my italics).
239 *Katapausis*, 92.
240 *Hebräer*, 69.
241 *New Temple*, 29.
242 Note that John of Patmos refers to the new Jerusalem as ''Mount Zion'' (14:1 indicates the earthly city which is the scene of the final battle).
243 Thompson, 41ff., focuses on Heb. 12:18–29 with regard to the ''shaking'' of heaven and earth and the ''intangibility'' of Mt. Zion. For a detailed rebuttal, see Hurst, ''Eschatology and 'Platonism,''' 69ff.

2 Qumran

1 Hebrews and Qumran were mentioned together as early as 1952, but without any systematic treatment, by K. G. Kuhn, *ZTK* (1952), 221, who linked the scrolls to Heb. 2:17f. and 4:15.
2 "Scrolls and Hebrews,'' 36–55.
3 *Ibid.*, 38.
4 *Ibid.*, 45f.
5 *Ibid.*, 48–53.
6 *Ibid.*, 53.
7 *Ibid.*, 53f.
8 *Ibid.*, 54f.
9 *Hebräer – Essener – Christen.*
10 *Ibid.*, x.
11 *Ibid.*, 76–81.
12 *Ibid.*, 7–10.
13 *Ibid.*, 17–30.
14 See, e.g., Bowman, *Hebrews, James*, 9f.; Brown, ''Messianism,'' 77; Buchanan, ''Present State,'' 308 (who claims that a relationship

between Qumran and Hebrews is "so obvious that many scholars noticed it almost simultaneously"); Cullmann, *Johannine Circle*, 54f.; Daniélou, 11–13; Fensham, *passim*; Floor, 72; Flusser, "Dead Sea Sect," 215–66; Gärtner, "Habakkuk Commentary," 13 and 161; Schaeffer, 368; Spicq, "Hébreux, Apollos, Jean-Baptiste"; and de Waard, *passim*.

15 "Hebrews or Essenes?" See also his *Hebrews*, xxxi–xxv, and "Recent Contributions," 260–64.
16 "Affinitiés," 128–41, 257–82.
17 *Ibid.*, 29f.
18 *Qumran*, 241–78.
19 See, e.g., Batdorf, 16–35; Grässer, "Hebräerbrief, 1938–63," 171ff.; Kümmel, 278; LaSor, *Scrolls and the NT*, 180ff. (who calls Yadin's arguments "slanted"); McCullough, "Recent Developments," 145–48; Montefiore, 17f.; and Sowers, 65.
20 See, e.g., Michel, *Hebräer*, 1966 edition.
21 The phrase is taken from Batdorf, 20.
22 See, e.g., Lonegnecker, "Melchizedek Argument" (1978), 172, who attacks Coppens for lumping Kosmala's arguments with Yadin's, the latter of which he continues to find sound.
23 Bruce, "Hebrews or Essenes," 218.
24 "Scrolls and Hebrews," 45–48.
25 *Ibid.*, 48. On the cosmic role of angels at Qumran, see also Yadin, *Scroll*, 229–42, and Brownlee, "Cosmic Role," 83f.
26 "Hebrews or Essenes," 219.
27 See Hurst, "Christology of Heb. 1 and 2," 157–59.
28 *Theology*, 90.
29 According to van der Woude's reading of the text (cf. "Melchizedek," *passim*).
30 It would be incorrect to assume, as does, e.g., Baaker, "Christ an Angel?" 260ff., that the only "name" by which *Auctor* distinguishes Christ from the angels is "son" – he also finds the ascription "God" and "Lord" of interest for the argument.
31 *Hermeneutics*, 65, n. 10.
32 "Scrolls and Hebrews," 44.
33 Daniélou, 112f.; Cross, *Ancient Library*, 166; Kosmala, 88ff.; Grässer, *Glaube*, 73–91; Lindars, 142; P.E. Hughes, 13ff.; Kistemaker, 86f.; Brown, "Messianism," 65; Barbour, 113; and Johnston, 85, 97 are among the many one could cite. The last two attack Montefiore for not giving the theory more attention.
34 "Hebrews and Qumran," 17 (my italics).
35 Cullmann, *Christology*, 107, n. 1, Hay, 135, and Bruce, "To Hebrews or Essenes?," 222ff. all set out the evidence but fail to make a connection (although Bruce does seem to accept it in "Kerygma," 7). Buchanan, *Hebrews*, 15, 97, Batdorf, 23, 32, and LaSor, *Scrolls*, 185ff. also fall short of suggesting a direct relationship.
36 See, e.g., Sowers, 119, n. 79, who rejects it as a background of Hebrews but accepts the doctrine at Qumran.

37 See, e.g., Brown, "Messianism," 54, n. 6; Liver, 152, and Kuhn, "Die Beiden Messias," 174, all of whom conjecture that the earlier form of the phrase in CD (e.g. 9^b:29 [20:1] or 8:2 [6:1]) was plural and that it was corrected to the singular by medieval scribes.

38 See also T. Levi 18:3, where the star, so often applied to the Davidic Messiah, refers to the priest from Levi. Van der Woude, *Die messiansichen*, 60f., Kuhn, "Two Messiahs," Beasley-Murray, and Schubert, "Zwei Messiasse," all see a priestly Messiah in the Testaments.

39 See, e.g. Kuhn, "Two Messiahs," 59f. (who sees 1QS 9:11 as final proof of medieval tampering with CD); Burrows, "Messiahs," 204; and Milik, *Ten Years*, 124.

40 See, e.g., Kuhn, "Two Messiahs," 54.

41 Silberman, "Two Messiahs," 79.

42 "Priest and Messiah," 332.

43 "Priestly Messiah," 244f.

44 "Use of 'Anointed,'" 132ff.

45 For a full discussion, see Villalón, 53ff.

46 "Two sons of oil," says Brownlee, *Meaning*, 99,

> is the literal expression which is correctly translated in the Bible as "the two anointed"; but it does not give us verbal agreement with the language of the *Manual of Discipline* ... even this minor discrepancy is bridged by the statement of I Chron. 29:22, "They anointed him (Solomon) as Prince for the Lord, and Zadok as Priest." Here the anointed stand side by side, the representatives of state and church.

See also Ezek. 40–48, the program for the new commonwealth, where apparently the Prince is subordinate to the priests, although the latter are by no means seen as "Messiahs" (42:13ff.).

47 Schubert, *Dead Sea Community*, traces Qumran's two Messiah theory back to the passage, saying that it "is in unusual degree both pro-Zadokite and pro-Davidic." But, comments Brownlee, Schubert's zeal has caused him to overlook the apparent textual suppression of Zerubbabel (see Brownlee's review of Schubert, 278f. and Brown, "Messianism," 63, n. 53). The suppression of the name of Zerubbabel is probably the result of Hasmonean interest that the royal succession devolves upon the priestly figure.

48 Fritsch, "Priestly Messiah," 244.

49 A. Reifenberg, *Ancient Jewish Coins*, table XIII, no. 169.

50 Smith, "What is Implied," 71f. Smith also notes the problems encountered by the Apostle Paul in keeping uniform eschatological ideas in the churches he himself founded. While such parallels are interesting, Smith is weak in citing evidence from Qumran literature itself.

51 Another problem is the dating of the documents. Burrows (quoted in Silberman, "Messiahs," 78) thinks that 1QS 9:11 points to a "change in the idea between CDC and 1QS." Wcela, 348, Liver,

182ff. and Priest, "Mebaqqer," 55ff. are among many who hold that the development was from two Messiahs to a single lay Messiah by the time of John the Baptist, and that those references which seem to speak of two Messiahs are the earlier ones.

52 "Les Quatre Etapes," 481–505.

53 Not only is the precarious argument from silence (stage a) invoked, but also there is the unwarranted assumption that in stage c it is the Levitical Messiah who usurps the function of the royal Messiah and assumes the title "Prince of the Whole Congregation." Why cannot it be the other way around? The controlling (unproven) assumption, of course, is that the Davidic references are the latest, and that stage c represents a period too early for them to exist.

54 Buchanan, *Hebrews*, 15, 97.

55 Batdorf, 23.

56 Higgins, "Priest and Messiah," 335, and "Priestly Messiah," 211ff., thinks that this suddenness indicates a belief already familiar to the readers.

57 Cf. Higgins, "Priest and Messiah," 335, and Bruce, "Hebrews or Essenes," 223.

58 "Scrolls," 53.

59 *Ibid.*, 53. See also Schnackenburg, 631ff., Black, "Qumran Messiah," 157ff., and Vermes, *Scrolls in English*, 48f., all of whom feel that the "prophet" of 1QS 9:11 is the Mosaic prophet of Deut. 18:18.

60 On the prophet at Qumran see, e.g., Vermes, *Jesus the Jew*, 94–97.

61 "Scrolls," 53f.

62 *Ibid.*, 54.

63 *Dead Sea Manual*, 35f., n.19.

64 Contra LaSor, "Messianic," 353.

65 Milik, *Ten Years*, 126. According to Milik, the prophet "seems scarcely to be mentioned elsewhere in the Qumran texts and little further can be said about his functions and person" (126).

66 "Messianism," 61. Some (e.g., Vermes, *Scrolls in English*, 87, and Gaster (67)) insist on adding the definite article to "prophet" in 1QS 9:11, as if the figure is "the prophet" of Deut. 18:18.

67 Other figures who have been conjectured to be "the prophet" are the herald of Isa. 52:7 spoken of in 11Q Melch, lines 15–18 (so de Jonge and van der Woude, 307) and the *Geber* of IQS 4:20–22 (see, e.g., Vermes, *Scripture*, 56–66).

68 "Scrolls," 53, n.47.

69 *Ibid.*, 38.

70 The adversative is found in Moffatt, *Hebrews* (upon which Yadin builds his case – *ibid.*, 39, n.6), the RSV, NEB and REB, but not in the KJV.

71 Caird, "Exegetical Method," 47, points out that the spread of quotations from the various divisions of the Hebrew Bible indicates "that the author regarded the whole of the Old Testament as a prophetic work."

72 Heb. 8:6, 9:15, 2:24.

73 "Scrolls," 40f.
74 Cf., e.g., Flusser, "Dead Sea Sect," pp. 236–41.
75 This is not as far-fetched as it may appear. Scharlemann, 169, notes that both Jews and Samaritans thought of the Messianic age as a time when the tabernacle and its furnishings would be restored.
76 See, e.g., Sowers, 119.
77 Batdorf, 25.
78 "Melchizedek als himmlische Erlösergestalt."
79 See de Jonge and van der Woude, Fitzmyer, "Further Light," and Carmignac. Yadin published a note on the discovery and briefly reaffirmed his theories regarding Hebrews in *IEJ* 15 (1965), 152f.; Horton, 64–82, gives a thorough analysis of the text and its implications.
80 Van der Woude's reading of the text puts Melchizedek in a similar position to that of Michael as the head of the heavenly host, which accounts for the identification, which was known in medieval times.
81 This interpretation is generally followed by Yadin (with minor variations), Fitzmyer, Laubscher, and Horton. The identification with Michael is still open to debate among these writers.
82 Hay, 137, n. 37, finds Carmignac's reconstruction "certainly possible," while LaSor, *Scrolls*, 183f., thinks Carmignac is correct. The majority of writers, on the other hand, have decided in favour of van der Woude (see e.g., Fensham, 17f.; Longenecker, "Melchizedek Argument," 167ff.; Buchanan, "Present State," 309; Wülfing von Martitz, 388; Batdorf, 28f.; and P. E. Hughes, 80).
83 Another text (from Cave 4) mentions "Milki-sedek" along with the Prince of Darkness, "Milki-resă'," who rule light and darkness, respectively. See Milik, "Milkî-sedeq et Milkî-resha'."
84 De Jonge and van der Woude, 321f.
85 "The tradition is not the same, but what we have in 11Q Melch at least furnishes a new light on the comparison" (Fitzmyer, "Further Light," 253). So also Buchanan, *Hebrews*, 99f.
86 For studies of Melchizedek in Hebrews, see, in addition to the above, the following: Burch, 85–112; Del Medico, 160ff.; Dimmler; Fitzmyer, "Further Light," and "Now this Melchizedek"; Hay, 143–52; Horton; P. E. Hughes, Excursus I, 237–45; Jérôme; Mackay, "Order"; Michel, "μελχισεδέκ"; Rusche; Schille; Sowers, 119–26; Spicq, *Hébrews*, II, excursus V, 203–14; Westcott, 201–205; Wuttke; and Zimmermann.
87 Caird, "Exegetical Method," 48; Longenecker, *Biblical Exegesis*, 183.
88 "11Q Melchizedek," 321, n. 4.
89 *Ibid.*, 321, n. 4 (my italics).
90 "There is no danger, therefore, that Melchizedek will overshadow Jesus Christ" (*ibid.*, n. 5). This danger, however, does not seem to have occurred to *Auctor*.
91 "Melchizedek Argument," 177, n. 51.
92 *Beginnings*, 119: "Melchizedek is a heavenly being, not a part of the world of sense perception."

93 *Hebrews and Qumran*, 18.
94 *Jesus Christ in the OT*, 65ff.
95 According to Hanson, Melchizedek is called a "type" by Westcott, 202, Nairne, *Priesthood*, 334, and Lampe and Woolcombe, among many others.
96 G. Howard, in his review of Williamson's *Philo and Hebrews*, accuses Williamson of misrepresenting Hebrews, and describes the Levitical priesthood in Hebrews as "a shadow of an eternal heavenly priesthood as prior in time to Levi." But it is Howard, by attributing to Melchizedek the term "heavenly," who distorts Hebrews. Horton, 155ff., 272f., rightly denies Melchizedek such terms as "divine," "heavenly" or "angelic."
97 So Kennedy, *Theology*, 193, 211; Mackay, "Order," 176 (who attributes it to his "faith"); Longenecker, "Melchizedek Argument," 177f.; Horton, 161 (although he assumes without argument that the subject of 7:16 is Melchizedek rather than Christ, which is hardly certain).
98 The phrase is Nairne's (*Priesthood*, 152).
99 It would take us beyond our brief to deal extensively with the question of whether or not Heb. 7:3 is derived from a previous oral or written "hymnic" source. Many, such as Longenecker, "Melchizedek Argument," 177, Fitzmyer, "Now this Melchizedek," 236, n.48, and de Jonge and van der Woude, 319, have felt so. The position maintained in this study will be that even if such is the case, the passage nonetheless represents what *Auctor* wished to say within the context of his understanding of Gen. 14.
100 For a good summary, see Thompson, *Beginnings*, 119.
101 See A. Vaillant, *Le Livre des secrets d'Hénoch. Texte slave et traduction française* (1951), 69ff., referred to in Hengel, *Son of God*, 82, n.144.
102 Cullmann, *Christology*, 305, claims that "the addition of 'without mother' verifies the assertion that one can hardly find evidence for the virgin birth in the environment of this writing."
103 *Hebrews*, 119.
104 *Hebräer*, 162f., and "μελχισεδέκ," 570.
105 *Beginnings*, 119.
106 "11Q Melchizedek," 322.
107 See Mackay, "Argument of Hebrews," 332.
108 It would be an exhausting exercise to attempt to list those writers who are satisfied with an appeal to scriptural silence in explaining *Auctor*'s treatment of Melchizedek. Its most famous expositor is probably Westcott, 201ff. On the principle in the rabbis, cf. Strack–Billerbeck, III, 694f., and Longenecker's discussion in "Melchizedek Argument," 184f., n.50.
109 E.g., Fensham, 18; Longenecker, "Melchizedek Argument," 184f.; Fitzmyer, "Now this Melchizedek," 235f., etc.
110 This seems to cancel out much of Fensham's thesis. His rejoinder that "in the arguments of Hebrews we might discover a polemical

tendency built on a firm Old Testament basis against heterodox Jewish conceptions' (18) is singularly unconvincing.

111 E.g., Bruce, "To Hebrews or Essenes," 223f.; Horton, 153ff.; and Hay, 147.

112 F.F. Bruce, *Hebrews*, 138 (my italics). See also Nairne, *Priesthood*, 345: "He would consider the type to represent life before the incarnation as well as after it."

113 With this in view it might be better to substitute the terms "homologue" and "homology" for "type" and "typology."

114 *Jesus Christ in the OT*, 67f.

115 "11Q Melchizedek," 320f. For them "being made like the Son of God" (7:3) is not an attempt "to limit the statements of Hebrews to the *description* of Melchizedek (as opposed to the real person) or his office."

116 *Ibid.*, 320f.

117 See Hurst, "Christology of Hebrews 1 and 2."

118 *Hebrews*, 7. For a different treatment of the question of when Christ "became" priest, cf. Peterson, 191ff.

119 Longenecker, "Melchizedek Argument," 178, comes close to saying this when he describes the priesthood of Melchizedek as "based on character apart from lineage and *ordained by God* apart from law" (my italics).

120 *Beginnings*, 119ff.

121 *Hebrews*, 138.

122 *Melchizedek Tradition*, 162.

123 "11Q Melchizedek," 319, n. 2.

124 I dispute Thompson's claim (*Beginnings*, 121) that ζῆ is a comment on both phrases.

125 In this case "no beginning of days" would mean "no point at which his priesthood begins," and would imply a contrast to the Aaronic priests, who, when they reached a certain age, begin their days as priests (at twenty-five years of age, continuing to the fiftieth year, when they entered semi-retirement with limited duties – Num. 8:24–26). *Auctor's* argument appears to be that, rooted in God's eternal purposes, Melchizedek's priesthood has no point in time when his qualifications for office actually begin.

126 See Hay, 147; Michel, *Hebräer*, 261; Spicq, II, 210 and Peterson, 107. That *Auctor's* interest in this section is primarily in genealogical credentials vis-à-vis *those of the Aaronic priests* is indicated by 7:6 ("But Melchizedek, although he does not trace his descent *from them*"). On the importance of the correct genealogy for Aaronic qualification for the cultus, see Johnson, 79f. "Without genealogy" in 7:3 can thus only be read as referring to miraculous generation (along with "without father, mother") if it is read *in vacuo* (e.g., as a "hymn" which *Auctor* has taken over). If it is read in its context in Hebrews, however, it is clear that *Auctor's* sole interest in Melchizedek's genealogy is in the context of priestly credentials. As elsewhere in Hebrews (e.g., chs. 1 and 2), *Auctor's* theological argument might be better understood if it were read

backwards (in which case 7:6 would pave the way for 7:3b ("without genealogy"), and 7:3b would pave the way for 7:3a ("without father, mother"). For the value of this method of reading the NT, see Fenton, 'Respice Finem."

127 See J. A. T. Robinson, *Human Face*, 160.
128 Fitzmyer, "Now this Melchizedek," 226f.
129 "Melchizedek Argument," 178.
130 *Ibid.*, 175.
131 *Biblical Exegesis*, 170 (my italics).
132 "Melchizedek from Genesis to the Qumran Texts," 126, quoted with approval by Longenecker, "Melchizedek Argument," 173.
133 "Hebrews and Qumran," 18.
134 Fitzmyer, reviewing Horton in *CBQ* 39 (1977), says that "I think that he is right in saying that Melchizedek is not an angelic figure, but I hesitate about saying that he is not a 'heavenly' figure."
135 *Ibid.*, 437.
136 "11Q Melchizedek," 317f.
137 Cf. Perry, 70, who correctly says that "Hebrews consistently plays down analogies between Jesus and the angels, whereas the analogy with Melchizedek is something on which he wants to build." Horton, 155f., agrees.
138 This is a revised form of the list found in Batdorf, 31, with my own additions.
139 See de Jonge and van der Woude, 322, n. 4.
140 See the valuable discussion of Hay, 138.
141 Batdorf, 31.
142 Hay, 138.
143 Thompson, 120.
144 *Ibid.*, 32.
145 Hay, 152, n. 99.
146 *Ibid.*, 152f.
147 *Ibid.*, 152. See also McCullough, " Recent Developments," 148.
148 So Hengel, *Son of God*, 80f.
149 "Hébreux, Apollos," 383–86.
150 "Some Thoughts," 32.
151 *Psalm Citations*, 74, 141.
152 *Hebrews and Qumran*, 15.
153 Cf. also R. P. C. Hanson, 17–20, 125; de Waard, 82; and Gärtner, "Habakkuk Commentary."
154 *Psalm Citations*, 74.
155 Cf. Bruce, *Biblical Exegesis*, 12.
156 "Hébreux, Apollos," 383ff.; see also Batdorf, 18.
157 Dunn, *Unity and Diversity*, 88, claims that "following the quotation the key features of it are taken up and explained in pesher fashion"; see also Sowers, 83.
158 Fitzmyer, "Now this Melchizedek," 222, who argues that Heb. 7 answers perfectly R. Bloch's five features of "midrash" and that it has close affinities with "classic midrash" such as Genesis

Rabbah 43:6. For the numerous rules for midrash from rabbis Hillel to Eliezar, see Kistemaker, 62ff.

159 See Ellis, *Prophecy and Hermeneutic*, 193, who, after comparing it with 1QpH, describes it as a "Christian *pesher*-type midrash." Bruce calls it "the most striking biblical parallel" between Hebrews and Qumran ("To Hebrews or Essenes," 221).

160 On the combination of Ps. 2:7 and 2 Sam. 7:14 in Hebrews and 4Q Testimonia, see Bruce, "To Hebrews or Essenes," 221, and *Hebrews*, 14; Wülfing von Martitz, 361f.; Kistemaker, 75f.; Fensham, 14f.; Fitzmyer, "Now this Melchizedek," 222f.; Longenecker, *Biblical Exegesis*, 177; and Buchanan, *Hebrews*, 14f., 29.

161 Longenecker, *Biblical Exegesis*, 185, and "Melchizedek Argument," 175.

162 *Hebrews*, introduction 1.

163 See Caird, "Exegetical Method," 48, who describes *Auctor*'s treatment of Ps. 110 and Gen. 14 as "very modern," against most contemporary scholarly opinion.

164 Combrink, 32.

165 "OT Citations," 320f.

166 See Stendahl, 157ff., especially in relation to the apparently conflated OT texts which develop the theme of the treachery and death of Judas.

167 Buchanan, "Present State," 317f.

168 Kistemaker, 13–60 (although he admits that this is not successful in the majority of cases); Barth, 73; Guilding, 100.

169 *Unity and Diversity*, 91.

170 "OT Quotations," 363–79, especially 378f. T. W. Manson, "Argument from Prophecy," 135f., argues that the NT writers in general felt free to change the wording of OT texts in order to give what they had already determined was its sense.

171 See Hurst, "Christology of Heb. 1 and 2," pp. 156–62.

172 See below, pp. 110f.

173 See below, p. 71.

174 See above, pp. 53–58.

175 *Verfasser*, 259ff.

176 Sowers also thinks that since *Auctor* "could never think that the same OT containing sacrificial ordinances also contains prophetic protests against their use," Ps. 40 is referred by *Auctor* to a "later time," i.e., the time of Christ. It apparently did not occur to Sowers that for *Auctor* the OT itself contained warnings against the taking of it as ultimate (see Caird, "Exegetical Method").

177 See *Cambridge Greek Testament*, 98, and *Priesthood*, 311. Schröger's placing of Heb. 2:6–8 (Ps. 8:5–7) in the *midrash-pesher* group, while designating 1:8f. (Ps. 45:7f.) in the category of "indirect messianic promise-fulfilment," is similarly difficult.

178 *Verfasser*, 269–93.

179 For treatments of rabbinic exegesis, cf. Bonsirven; Doeve; Ellis, *Paul's Use*, 39–45; Daube, *NT and Rabbinic Judaism*; and Strack,

Einleitung. Regarding Qumran *pesher* exegesis, see especially Fitzmyer, "Use of Explicit Quotations," 185ff.; and Gärtner, 1–24. Thyen is still the best treatment of the subject.

180 On the problem of defining the various categories of OT interpretation at Qumran, see Brooke, "Qumran Pesher," and Friebel.

181 See "Christology of Hebrews 1 and 2," 157ff.; also Braun, 243.

182 See in addition to the full-length study of Brooke (*Exegesis at Qumran*), Allegro, "Further Messianic Reference," 186f., and "Fragments," 350–54; and Yadin, "Midrash," 95–98.

183 See Kistemaker, 75f.

184 This coupling has been compared to the "begetting" by God of the Messiah in 1QSa (Cf. Vermes, *Jesus the Jew*, 197ff.; Wülfing von Martitz, 361f.; and Gordis.

185 Fuller, *Foundations* 32.

186 E.g., Sowers, 87.

187 So Fitzmyer, "Now this Melchizedek," 222f.

188 I.e., the recipient of the oracle of 2 Sam. 7:14 is "the shoot of David who will function in Zion in the last days."

189 Wülfing von Martitz, 361f.

190 Buchanan, *Hebrews*, 14f., 29.

191 Fitzmyer, "Now this Melchizedek," 222f. This is not to deny that Hebrews uses main and subsidiary texts; it merely observes that the literary structure of Heb. 1 and 4Q Flor is not identical. Cf. also Lane, 343f.

192 On the use of Hab. 2:3f. in Heb. 10:37f., see below, pp. 122f.

193 *Psalm Citations*, 74.

194 *Prophecy and Hermeneutic*, 193.

195 *Hebrews*, 175.

196 *Prophecy and Hermeneutic*, 193, n. 29.

197 The placing of μου after δίκαιος rather than πίστεως does not come into consideration here, since both readings are well attested in LXX manuscripts. It looks as though *Auctor* was following the A text (cf. Lindars, 231, and McCullough, "OT Quotations," 376f.).

198 *NT Apologetic*, 231, n. 1.

199 This suggestion is similar to that of B. W. Bacon with reference to Ps. 102:23–27LXX (see Hurst, "Christology of Hebrews 1 and 2," 160).

200 McCullough does not consider the above evidence in his treatment of the addition of the definite article in v. 37, although it would have lent considerable strength to his thesis.

201 This is the normal interpretation; see Westcott, 350, and Bruce, *Hebrews*, 274.

202 See Lewis, "And if he Shrinks Back," 88ff.

203 F. F. Bruce, *Hebrews*, 274.

204 See, e.g., Batdorf, 22.

205 See below, p. 123.

206 Other points of contact which, for reasons of space, have not been treated here are adequately dealt with elsewhere. See, e.g., Qumran ritual baths and Heb. 6:2, 9:10, 10:22 (F. F. Bruce, "To Hebrews

or Essenes," 224ff.; Kosmala, 33ff.).; Qumran ritual meals and Heb. 13:10 (Williamson, "Eucharist," 200ff.); Qumran dualism and Hebrews (Flusser, "Dead Sea Sect," 254; Batdorf, 34); the focus on the wilderness period (F. F. Bruce, "To Hebrews or Essenes," 219ff., and Robinson, *Redating*, 201f.; heavenly temple and sacrifice (Yadin, "Midrash," 93ff.; the new covenant (Flusser, "Dead Sea Sect," 236ff.) and Qumran discipline and the severity of Hebrews (Fensham, 14; Buchanan, *Hebrews*, 109, 174; and Batdorf, 22ff.).

3 Other Non-Christian Backgrounds

1 *Hebrews*, 37f.
2 See, e.g., Kennedy, *Theology*, 214: "As soon as the conscience is unburdened of its sin, it passes out of the sphere of death into that of life, which is the sphere of God. For the first time the human spirit finds *its real home*" (my italics).
3 *Das wandernde Gottesvolk*, translated in 1984 as *The Wandering People of God*. For the sake of convenience I shall refer in what follows to the English version.
4 Michel, *Hebräer*, 75 (see also below, n. 60).
5 Käsemann, *Wandering*, 101ff.
6 *Ibid.*, 202ff.
7 *Ibid.*, 151f.
8 See above, pp. 35ff.
9 Michel, Hebräer, newly revised edn (1949), *passim*.
10 See especially vol. I, 100, 107, 109, 111f. and 174ff.
11 *Saint Paul*, 216.
12 For other literature regarding Hebrews and gnosticism since Käsemann, see Hofius, *Katapausis*, 5–12.
13 Eccles, "Mysticism," *passim*; Johnsson, "Cultus," *passim*; and Thompson, who argues repeatedly for a gnostic–Platonic background for Hebrews.
14 T., W. Manson, "Problem."
15 Many feel that it rests primarily on the isolation of 13:9 and *Auctor*'s arguments regarding angels in ch. 1 from their contexts (e.g., C. P. M. Jones, 115, and W. Manson, 12f., 24).
16 W. Manson opposes Scott's view that Hebrews constitutes a "gnosis" for any intellectually elite group (7, 60), and admits no gnostic influence in his assessment of Hebrews.
17 Barrett, "Eschatology," 389, who claims the Christ of Hebrews to be "rather a priest who makes atonement for the sin of mankind than a gnostic mediator who procures their passage from the material world to the spiritual."
18 Review of Grässer, 149.
19 *Hebrews and Hermeneutics*, 137–42.
20 American opinion, on the other hand, tends to follow German scholarship more closely than British. A gnostic background for Hebrews thus continues to enjoy considerable popularity in

America. This enthusiasm will undoubtedly be enhanced now that both Käsemann's *Gottesvolk* and Koester's *Einführung* have been translated into English. As the translators of Käsemann say, "this early work of a master of biblical interpretation will ... enlist admirers from a new generation of readers" (translators' preface, 13). Koester, for whom Käsemann's study is a "classic monograph which gave directions for modern research" (272), claims that "Gnostic concepts are found frequently in Hebrews and are crucial for understanding its argument." This curious scholarly divide is apparently becoming wider. The British scholar R. McL. Wilson, himself a recognised authority on gnosticism, in his recent commentary on Hebrews (1987) examines the gnostic background extensively, and concludes that if there is any gnostic influence it is "at most very slight, and limited to a few terms and concepts which may have already begun to have taken on a gnostic colour" (26). The tone of his statements throughout the commentary makes it clear that even this slight concession is more the result of caution than conviction.

21 *Wandering*, 17ff.
22 *Ibid.*, 19.
23 See Barrett, "Eschatology," 378, and Williamson, "Eucharist," 312, who translate "die Wanderschaft" in Käsemann as "pilgrimage." This is disputed by Johnsson, "Pilgrimage Motif," 243, who thinks "wandering" to be the more accurate term. Yet this is a barren distinction; a heavenly pilgrimage inevitably involves what appears as "wandering" in this world, since it presupposes the habitual leaving of earthly security and present fixtures.
24 E.g., *Wandering*, 225.
25 *Ibid.*, 23, n. 10.
26 See below, pp. 72f.
27 *Wandering*, 73–75.
28 *De cher.* 87; see also *Leg. all.* I.16–18. But note *Quod Deus* 12, which speaks of the Seven as "a soul which rests in God and toils no more at any mortal task." Chadwick, 305, thinks that Philo has here influenced later gnostics such as Valentinus.
29 See *Katapausis, passim*, especially 53, 60, 102, 110.
30 *Untersuchungen*, 125ff.
31 See Käsemann's references in *Wandering*, 97–108.
32 *Ibid.*, 108–17. See also Bultmann, *Theology*, I.176, who adds, however, that the gnostic redeemer myth "is modified in the direction of Jewish–Christian eschatology by postponing the total subjection of the cosmos to him until the future parousia."
33 *Wandering*, 130ff., following an earlier interpretation of J. Kögel.
34 *Ibid.*, 207ff.
35 *Ibid.*, 208.
36 *Ibid.*, 192.
37 *Ibid.*, 133. He cites, e.g., Odes Sol. 14.4 ("Stretch out to me, O Lord, at all times thy right hand: and be my guide even unto the end"); the Naasene Hymn, which speaks of Adam (*qua* Hermes)

as ψυχαγογός and χυχῶν αἴτιος; Mandaic literature, which speaks of Jokabar-Ziwa as "leader"; and numerous citations from the *Acts of John* and the *Acts of Thomas* which speak of various aspects of leadership.

38 *Wandering*, 202ff. That Heb. 7:1–3 is based upon proto-gnostic speculations is met with approval by, among others, Cullmann, *Christology*, 85; Michel, "Μελχισεδέκ," 570, n.8; and Hay, 142.
39 "Doctrine of Faith," 14.
40 Cf. *Wandering*, 37ff.
41 *Der Glaube*, 115.
42 As observed by Filson, "Hebrews," 25.
43 See Oepke, 58ff.
44 Michaelis, "ὁδός," 78, n.127.
45 *Ibid.*, 78.
46 *Der Glaube*, 111, n.283.
47 "People of God," 91.
48 Cf. Williamson, *Philo and Hebrews*, pp.490f.
49 See, e.g., Hengel, *Son of God*, 86, n.147.
50 E.g., Lombard, 62.
51 See Lohse, "σάββατων, κτλ.," 34.
52 "Trois ouvrages."
53 Hofius limits "rest" in Hebrews to a purely "local" sense, i.e., it is entry into the heavenly sanctuary. He rejects Käsemann's radical divide between spiritual and earthly, and emphasizes that the promise made to the readers of Hebrews was the same as that made to the OT Jews. Thus what the Jews under Moses forfeited through unbelief was immediate entry into heaven!
54 So Sowers, 131.
55 This is not to deny the extensive role of apocalyptic in Hebrews. It only questions whether, and to what extent, *Auctor* has consciously connected the "rest" of chs. 3–4 (Ps. 95) to apocalyptic notions. For further arguments against a gnostic background for "rest" in Hebrews, cf. Wilson, *Hebrews*, 75f., 83f.
56 For a helpful recent discussion, see Caird, *Paul's Letters*, 103.
57 See Rawlinson, 125ff.; Caird, *Paul's Letters*, 103f.; Colpe, *Gnostic Christology*; and Dodd, *Bible and Greeks*, 145ff.
58 Cf. Hatch–Redpath, 165.
59 See Moffatt, *Hebrews*, 31.
60 See Michel, *Hebräer*, 75, who, although citing certain texts also cited by Käsemann, looks instead to apocalyptic Judaism as the background of *Auctor*'s ἀρχηγός idea.
61 Sowers, 124, n.93.
62 "He is a figure who descends from the upper regions into the midst of the archons bearing the water of life" (150).
63 Cf. above, pp.53–58.
64 "Bekenntnis," cols.55–66. Bornkamm, however, generally approves of Käsemann's work, and thinks that it is the high priest concept which holds *Auctor*'s gnostic tendencies in check.

65 Hurst, "Christology of Hebrews 1 and 2," 153ff.

66 *Hebrews and Hermeneutics*, 137ff. Hughes reacts particularly to Grässer's perpetuation of the "word-concept" fallacy in his analysis of "faith" words in Hebrews, his distancing *Auctor* from Paul, his neglect of emphases in the epistle which clearly depict the present, realized benefits of Christianity, the late dating of Hebrews and consequent assessment of it in terms of *Frükatholizismus*, and the somewhat confused relations of *Auctor* to a theory of parousia delay.

67 Cf. below, pp. 119–24. See also Wilson, *Hebrews*, 192, for a denial that Heb. 10:23 is gnostic.

68 It has long been known that there is a "realized," "existential"-type aspect to salvation in gnosticism. Peel, 156, argues persuasively that, in addition to the traditional view of gnostic salvation as "instant eschatology" via the achievement of enlightenment plus the post-mortem ascent of the gnostic "spirit-self," gnosticism taught that the destiny of the individual spirit-self is linked to the destiny of the cosmos. Gnosticism may also have envisaged a future resurrection of a "spiritual flesh." What Peel demonstrates is that in later gnostic systems there is something of the same kind of tension which one finds also in the NT of "already–not yet." Grässer's elimination of the "already" aspect is thus suspect even in terms of his gnostic parallels. On final cosmic eschatology in gnosticism, see also Jonas, 45f.

69 See Jonas, 49ff.: "Equipped with this *gnosis*, the soul after death travels upwards ... thus the spirit stripped of all foreign accretions reaches the God beyond the world and becomes reunited with the divine substance."

70 See below, 177, n. 67.

71 See van der Waal, 90.

72 *Glaube*, 112, n. 285.

73 See Hurst, "Eschatology and 'Platonism,'" 69ff.

74 *Hebräer*, 69.

75 *Beginnings*, 100.

76 "Pilgrimage Motif," 241.

77 The best treatment of Pauline echoes of Christ's relationship to believers in Hebrews remains that of Nairne (both commentaries).

78 See Gen. 6:13, where "all flesh" means, simply, "everyone."

79 See, e.g., T. W. Manson, *Paul and John*, 32ff., and Bultmann, *Theology*, I, 191ff. In Paul "flesh" is probably a neutral area which can be invaded by sin, which means that, as with the law, Paul can speak of "flesh" in a negative way (see Rom. 7:5, 18, 25). This negative usage, however, does not appear in Hebrews.

80 In Heb. 4:12 the distinction between ψυχή and πνεῦμα is probably hyperbolic – a rhetorical flourish which should not be pressed overly for "philosophical" distinctions. G. Hughes, 42, and R. McL. Wilson, *Hebrews*, 188f., correctly deny the presence of an anthropological "flesh–spirit" dualism in Hebrews.

81 See McKelvey, who states the problem for those who attempt to "gnosticize" Hebrews at this point:

The word "spiritual" is not altogether satisfactory for our purpose. The opposition in character and in quality to what is bodily, material, and earthly which the term normally implies does not apply to the Biblical and ancient tradition, which never divorced the material and the spiritual. Spiritualization of worship means its interiorization, inasmuch as the emphasis is on the intention, disposition, and motivation of the worshipper, but it means more than this, for the ancients were not only concerned *why* a certain thing was done but *that* it should be done. Perhaps "integrity" is the word we should have in mind when we think of spiritualization at least in regard to the Old Testament (42, n. 1).

82 See R. McL. Wilson, *Gnosis, passim.*
83 "Hebrews and Qumran," 33f. See also Peel, 142.
84 "Hebrews and Qumran," 33f.
85 See Chadwick, 302.
86 *Wandering,* 210.
87 "Hebrews," 186.
88 See Reicke, "Traces of Gnosticism," and Batdorf, 26.
89 See Chadwick, 302–306.
90 "Hebrews and Qumran," 35.
91 See above, ch. 2.
92 *Son of God,* 33, n. 66.
93 "Samaritans and Hebrews."
94 *Ibid.,* 187.
95 *Ibid.,* 193.
96 *Ibid.,* 189.
97 *Ibid.,* 190.
98 *Ibid.,* 191.
99 *Ibid.,* 192f.
100 *Ibid.,* 193.
101 *Did the Samaritans?, passim.*
102 *Theology, passim.*
103 *The Dositheans,* 142, n. 54 (cited in Goulder, 85, n. 14).
104 "Origins and Development," 409–14.
105 *Ibid.,* 409–14.
106 E.g., Perry, 70, n. 2, who, acknowledging Scobie, looks to *Auctor*'s "divergencies from mainstream Judaism ... such that there seems to be a great deal to be said for E. A. Knox's suggestion ... that it may be addressed to Samaritan Christians"; Cullmann, *Johannine Circle,* 50 and *passim,* thinks that Acts 7, the Samaritans, Qumran, the Fourth Gospel and Hebrews all belong to the same circle. Goulder, 67, also treats the hypothesis favourably.
107 Scobie, 410.
108 *Ibid.,* 410. Scobie does not explain what he means by this. Does he mean that the recipients, *qua* Samaritan Christians, viewed Jesus as a second Moses? Or does he mean that they expected a Moses

redivivus, apart from Jesus, against which *Auctor* is polemicizing? According to the supposed background, either would be possible.

109 See MacDonald, *Memar Marqah*, 79, 136f.; Buchanan, *Hebrews*, 59.

110 MacDonald, *Memar Marqah*, 155, and *Theology*, 445.

111 See E. A. Knox, 189.

112 Scobie, "Origins," 411.

113 *Ibid.*, 411; see also Trotter, 23f.

114 See MacDonald, *Theology*, 128, 290: "According to the Samaritan idea of perfection, the origin of that which is perfect has its *form* or pattern in the real (invisible) world" (290).

115 Samaritan thought apparently interpreted Ex. 25:40 along Platonic lines. According to MacDonald, "Moses penetrated that cloud or veil and entered into the upper world where existed the true pattern of all things on earth" (*Theology*, 181; see also 201).

116 *Theology*, 128.

117 "Origins," 412.

118 *Ibid.*, 410.

119 *Ibid.*, 412. See also Theissen, 130ff.

120 Scobie, "Origins," 412; MacDonald, *Theology*, 445; Trotter, 17f.

121 "Origins," 412f.

122 *Ibid.*, 413.

123 *Ibid.*, 413.

124 See also E. A. Knox, 192f.

125 Cf. Hurst, "Christology of Hebrews 1 and 2," 154ff. The points I raise there will make it clear that I regard as unsatisfactory Thurston's ("Philo and Hebrews," 137) revival of Allen's old idea that *Auctor* is attempting to refute an angel christology.

126 Heb. 2:2.

127 Macdonald, *Theology*, 400.

128 *Ibid.*, 287 (my italics).

129 *Ibid.*, 400.

130 Knox and Scobie do not treat this difficulty. In particular Scobie's silence concerning Acts 7:53 and Heb. 2:2 is telling. Elsewhere (*Theology*, 402) MacDonald thinks that Heb. 12:1 (the "cloud of witnesses") "expresses the same basic concept as *Amram Darah* C. p. 43.26–28, where angels are present wherever men pray, since it pleases them to hear their Lord praised at all times." This is in fact irrelevant to Heb. 12:1, which is referring to human beings, but it does illustrate the *passive* role of angels in the relations of God and human beings in Samaritan theology (unlike, e.g., Qumran, where angels actually participate in the community's worship – see Strugnell, "Angelic Liturgy").

131 The latter premise is somewhat doubtful, for Philo's view of Moses is probably as high as that of the Samaritans (see Williamson, *Philo and Hebrews*, 449ff.).

132 On the pre-existence of Moses in Samaritan thought, see MacDonald, "Samaritan Doctrine of Moses," 151f., and Bowman, "Fourth Gospel," 302f.

133 "Samaritan Doctrine of Moses," 151f.
134 *Ibid.*, 151f.
135 See Hurst, "Christology of Heb. 1 and 2."
136 MacDonald, *Theology*, 154ff., 362f., etc., and Trotter, *passim*, in contrast to Scobie, "Origins and Development," 410.
137 See Williamson, *Philo and Hebrews*, pp. 449–91.
138 Cf. Reid, 158–62.
139 See above, ch. 1.
140 See below, ch. 4.
141 See S. G. Wilson, 148. Also, the suggestion of Kahle (quoted with approval by Scobie and Cullmann (*Johannine Circle*, 114, n. 59) relating the altar of incense of Heb. 9:3f. to the SP description of the tabernacle is unconvincing. If *Auctor* were following the SP order, that he would have blundered so badly as to place the altar within the Holy of Holies, when his whole burden is to demonstrate that this shrine was entered only once a year (the SP clearly states that Aaron shall burn fragrance upon it *each morning and evening of the year*), is extremely unlikely. Westcott, Nairne (both commentaries), and Montefiore (q. v.) provide more probable explanations of *Auctor's* peculiar wording in 9:3f.
142 It is remarkable that modern writers are willing to ignore clear statements by NT writers concerning their motives for conjectured motives for which there is absolutely no evidence in the text.
143 MacDonald, *Theology*, 362f. See also Bowman, "Early Samaritan Eschatology," 72 ("God ... does not delegate his authority – not even to a Messiah ... God alone is king and his authority is never challenged") and "Faith in Samaritan Thought," 311 ("At the earliest stage there was no agent but God himself who would effect deliverance ... later the Taheb, Returning One, or Restorer, appears as God's agent").
144 If Trotter is correct, the picture of Christ as God's appointed ruler in Hebrews may have influenced later (more exalted) Samaritan depictions of the Taheb.
145 See Hurst, "Christology of Hebrews 1 and 2," 153ff.
146 See Bowman, "Samaritan Eschatology," 66, in treating the eighth stanza of Abisha's hymn. Although the hymn is late (c. A.D. 1370), Bowman claims that Abisha was a systematizer of earlier Samaritan traditions.
147 See MacDonald, *Theology*, 42, who claims *Memar Marqah* "shows the first clear traces of the influence of the NT" (see also 362f.).
148 "Early Samaritan Eschatology," 63.
149 "Origins," 411.
150 See MacDonald, *Theology*, 362f.
151 "Origins," 413.
152 Regarding the use of main and subsidiary texts in Hebrews, see Caird, "Exegetical Method."
153 "Erwägungen zum Rätsel," 433f.
154 "Background of Hebrews."
155 *Christushymnus*, 87f.

156 G. Scholem, cited in Williamson, "Background," 236, n. 7.
157 "Background," 236, n. 7.
158 Cf. Odeberg, *3 Enoch*, cited in Williamson, "Background," 234.
159 Williamson, "Background," 234f.
160 *Ibid.*, 233.
161 Scholem, 56f., cited in Williamson, "Background," 236, n. 18.
162 Williamson, 235.
163 *Ibid.*, 235.
164 *Ibid.*, 236.
165 *Ibid.*, 236 (my italics).
166 There may be a reference to the "everlasting kingdom" of Dan. 7:27 in the "unshakeable kingdom" of Heb. 12:28, but it is at best oblique.
167 Some have suggested that beneath Heb. 1:6 stands Ps. 97:7, "all gods bow down before Him," but this is probably to be rejected in favor of Deut. 32:43 (see Hurst, "Christology of Hebrews 1 and 2," 157ff.).
168 "Background," 236, n. 30.
169 *Ibid.*, 235.
170 Scholem, 42.
171 *Ibid.*, 43.

4 The Stephen tradition

1 See, e.g., Bacon; Barnard; Barrett, "Stephen and the Son of Man"; Bihler; Coggins, "Samaritans"; Dahl, "Abraham Story"; Davies; Foakes Jackson; Foerster; Hengel, "Zwischen"; M. Jones; Klijn; Kilgallen; O'Neill; Owen; Ropes; Scharlemann; Selwyn, "St. Stephen's Place"; Simon, *St. Stephen* and "St. Stephen"; Spiro; Stanton; and various commentaries on Acts, including those of F. F. Bruce, Conzelmann, Foakes Jackson and Lake, Haenchen, and Williams. For a fairly complete bibliography, see Scharlemann and Kilgallen.
2 See Bruce, *Commentary on Acts*, 142f., who calls Acts 7 "the first manifesto of Hellenistic Christianity."
3 Those who have advocated some form of relationship include Ayles (following Ritschl), 58f.; Badcock, *Pauline Epistles*, 190f.; Bruce, *Commentary on Acts*, 142ff. (see also his *Hebrews, passim*); Dunn, *Unity and Diversity*, 263; Filson, "Hebrews," 22ff.; Goppelt, *Christentum und Judentum*, 78, n. 1 (cited in Scharlemann, 166); Héring, *Hebrews*, 66; C. P. M. Jones, 123f.; Moule, *Birth*, 75f.; "Commentaries," 229; Scobie, "Origins," 414; Scott, *Hebrews*, 63; and Spicq, *Hébreux*, I, 203. Those who are skeptical of a relationship include Alexander, 17; Barnard, 34; Barrett, "Eschatology," 377, n. 1; Buchanan, "Present State," 307 (where he claims that the Dead Sea Scrolls have rendered W. Manson's views on Hebrews "obsolete"); Grässer, "1938–63," 191; Kümmel, 282; Moffatt, *Hebrews*, lxii; Montefiore, 18; Robinson, *Redating*, 219; Simon,

St. Stephen, 101ff.; and "Saint Stephen," 134f.; Scharlemann, 166ff.; Sowers, 64f., n. 6, and Thurston, "Midrash and 'Magnet.'"

4 *Hebrews*, 31 (his italics).
5 *Ibid.*, 25f.
6 *Ibid.*, 27.
7 *Ibid.*, 32.
8 *Ibid.*, 32f.
9 *Ibid.*, 35.
10 *Ibid.*, 46, quoting Scott, 63ff.
11 *Ibid.*, 44.
12 *Ibid.*, 42
13 *Ibid.*, 44.
14 *Ibid.*, 56ff.
15 *Ibid.*, 44.
16 See below, p. 94.
17 Simon, *Stephen*, 102.
18 E.g. Moule, *Phenomenon*, 93, 98, who agrees that Stephen is a guiding force behind the thought of *Auctor*, but does not feel that Manson's interpretation of "the Son of Man" will bear the weight which he has placed upon it (see below, pp. 105f.).
19 See, e.g., Scobie, "Origins," 396, and "Source Material," 399ff., for whom "the use of a source must now be considered proved." Dupont, *Sources*, also gives a thorough summary of the debate.
20 Cf., e.g., Dibelius, *Studies in the Acts*, 167, who thinks that Luke's source is a non-Christian synagogue homily with no relation of Stephen to the Hellenists.
21 For a useful discussion of these items, cf. the various commentaries, especially Foakes-Jackson/Lake and Haenchen (for rival views).
22 Stanton, 345ff.
23 *Ibid.*, 347.
24 See, e.g., Schmithals, *Paul and James*, 25 ("Stephen and his group declared the law as a whole, including circumcision, to be abolished for Jews and for Jewish Christians, as Paul also did"); for similar views cf. Simon, *Stephen*, 138; Bacon, "Stephen's Speech," 257f.; Barnard, 32; and Blunt, *Acts*, 162.
25 It is normally assumed that the persecution of Acts 8:1 affected only the Hellenists, in which case Luke's application of it to the church in general is an exaggeration (see, e.g., Scroggs, 180; Scobie, "Origins and Development," 398, and Dunn, *Unity and Diversity*, 274). Caird, however (*Apostolic Age*, 86f.), arguing that "Luke's account is remarkably confirmed by the evidence of Paul," points to, among other things, the reference in Gal. 1:22f. to Paul's persecution of the churches of Judaea, which, he feels, were "clearly ... established by Aramaic-speaking refugees from the city of Jerusalem." The taking of Acts 8:1 to indicate a church-wide persecution does not militate against a view of the Christian "Hellenists" having views distinct from those of the Christian "Hebrews," since it may be that the former group called attention to those elements of Jesus' teaching which, having been suppressed

by the latter group, made it dangerous for *anyone* who claimed association with the crucified leader.

26 Munck, 221, n. 1, feels that the speech's estimate of Moses ("the highest ... that we meet in the NT") must embrace also the customs delivered *by* Moses. M. Jones, 177, Scharlemann, 168, and Dunn, *Unity and Diversity*, 272f., all contrast Acts 7 with Paul in their view of the law. It has been argued that the quotation of Amos 5:25–27 in vv. 41ff. is used to attack the sacrificial system itself as idolatrous (see Simon, *Stephen*, 45f., followed by Gaston, 157). But, although it is a difficult passage and opinions differ, Munck is perhaps correct to assert that "in the context of the rest of Stephen's speech these words can surely only mean that because the Israelites were idolators, they did not sacrifice to God while they were wandering in the desert" (222, n. 1). See also Scroggs, 186f.; S. G. Wilson, *Gentile Mission*, 133; and F. F. Bruce, *Book of Acts*, 154–56.

27 Scroggs, 182; see also Schlatter, 86 ("they were frightened of the effect which such an attachment to Jesus would have on the authority of the Law").

28 Windisch, "Ἕλλην," 511f., citing the experience of Paul in Acts 9:29, speaks of "fanatical orthodox Jews of the dispersion," while Scharlemann, 111, points correctly, in my opinion, to their "sensitivity to such matters" as the result of the fact that, since they had more contact with Gentiles, they were constantly under suspicion.

29 *Ibid.*, 23 (my italics).

30 Cf. *De migr. Abr.* 89f., quoted, e.g., in Goodenough, 79.

31 Gaston, 154f.

32 *Birth*, 14.

33 Simon, *St. Stephen*, 84; see also Barnard, 82, who calls Stephen "more extreme than anything found in the Hebrew prophets or in sectarian Judaism"; S. G. Wilson, *Gentile Mission*, 148; and Cullmann, "New Approach," 39. Filson, "Hebrews," 24, on the other hand, sees Stephen as "still within the Jewish Christian framework"; Munck goes so far as to say that there is *nothing* in Stephen's speech which can in any way be seen as unusual from the rest of the early church (223f.); Bowman, *Hebrews*, 11, sees nothing in the speech which is not conducive to the viewpoint of Amos; and Schmithals, 21, sees the criticism of the temple as neither "Jewish" nor "un-Jewish." "After all, Judaism survived the destruction of the temple without a great convulsion." It may, of course, be a mistake to read the attitude of the post-destruction rabbis back into the tension-charged atmosphere of Jerusalem in A.D. 30.

34 Cf. Dunn, *Unity and Diversity*, 271; Simon, "Stephen," 134; Scroggs, 188; Klijn, 29; Scobie, "Origins and Development," 395, n. 1.

35 "Stephen," 133.

36 See also Scharlemann, 48, n. 134, for the targums of Ex. 29:43. Munck, 222, n. 1, agrees that the term cannot be pinned down in

this way. Haenchen, 285, n. 3, cites as a non-idolatrous reference the LXX of Isa. 16:12, but it is not clear how this can mean anything there other than "idols."

37 Haenchen, 284, n. 3, points out that in Acts 7 it might also have been mentioned that the tabernacle was made with hands, except that it did not occur to the author!

38 W. Manson, *Hebrews*, 34.

39 Stanton, 350ff.

40 W. Manson, *Hebrews*, 34.

41 See Bruce, *Book of Acts*, 160, n. 78, and S. G. Wilson, *Gentile Mission*, 133f.: "It is a denial of ... the exclusive confine of God's presence and activity."

42 Cp. Paul, for whom the law, while itself being holy and good, "tempts" men to commit the very deeds it forbids (Rom. 7:7f., 1 Cor. 15:56). For Paul to say "the power of sin is the law" is more "revolutionary" than for Stephen to say that the idea of God's presence in the temple is a denial of his nature.

43 Stanton, 352.

44 Scroggs, 188.

45 S. G. Wilson, *Gentile Mission*, 134.

46 Stanton, 348.

47 See Thornton, who suggests that the legend of Isaiah's murder would have involved the belief that it took place immediately after his last prophecy – Isa. 66. If this had been known in Stephen's time, he claims, it would provide a believable transition from "words against the temple" to the murder of the prophets. The view that Stephen was interrupted after v. 50, with verse 51 indicating his reaction, is rightly rejected by Haenchen, 286, who observes that Luke always informs the reader of such interruptions.

48 S. G. Wilson, *Gentile Mission*, 133f. (my italics).

49 *Unity and Diversity*, 273.

50 S. G. Wilson, *Gentile Mission*, 135, correctly observes that while a condemnation of the Jews similar to that of Stephen in Acts 13:46, 18:6, and 20:28 is linked to a turning to the Gentiles, no such idea can be found in Acts 7. The most that can be found there is a turning *away* from the Jerusalem Jews (136). Scobie, "Origins and Development," 399f., suggests that in the speech one finds "the great prophetic hopes (Jeremiah, Ezekiel, Zechariah) for a reunion of North and South," but there is scarcely more evidence for this than there is for a Gentile mission. Yet, while Gaston, 156, n. 2, is *technically* correct to view a turning to the Gentiles in Acts 7 as "an anachronism," one should remember that the speech is represented by Luke as being terminated abruptly (prematurely?), and that the themes which are preserved in it (especially the spiritual nature of God and his demands, together with the rebelliousness of the Jews) are, in *other* biblical contexts (cf. especially Jonah, Amos 9:7f., Mat. 21:43, Rom. 9–11, etc.), linked with a Gentile concern. A more balanced approach is that of Moule, *Birth*, 44, who says that it was a "courageous *application* of Stephen's arguments" which led to

the Gentile Mission (my italics). The claim of Bowman, *Hebrews, James,* 11, that the emphasis on Moses' Egyptian culture in vv. 17–22 points to God's revelation being "independent of cultural backgrounds" is somewhat wobbly, although the phrase "wisdom of the Egyptians" (v. 22) *is* tantalizing.

51 Cf. Spicq, *Hébreux,* I, 203, n. 2, who feels that Acts 13:16–41 is a "remarkably faithful echo" of Acts 7.

52 Cf. O'Neill, 93f. who thinks that Stephen's followers "had drawn the conclusion from his theology that the Gentiles must also be spoken to."

53 W. Manson, *Hebrews,* 36.

54 I do not, however, go as far as O'Neill, 89ff., who actually denies that the historical Stephen was a Christian! O'Neill's case depends too much on a theory of composite sources and Christian interpolations at two crucial places in Acts 6 and 7.

55 168. Scharlemann claims that the speech 'interprets the story of both the period of the OT and the age of Judaism as consisting almost wholly of Israel's rebellion against this law. Nothing of this kind occurs in Hebrews," O'Neill, 85, while not making the point of issue obedience to the law, says essentially the same thing by claiming that in Acts 7 the OT is used "to prove that the Jews have never accepted the prophets."

56 See, e.g., O'Neill, 91, for whom the second person pronoun in Acts 7 "embraces every generation."

57 Stanton, 353.

58 Cf. Filson, *Matthew,* 248: "These contemporary wrong-doers, who continue the wrong-doing of their ancestors, are held to participate in the sin and guilt of those earlier generations."

59 Stanton, 349.

60 Cp. John 8:42ff., where the attribution of a similar pedigree leads to the identical homicidal reaction of the audience.

61 Note the similarity of this interpretation of Acts 7:52 to the device of Heb. 7:9, which would allow one to paraphrase Stephen: "You who received the law through angels and did not keep it, since you were in the loins of your fathers who disobeyed!"

62 *Hebrews,* lxii.

63 Contra J. A. T. Robinson, *Redating.*

64 Ayles, 60, notes that a difference of purpose would account for *Auctor*'s omission of "the repeated instances of disobedience on which so much stress is laid" by Acts 7.

65 Similarly, the speech at Pisidian Antioch, although it represents Paul as rejecting the Jews and turning to the Gentiles (13:46f.), does not preclude Luke from depicting Paul at the *end* of Acts preaching to Jews in Rome "the hope of Israel" (28:20). See also Romans ("what advantage hath the Jew?" – Rom. 3:1). There are those (e.g., Alexander, 17) who find Stephen much closer to Paul than to Hebrews.

66 See, e.g., Simon, *St. Stephen,* 102ff.; Reid, 144f.; Barrett, "Eschatology," 392 and note; Scharlemann, 168f.; and Montefiore, 137f.

67 Simon, *St. Stephen*, 102ff., argues that, although "from his very silence" he probably valued the temple less than the tabernacle, "it cannot be asserted that he utterly condemned it."

68 There is an inconsistency in Simon's treatment of the term χειροποίητος; on the one hand, he argues that, because it normally means idolatry, this is the meaning it *must* bear in Acts 7:48. Yet in Hebrews, although "the tabernacle is repeatedly described as made with hands, ... the writer does not go so far as to condemn the earthly tabernacle: for it was made as a copy of the heavenly one" (*Stephen*, 103). For Stephen *and* Hebrews both the tabernacle and temple would undoubtedly be "made with hands."

69 Scroggs, 206.

70 So Bruce, *Hebrews*, 182.

71 See Cole, *New Temple*, 38.

72 Bruce, *Hebrews*, 219.

73 See McKelvey, 87.

74 See below, p. 104.

75 Haenchen, 284, n. 3, rightly believes that Wendt has gone beyond the evidence when he says that for Stephen "this tabernacle was a direct replica of the heavenly original, whereas the Temple was merely a copy of the copy." McKelvey is curiously ambiguous at this point. While stating that there is in Acts 7 no place for a dwelling of God in a temple made without hands, he argues that for Stephen the counterpart of the earthly temple is "the heavenly temple, the pattern that Moses saw on the mount" (87). Would not this constitute a temple "made without hands," and, if so, would God not dwell in it? Ayles, 58, thinks that Stephen believes in a "true sanctuary of God ... in heaven and not on earth," but he does not relate this to Ex. 25:40.

76 *Johannine Circle*, 45.

77 Reicke, *Glaube und Leben*, 129ff.

78 Scroggs, 189, argues that "from the call of Abraham to the building of the Temple, many of the important *heilsgeschichtliche* events narrated in the Bible *do* occur outside of the promised land."

79 C.P.M. Jones, 124.

80 Nixon, 25.

81 *Birth*, 75.

82 *Book of Acts*, 143.

83 *Paul*, 222f.

84 *Land*, 270ff.

85 Scharlemann, 172.

86 See Stanton, 357, who, referring to O'Neill, points out that "Abram's journey into Egypt, which would have been grist to this mill, is passed over in silence."

87 Simon, *Stephen*, 101; see also 83; and S. G. Wilson, *Gentile Mission*, 135f.

88 As Moffatt (*Hebrews*, lxii) has put it, in Hebrews "the κληρονομία of Palestine is spiritualized, whereas Stephen merely argues that its local possession by Israel was not final."

89 Simon, *Stephen*, 101f.
90 172f. The same criticism is made by Michaelis, "ὁδός," 78.
91 *Gottesvolk*, 9, n. 1.
92 Scharlemann, 172f.
93 *Ibid.*, 172f.
94 *Ibid.*, 171f.
95 "The oath which he swore to our father Abraham, to grant us that we, being *delivered from the hand of our enemies, might serve him without fear.*"
96 Cf. Acts 7:7, where the words "they shall come out with great possessions" in Gen. 15:14 are substituted with "And after that they shall come out and worship me in this place" (cf. Ex. 3:12). Dahl, "Abraham Story," 145, thinks that "worship in this place" refers in the speech to worship in Jerusalem rather than Sinai. But because of the amount of space (vv. 30–44) devoted by Stephen to events in the Sinai region, I find this unconvincing.
97 Cf. Dahl, "Abraham Story," 143 (who connects this with Hebrews but does not elaborate), and Davies, *Land* 269f.
98 Cf. Munck, 222.
99 ἐξέρχομαι (vv. 3, 4, 7), μετοικίζω (vv. 4, 43), ἐξαποστέλλω (v. 12, with Jacob as subject), ἀποστέλλω (v. 34), καταβαίνω (vv. 15, 34), φεύγω (v. 29), ἐξάγω (vv. 36, 40), and εἰσαγω (v. 45).
100 Cf. 8:8, quoting Jer. 38:32 LXX, which makes mention of Israel being "led out" of Egypt; Jesus is an ἀπόστολος in 3:1, possibly a second Moses motif (cf. the ἀποστέλλω of Ex. 3:10 – reflected also in Acts 7:34 – which would explain the unusual term); the readers are to "leave behind" (ἀφίημι) the primary things and "press on" (φέρω) to maturity; Moses' flight (Acts 7:29) resembles that of the readers in Heb. 6:18 (καταφεύγω); and Jesus is depicted as ἀρχηγός in 2:10 and 12:2. It is ch. 11, however, where a concentration upon movement similar to that of Acts 7 becomes most clear: by faith Noah jettisoned old ties in favor of the future (v. 7); Abraham heeds God's call to "go out" (v. 8f., cf. Acts 7:3, 4) and lived as an alien in the land of promise; the patriarchs "went out" (ἐκβαίνω, v. 15) and are "reaching out" (ὀρέγομαι, v. 16); Joseph looks to the Exodus (v. 22); Moses "passes through" (διαβαίνω, v. 29); the heroes "escaped" (φεύγω, cf. Acts 7:34), "went about" (περιέρχομαι, v. 37), and "wandered" (πλανάω, v. 38). Likewise the people of the new covenant are to run the race before them (12:1), and, following their leader, who likewise kept his eyes on what went before (12:2), are to make "straight paths for their feet" (12:13), engage in pursuit (12:14, although with "peace" as object), approach (προσέρχομαι, 12:18, 22) the heavenly city, and "go forth to him outside the camp" (13:13). In the latter case the use of ἐξέρχομαι exemplifies one of the leitmotifs of the epistle, and the choice of this verb to describe the believer's response in the face of the lure of earthly allegience may be drawn from the example of Abraham (11:8).

101 For other hints in the speech that possession of the land is being de-emphasized, cf. Davies, *Land*, 270f.

102 Cf. C.P.M. Jones, 124.

103 Scharlemann, 46f., cites the Samaritan Tenth Commandment, the context of which speaks of "the voice of the living God," and *Memar Marqah* IV, which calls the law the spring from Eden which gives forth "living waters." "Once more," he claims, "the conclusion seems inescapable that Stephen had come under the influence of Samaritan theology." But see Dodd, *Interpretation of Fourth Gospel*, 56, for numerous parallels from Philo where God and the Logos are depicted as life-giving waters. Strangely, Scharlemann makes no mention of either Deut. 32:47 LXX or 1 Pet. 1:23. Williamson, *Hebrews*, 36, cites as parallels Gen. 1:3–31, Deut. 18:18f., 32:46f.; Ps. 147:15, 33:9, and Heb. 11:3.

104 Cf. Foakes Jackson and Lake, IV.78. Philo also speaks of ψευδέσι μαντείαις (*Quod. Deus* 181).

105 See also Isa. 55:10f.

106 Cf. Arndt–Gingrich, 137.

107 *Stephen*, 174.

108 *Stephen*, 102.

109 Selwyn, *1 Peter*, 152.

110 See Dodd, *Interpretation of Fourth Gospel*, 83.

111 See also C.P.M. Jones, 124, and Dahl, 146, both of whom find Acts 7 and Hebrews very close at this point.

112 See above, pp. 98–100.

113 There is a certain attractiveness to the thesis of Thurston that Isa. 66:1 has more significance for the argument of Stephen and *Auctor* than has been noted. Thurston claims that in Acts 7 and Hebrews a midrash on Isa. 66:1ff. is preserved, with its key words becoming "magnets" for other OT texts containing the same words. He cites the terms "throne," "heaven," "earth," God's "hands," "footstool," "house" and "resting place" as terms in Isa. 66:1ff. which are prominent in other OT texts quoted by *Auctor* (cf. Heb. 1:8, 10, 13, 3:2, 11, 4:4, 8:1, 10:12, 12:21, etc.).

114 Contra Scharlemann, 174.

115 See Thurston, 27f.

116 See Bowman, *Hebrews*, 12.

117 So Bruce, *Hebrews*, 28, n.3.

118 This, of course, is not to deny that *Auctor*, in comparing the New Covenant with the Old, uses the idea that the Old was mediated by beings over whom Christ is now exalted in order to support his argument for the superiority of the New Covenant (see G. Hughes, 147, n.20). There is nothing to indicate, however, that *Auctor* would not have agreed with Stephen that *in its time* the giving of the law by God's "ministering spirits" (1:14) was a manifestation of divine graciousness, just as there is nothing to indicate that Stephen would not have agreed with *Auctor* that the second covenant was accomplished by a mediation even greater than that of the first. The "difference" is probably illusory, arising from the simple fact that

Stephen's purpose would not have been served by venturing into a discussion of the two covenants. In this case Stephen and *Auctor* stand apart from Paul, for whom the concept of mediation *itself* indicates inferiority (Gal. 3:19f.).

119 *Stephen*, 174.

120 *Ibid.*, 174 (my italics).

121 The problem is, as Hooker, *Son of Man*, 197, observes, that apparently in the martyrdom Luke is drawing a parallel between Jesus and Stephen in which both are vindicated through suffering. The vindicated Son of Man, in other words, vindicates his first martyred follower. Simon, *Stephen*, 71f., adduces the account of Hegesippus of the death of James (*Hist. eccl.* II.23), where James, before his martyrdom, speaks of the "Son of Man" who "sits in heaven at the right hand of the Mighty Power." This, claims Simon, indicates both martyrdom accounts to be historical. But for a less positive estimate of the account of Hegesippus, see Bruce, *Spreading Flame*, 151. Scobie ("Origins and Development," 397) feels that "distinctive features of a source can still be discerned" in the martyrdom account of Stephen, although he neglects to say what those features are. Similarly, Cullmann (*Johannine Circle*, 44) argues that the vision is based on "another Hellenist source in Luke's possession," for the picture of the Son of Man there "is not Lukan." The latter, however, cannot be supported (cf. Luke 12:8, where the Son of Man confesses in heaven those who confess him on earth). It is, of course, improbable that Luke has created the martyrdom story *ex nihilo*, but how or to what extent he has edited it for his own theological purpose is difficult to determine with precision.

122 Although the use of the simple name "Jesus" in Acts 7:55 and Heb. 12:2, both in connection with his place at God's right hand, *is* somewhat tantalizing.

123 C.P.M. Jones, 123, 141, has emphasized that in both the martyrdom story and Hebrews the *imitatio Christi* theme is strong, as is an emphasis upon the glory of God in relation to Jesus' exaltation.

124 Scharlemann, 169.

125 W. Manson, *Hebrews*, 54.

126 Review of Manson, 97.

127 Jesus could be standing to receive his first martyr.

128 "Stephen," 135; *Stephen*, 104.

129 At the other end of the scale, see Hanson, *Allegory and Event*, 95, for whom Christ in Acts 7 is prefigured in the Inheritance, the Seed, and land, the place-names Emmor and Shechem, the figures of Jacob, Moses and Joshua, the tabernacle and the House of God!

130 See Richard, "Polemical Character," for a good exposition of Joseph as a type of Christ in Acts 7.

131 Contra also Hanson, *Allegory and Event*, 95, for whom Stephen's speech is "full of typology which is just ready to slip over into allegory." Haenchen is correct to say "the text treats the persons and events as τύπος, not allegorically" (*Acts*, 282, n. 1).

132 E.g. Owen, 224ff., who thinks that Christ is standing because the

time had come for the gospel to be preached to the Gentiles, an event which heralds Christ's imminent return. "Christ rises in preparation for his parousia" (*ibid.*, 225), and this is meant to be a sign to preach the gospel universally. "And if anyone knew that it was surely Luke, the companion of Paul and the evangelist to the Gentiles." The difficulty with this is that in his version of the eschatological discourse (Luke 21:5ff.) Luke omits the key passage of Mark 13:10 (see also Mat. 10:18) that the gospel must first be preached to all nations. A more satisfactory approach is that of Barrett, "Stephen and the Son of Man," who argues that vv. 55f. are Luke's own distinctive use of the Son of Man tradition for a *personal* eschatology: "Christ is standing in order to come to Stephen in his distress" (36).

133 W. Manson, *Hebrews*, 32.
134 "Just as the beasts stood for the pagan empires, so the Son of Man stands for Israel or for the Godly Remnant within Israel" (T. W. Manson, "Son of Man in Daniel, Enoch and the Gospels," 171).
135 *Phenomenon*, 97.
136 *St. Stephen*, 68. Rather than Dan. 7:13f., Simon (70f.) chooses to relate Stephen's vision directly to "imminent parousia" texts in Luke's gospel (e.g., Luke 22:69). But he does not recognize the significance of Luke 22 of the phrase ἀπὸ τοῦ νῦν, which seems to indicate, not a once and for all event, but some kind of continuous reality.
137 Kilpatrick, 56, argues that originally Acts 7:56 read "Son of God" rather than "Son of Man," and that it was altered to avoid repeating the word "God" four times in two verses and to assimilate the text to Luke 22:69. But in view of the lack of textual evidence and the apparent parallel Luke is attempting to draw between Jesus and Stephen, this is to be rejected.
138 *Phenomenon*, 93.
139 Although see W. D. Davies, *Land*, p. 272, who postulates that Acts 7 must represent Luke's mind, and not Stephen's, because the question of the land which is raised by the speech could not have emerged in Jerusalem as early as Luke presents it. His reasons, however, I find unconvincing; certainly diaspora Jews who had settled in Jerusalem circa A.D. 30 could have been less fanatical toward the land and temple than about obedience to the Law, and this is precisely how Stephen is depicted by Luke.
140 Scharlemann's (*Stephen*, 170) objection that Stephen lacks any concern for the "over-and-over againness" of the cultic ritual, or his insistence that the lack of any allusion in Acts 7 to the sacrifice of Isaac means "it is impossible to speak of any similarity in point of view" between Acts 7 and Hebrews are good examples of this approach.
141 Contra Thurston, "Midrash and 'Magnet,'" who claims that the similarities between Acts 7 and Hebrews may be explained by the common use of a Book of Testimonies.

5 Pauline theology

1 *Théologie*, 197. Milligan, generally endorsing Ménégoz's findings, concludes similarly: "Not only can Paul not be the author ... it is extremely unlikely that the writer is to be sought in the immediate circle of his followers or friends: otherwise he would have reproduced more closely his master's teaching" (26). This comment, however, is difficult to harmonize with Milligan's claim (on the same page!) that "there is no real inconsistency between the two writers. On all fundamental points there is complete harmony between them." Could not this be said of a member of Paul's circle?

2 *Hebrews*, 192ff.

3 See Williamson, "Eucharist and Hebrews."

4 See below, pp. 122f.

5 *Hebräerbrief*, 128f.

6 E.g., "the God of peace," v. 20, found only in the NT elsewhere in Rom. 15:33 and 16:20; the link of "Lord" to the name of "Jesus" – e.g., Rom. 4:24; "equip you with every good thing to do his will," v. 21a, cf. Rom. 12:2; "through Jesus Christ," v. 21, cf. the repeated usage in Romans; and the ascribing of glory to God, v. 21, cf. Rom. 1:25, 11:36, etc.

7 See Nairne, *Priesthood*, 394, who thinks κατὰ πίστεως in 11:7 "is no doubt the same as the righteousness which S. Paul saw 'springing out of faith' (ἐκ πίστεως, Rom. ix.30, x.6; cf. Rom. ii.22, iv.11, Phil. iii.9)."

8 For the latter option, see Scott, *Hebrews*, 59.

9 For a full discussion, see Hurst, "Apollos, Hebrews and Corinth."

10 For the view of Lohmeyer, Hofius and others on Hebrews and Phil. 2, see below, pp. 115–19.

11 Barnett adduces numerous places where he feels that *Auctor* displays a direct literary dependence upon the Pauline letters, including: Heb. 1:2, Col. 1:16f.; Heb. 1:3 ("radiance" and "impress"), Col. 1:15; Heb. 1:3f. (Ps. 110:1), Eph. 1:20f.; Heb. 1:6 ("Firstborn"), Col. 1:15; Heb. 2:8, 1 Cor. 15:24–28; Heb. 3:6 (the church as a "house"), Eph. 2:19, Rom. 5:2; Heb. 3:6–4:2 (Ps. 95), 1 Cor. 10.1–11, etc.

12 *According to the Scriptures*, 110.

13 The problems concerning the phrase "pre-Pauline" are well stated by Caird, "Development," 66. For a stimulating discussion of the relationship of Paul to the shaping of the rest of the Christian tradition, see Hunter, *Paul and his Predecessors*.

14 This position was apparently begun toward the end of the last century among German commentators (cf., e.g., Wrede, 3ff. and *passim*). E. D. Jones, 562–67, argues that ch. 13 is a missing leaf of Paul's "severe" letter to the Corinthians.

15 This has been well stated elsewhere and need not be argued here. See Spicq, "L'Authenticité," and Filson, "*Yesterday*," both of whom argue persuasively that the chapter is authentic and that its themes are found in the epistle elsewhere.

16 According to Michel, *Hebräer*, 70f., who, citing 3 Enoch 5:10, says that it was made Messianic in apocalyptic Judaism. Buchanan, *Hebrews*, 39, chides Michel for denying that Ps. 8 was held to be Messianic by the rabbis; but he supplies no rabbinic references.

17 See, e.g., Bowman, *Hebrews*, 26; A.B. Bruce, *Hebrews*, 72ff.; Caird, "Exegetical Method," 49, and *Language and Imagery*, 27; Kistemaker, 16f.; Lindars, 168f.; Moffatt, *Hebrews*, 23; Montefiore, 57f.; Riggenbach, 36ff.; Robinson, *Human Face*, 159f.; Spicq, *Hébreux*, II, 32; Vanhoye, *Situation*, 265ff., 275ff.; Windisch, 20; and Westcott, 42f.

18 See, e.g., Anderson, 168f.; Buchanan, *Hebrews*, 26; Childs; Colpe, "ὁ υἱός," 464; Cullmann, *Christology*, 188; Delling, "τάσσω, κτλ.," 42; Davies, *Hebrews*, 27; Ellis, *Prophecy and Hermeneutic*, 193f.; Giles; Hanson, *Jesus Christ in OT*, 163, 166; Héring, *Hebrews*, 15ff.; Lünemann, *Hebrews*, 115f.; Michel, *Hebräer*, 70ff.; Peterson, 52; Reid, 131; Sowers, 80f.; Williamson, *Hebrews*, 11; Zuntz, *Text*, 48.

19 See Buchanan, *Hebrews*, 38–51.

20 Hurst, "Christology of Hebrews 1 and 2," 153ff.

21 "His presence at the right hand of God necessarily entails the conquest of the spiritual powers" (49f.).

22 *Hebräer*, 59. Michel considers the possibility that the enemies are the (human) enemies of the community to which *Auctor* is writing, but since there is virtually nothing said in the epistle about the persecutors, he rightly rejects it.

23 According to Sowers, the passage means that "all humanity will be under his rule in the coming age" (81, n. 22). Although this might be logically extrapolated, it is difficult to believe, since *Auctor* interprets Ps. 110:1 in the light of Ps. 8, that the thought could have been in his mind. The idea of co-rule, implied by his comment on Ps. 8 in 2:10 ("many sons" – cf. Mat. 19:28; Luke 22:30; Rev. 15:17; 1 Cor. 6:2; 2 Tim. 2:12) is probably more to the fore.

24 Contra Schneider, "τιμή," 175, who, denying that Ps. 8 in ch. 2 refers to humankind, follows Strathmann in referring the δόξα and τιμή not to the exaltation, but to "the position of honour which He assumes as the heavenly High Priest." See also Schaeffer, 383.

25 The author takes the adverbial phrase βραχύ τι not as an expression of degree but as a period of time according to the Jewish two-age theory. See Kistemaker, 105f.

26 For recent opinion on 1 Cor. 15:20–28, cf. Schweizer, "1 Korinther 15.20–28."

27 Fuller, 188, compares "the kingdom of Christ" here with "the kingdom of his Son" in Col. 1:3. Paul normally prefers to speak of "the kingdom of God" (Rom. 14:17; 1 Cor. 4:20, 6:9, 15:50; Gal. 5:21, etc.).

28 Hay, 61.

29 Héring, *1 Corinthians*, 168, asserts that ἐν πᾶσιν must be neuter and mean "in the whole universe," but this does not alter my point.

30 Does Christ continue to reign after it has been handed back? Robertson and Plummer think so, since the handing over means only the end of the dispensation during which his special task is to eradicate all which opposes God (355). See also Pannenberg, 368f., who claims that, since there can be no competition between the kingdoms of Christ and of God, God does not establish his kingdom "after" that of Christ, nor does Christ's lordship "end," since "subjection was its essence from the beginning." But does Pannenburg, who is concerned dogmatically to identify "the kingdom of God with Jesus Christ himself" (370), take Paul's wording seriously? Cullmann, *Christology*, 225, speaks emphatically of the "end" of Christ's lordship, as does Héring, *1 Corinthians*, 168 ("the final extinction of the dignity of *Kurios*"), although this does not involve "the loss of His nature as the Son of God and the Image of God, which He has had since His pre-existence"; see also Moffatt, *I Corinthians*, 249.

31 For another view, namely that the "handing over" of the kingdom of v. 24 reflects the tradition reflected in Pirke Eliezer 11:6, see Moffatt, *1 Corinthians*, 250.

32 That this cannot be construed as God's exclusive reign, independent of his vice-regent, humankind, is suggested by passages in which Paul speaks of humankind's inheriting the kingdom of God (e.g., 1 Cor. 6:9f., 15:50; Gal. 5:21, etc. – cf. Barrett, *From First Adam to Last*, 99f.).

33 Barrett, *From First Adam to Last*, 101: "in him Man will regain the lordship (even over death) that was originally entrusted to him."

34 See also Rom. 8:20, which at first blush does not seem relevant. But who is the ὑποτάξαντα? Humankind, Satan and God are possibilities (see Sanday and Headlam, 208, for a useful discussion). Yet 'εφ' ἐλπίδι seems decisive here: Satan does not subject humankind to futility "in hope," nor does humankind do this to itself. God must be the subjector, which makes Rom. 8:20 almost certainly an echo of Ps. 8. Creation is subjected to futility by the will of God, who (Ps. 8:6) said "let all things be subject to man." It is thus *because* creation is subject to humankind that it falls and becomes subject to futility with it. In this case the psalm is taken as a reference to humankind apart from its fulfilment in Christ. It is, in other words, as in Hebrews, an extremely anthropological understanding of Ps. 8.

35 Reference will inevitably be made here to Phil. 2:10 and 3:21, where it appears that the subjecting is done by Jesus alone. But these texts should be compared with a passage which, while not occurring in an epistle which is indisputably Pauline, also combines Ps. 8:6 with Ps. 110:1 – Eph. 1:20–22. Here, again, it could be claimed that the dignity belongs exclusively to Jesus. He, having been elevated to God's right hand, has a name above any other (cp. Phil. 2:9), not only in this age but in the age to come; he also (contra 1 Corinthians) appears to have absolute and unlimited authority (cf. W. D. Davies, *Paul*, 296, n. 4, who quotes Charles to the effect that,

in distinction to 1 Corinthians, "in his later epistles the Apostle conceives of this reign as unending"), while the subjection which was in 1 Corinthians a Scripture awaiting fulfilment is now an accomplished fact. (Similarly, Col. 1:20 speaks of "every knee" and "every tongue" acknowledging Christ's complete authority.) The impression here is that the "all things" subjected to Christ includes humankind, and that total cessation of opposition has already taken place (see, e.g., Fuller, 213, Dunn, *Unity and Diversity*, 54, and Montefiore, 56). It should, on the other hand, be noted that in Eph. 1:20–22 Christ's supreme status in this age *and* in the age to come only appears to be at variance with 1 Cor. 15:24ff. In 1 Corinthians the handing over of the kingdom in v. 24 and Christ's subjection in v. 28 is the complete fulfilment of the psalm for humankind. In Ephesians this is *presupposed*, and Christ's superior position in the age to come (v. 21) is as humankind's representative and vis-à-vis the powers. This is made certain by v. 22, where the church, i.e., redeemed humankind, is spoken of not in terms of subjection but in terms of Christ's "body." The idea that total cessation of opposition has already taken place in Ephesians, furthermore, fails to appreciate the tension of all eschatology. The powers have already been reconciled and subjected; but the consummation of the subjection is yet future (cf. Rom. 5:10, 18, where all have been reconciled through Christ's death, yet not all have turned, Rom. 10:11). The problem lies in determining whether the subjection of Eph. 1 is in actuality, in God's eternal decree, or in the corporate representation of the cross. That the work is not yet done is seen in the church's task of demonstrating to the powers the many-splendored wisdom of God (Eph. 3:10) and in fighting against the same world rulers (9:12). Similarly in Colossians, although the things in the heavens have been reconciled, the powers still exercise a tyranny over the world (2:8, 20). Thus in 1 Corinthians, Ephesians, Colossians and Hebrews both sides of the eschatological tension are maintained in approximately the same way.

36 See, e.g., Longenecker, *Biblical Exegesis*, 181, n. 62.
37 Cf. Hay, 36f., for the importance of the word "all" (occurring eleven times) in 15:20–28.
38 Cf. Ellis, *Paul's Use*, 96, who speaks of "the essential unity" of Paul's exegesis in 1 Cor. 15 with that of *Auctor* in 2:5ff.
39 See Kistemaker, 107f.; Dodd, *According*, 120–22; Hay, 36, 60–62; Anderson, 169, n. 56.
40 See Thornton, *Common Life*, 379, n. 1.
41 See below, p. 127.
42 Caird, "Son by Appointment," 74. For recent examples of this unexamined usage in discussions of the christology of Hebrews, cf. Williamson, "Incarnation," who argues that Hebrews enshrines a Johannine-like incarnation of the Logos, and Pryor, 49, for whom "by the time of the writing of this letter ... Christological development had already reached the stage where the divine status and

pre-existence of the Christ were accepted beliefs." Meier, 531ff., at least faces the question of personal vs. ideal pre-existence in Hebrews, although he opts for the former.

43 J.A.T. Robinson, *Human Face*, 155ff.

44 "Son by Appointment," 73ff.

45 Dunn, *Christology*, 206ff.

46 "Christology of Hebrews 1 and 2."

47 *Human Face*, 156ff.

48 "Christology of Hebrews 1 and 2," 155ff.

49 "Exegetical Method."

50 *Psalm Citations*, 78. Kistemaker points out numerous verbal links in the contexts of passages such as 2 Sam. 7:14 (Heb. 1:5) and Ps. 45:6 (Heb. 1:8) which *Auctor* exploits, thus ruling out the "proof–text" model.

51 See the authoritative survey of the history of the interpretation of the passage in Martin, *Carmen Christi*.

52 E.g., Murphy-O'Connor; Robinson, *Human Face*, 162ff.; and Dunn, *Unity and Diversity*, 134–36 and *Christology*, 114–25.

53 E.g., Hurst, "Re-Enter," and Wanamaker, "Phil. 2:6–11."

54 *Carmen Christi*.

55 *Son of God*, 88.

56 *Ibid.*, 87, following Lohmeyer, 77ff.

57 Käsemann, 63ff.

58 Michel, *Hebräer*, 36, n.3, argues for an affinity between Phil. 2 and Heb. 12:1–3.

59 *NT Christological Hymns*, 92ff.

60 *Hébreux*, I, 162–65.

61 Hofius, *Christushymnus*, 75.

62 *Ibid.*, 79. See also 93: "He becomes the enthroned sovereign Lord who already as the pre-existent Christ holds the whole universe."

63 *Ibid.*, 93f.

64 "Bekenntnis," 197ff. See also J.T. Sanders, 19.

65 Jeremias, 871, claims that in 11:25f., where Moses "renounced his glory as the son of the king's daughter in order to suffer with his people (v.25)," an explicit comparison is being drawn with the pre-existent Christ, who "in his incarnation freely surrendered the heavenly glory of the Son of God and accepted the shame of abasement (2:7, 9, 14)." While the case of Moses certainly would have supplied *Auctor* with an excellent parallel for the thought of Phil. 2, this is an opportunity which is passed by. Jeremias is apparently reading Hebrews through the spectacles of Phil. 2.

66 Hofius, *Christushymnus*, 92, n.71, is correct to claim, following Lohmeyer, that the name which Jesus is given in Phil. 2 is *kyrios*; but I cannot agree that this is equivalent in Hebrews to being "heir of the whole universe," as Hofius suggests. In Hebrews Christ is made heir because, as the ideal human, he constitutes what God had purposed in eternity for humankind, thus fulfilling Ps. 8 (cf. 2:5–10; cp. Rom. 4:13, 8:17, etc.). In Phil. 2:9, on the other hand, Christ's exalted name is apparently

a reward for his self-humbling from a previously exalted state, and is his alone.

67 Another passage which is often compared with *Auctor* at this point is Col. 1:15–20. I cannot here treat any similarities in depth, but certain points may be noted. Lightfoot's treatment (*Colossians*, 141ff.) has made it difficult to read the passage apart from the traditional "pre-existence" interpretation. Recent studies, however (e.g., Dunn, *Christology*, 187ff., Robinson, *Human Face*, 154, 162, and Caird, *Paul's Letters*, 174ff.), have produced compelling arguments that the figure in view is from start to finish the crucified and risen Jesus, and that the language which attributes creative activity to Christ is "the writer's way of saying that Christ now reveals the character of the power behind the world ... without the implication being intended that Christ himself was active in creation" (Dunn, *Christology*, 190). In this light the similarities with Hebrews are striking: (a) Both show an interest in the title "firstborn." (b) "In him all things hold together" (v. 17b) resembles Jesus' superiority to the angels in Heb. 1:4ff. (c) "Making peace by the blood of his cross" (v. 20b) resembles Heb. 1:3c ("made purification for sins"). (d) The ἀρχή root coupled with resurrection resembles the ἀρχηγός of Heb. 2:10. (e) Jesus' primacy over the principalities and powers (v. 16) resembles Jesus' superiority to the angels in Heb. 1:4ff. Differences, however, are also evident: (a) If, according to Caird and others, "image of the invisible God" (v. 15) is best taken as Christ the ideal human being, this would differ from "the effulgence of the glory of God and the stamp of his being" of Heb. 1:3, which is best taken as a reference to pre-cosmic Wisdom. (b) The qualification of πρωτότοκος in both occurrences ("of all creation," v. 15, and "from the dead," v. 18) differs from Hebrews (1:6; cf. 11:28 and 12:23), where it is unqualified. (c) The identification in Col. 1:16 of those to whom Christ is superior as "the principalities and powers" diverges from their status in Hebrews as "ministering spirits sent forth to serve those who are to inherit salvation" (1:14). (d) In Colossians Christ's superiority to the powers is rooted in his involvement in their creation, whereas in Hebrews it is based upon a name superior to theirs which he "inherits" (1:4). (e) Colossians has the "eschatological" phrase εἰς αὐτόν as well as the "protological" ἐν αὐτῷ and δι' αὐτοῦ, only the latter of which is reflected in the δι' οὗ of Heb. 1:2b. (f) The σῶμα metaphor for the church (v. 18) is not used in Hebrews. Thus, while the hymn of Colossians is closer to Hebrews than is Paul in Philippians, Colossians and Hebrews cannot be placed into any relationship of literary dependence at this point.

68 Cf. Dunn, *Christology*, 54.

69 See Caird, "Development," 80, who observes that Phil. 2, representing perhaps the highest christology of the NT, is also the earliest.

70 For the topic of faith in general, see the helpful discussion of Dodd, *Bible and Greeks*, 65–68, 198–200, and *Interpretation of Fourth*

Gospel, 179–86; Filson, "Nature of Biblical Faith," 223–27; Bacon, "Doctrine of faith," 12–21, and Williamson, *Philo and Hebrews*, 309–85.

71 See above, ch. 1.
72 *Philo and Hebrews*, 309ff.
73 So, e.g., Macrae, 192.
74 *Ibid.*, 194.
75 Snell, *New and Living Way*, 159: "Verse 8 is primarily meant to support verse 7, or at least is more closely connected with it than with what follows."
76 So A. B. Bruce, *Hebrews*, 395.
77 See Leonard, 85.
78 *Christology*, 98.
79 Macrae, 192.
80 So Grässer, *Glaube*, 64ff. 117.
81 Bultmann and Weiser, 207f.
82 *Ibid.*, 200.
83 See Williamson, *Philo and Hebrews*, 340ff., who underscores that nowhere in Philo's extensive treatment does one find anything equivalent to *Auctor*'s statement that faith gives substance to hope. G. Hughes, 160, n. 41, records the view of A. J. M. Wedderburn that "the extent to which Philo can speak of 'futurity' is in some ways a measure of his Judaism rather than his Hellenism."
84 "It is dyed through with the colours of ... hope" (87). See also Käsemann, 37ff., who argues that the predominant sense of faith in Heb. 11 is hope.
85 *Hebräer*, 128f.
86 For Heb. 11:3 as a statement of creation *ex nihilo*, see Williamson, *Philo and Hebrews*, 377ff.
87 See Bruce, 302. Barnett, 81, sees this as a pointer toward literary dependence.
88 Contra, e.g., Buber, 67.
89 Cf. McNeile, 256: "Only in reference to the future do the two halves of the definition [11:1] become identified."
90 It is, of course, true that Paul's language in 2 Cor. 5:1ff. appears to suggest that this "tent" already exists (note the present tense ἔχομεν and the description of the tent as "eternal," v. 1), but this is most likely a reflection of the Jewish notion of eschatological entities being "stored" in heaven, i.e., existing within God's purpose for the future.
91 See Williamson, *Philo and Hebrews*, 362, n. 6; also 369.
92 It is generally felt that in Romans 1:17 the passage means "he who is righteous by faith shall live" in order to support the concern there with the question of what constitutes one as "righteous" (Dodd, *Bible and Greeks*, 69; Milligan, 201f., n. 2; Purdy, "Hebrews," 717; Lindars, 232; Ellis, *Prophecy and Hermeneutic*, 192f., etc.). Sowers, 85f., significantly points out that by the shift of the possessive pronoun from "faith's" to "righteous one," as opposed to the LXX, *Auctor*'s text has been revised "in the direction of Paul's

interpretation of the passage." While this cannot be proven, it sheds interesting new light on the question. It is not entirely certain, however, whether the normal understanding of Paul's use of the text in Rom. 1 can be sustained. In Gal. 3:12 the text is linked with Lev. 18:5, "He who does them shall *live* by them," and it is by no means certain whether this means "live" in the sense that the term has normally been understood in Rom. 1 or in the sense of a *way of life*. Lindars, 229, takes it to mean the latter, so that in Rom. 1:17 the Habakkuk text could be translated as "the righteous shall live by his faith" – i.e., make faith his way of life. This would mean that Paul and *Auctor* understand the passage in the same way. Synge, 33ff., puts forth the bizarre view that Hab. 2:4b in Heb. 10:37ff. means "the righteous by faith will live." He bases this on the claim that the main theme of ch. 11 is "life," a theory then supported by an extraordinary eisegesis of that chapter. Although it brings *Auctor* into line with the predominant understanding of Hab. 2:4b in Rom. 1, this is to be rejected.

93 See Moule's review of Grässer, 148. Sowers, 133, makes capital of the fact that in 11:1 "God is not even mentioned," concluding from this that 11:1 "is not a definition of faith in God." But this rests on an isolation of 11:1 from ch. 10 and the rest of chapter 11. As with many others, Sowers tries to use this to prove that *Auctor* has a "Hellenist" view of faith which has its closest parallel in Philo. Slick distinctions between the "Hebrew" and "Hellenistic" view, however, are discouraged by Dodd's citation (*Bible and Greeks*, 66f.) of Xenophon (*Mem.* I.i.1–5), who speaks of πιστεύειν θεοῖς in a way which makes it clear that what is involved is much more than intellectual assent – to "believe in the gods" is to believe that their word is true, an idea which comes close to the main thrust of Heb. 11 in its emphasis upon faith as trusting God's promises.

94 See Grässer, *Der Glaube*, 27ff., 121ff.

95 Cf. Mat. 27:43, where Jesus' enemies say "he trusted in God."

96 Bultmann and Weiser, 210f., observe that in the NT faith in relation to God "is practically never" expressed in terms of πιστεύειν εἰς; but such linguistic observations, while necessary for NT study, should not be elevated to a place of scientific law in interpreting passages such as Heb. 11.

6 First Peter

1 Grässer, "1938–63," 195.

2 For a list of writers who advocate these various positions, see Ayles, 64.

3 "Comparison of 1 Peter and Hebrews."

4 Selwyn, *1 Peter*, 465f.

5 Grässer, "1938–63," 196f.

6 *Hébreux*, I, 139–44.

7 Moffatt, *Introduction*, 440.

8 Some of the more eccentric points offered by Ferris have been eliminated.

9 Wand, 25f.

10 Masterman, 36ff.

11 *1 Peter*, 465f.

12 See above, ch. 5.

13 I.141. See also Robinson, *Redating*, 161, who thinks that parallels between Hebrews and 1 Peter are "too sketchy or too general" to assert literary dependence either way.

14 *Hébreux*, I, 142.

15 *NT Apologetic*, 50f.

16 *Hebrews*, 5.

17 *Date, Destination*, 66.

18 Cf. Selwyn, 363–466, who argues that most of the similarities between Paul and 1 Peter are undeveloped and result from dependence upon common material, and Wand, 19–21, who concludes that "the distinctive features of Paulinism are conspicuous in 1 Peter by their entire absence ... what is common to the two teachers is just essential Christianity" (20). Selwyn's arguments are disputed by, among others, Beare, 195, and Mitton, *Ephesians*, 176ff. and "Relationship," 67ff., both of whom argue for literary dependence of Hebrews upon Paul. It would be impossible here to weigh the intricacies of such issues, but in my view Selwyn's case remains the more convincing.

19 Cf. Dunn, *Christology*, 236, who points out that the verb φανεροῦσθαι "regularly has the connotation of a manifesting of what was previously hidden (Mark 4:22, John 1:31, Rom. 16:26, Eph. 5:13, Col. 1:26, 3:4, 1 John 1:2)."

20 Most writers take it so (cf., e.g., Selwyn, 146; Beare, 80, Wand, 56), although Kelly, 74f., thinks that it may also refer either to the sacrifices of Ex. 29:1 and Lev. 22:17ff. or to the lamb of Isa. 53.

21 Cf. Kelly, 89, who states that "here, as frequently in the LXX ... *house* also specifically denotes 'temple.'"

22 Taylor, 34. For interesting literary links between the "spiritual sacrifices" and Qumran, see Flusser, "Dead Sea Sect," 233–35.

23 This draws attention to the NT's puzzlingly diverse treatment of priesthood. Ex. 19, quoted in 1 Peter, speaks of the "priestly nation." In Hebrews the focus is upon an individual priesthood of which Christ and Melchizedek are representatives. In Rev. 1:6 Christians are "kings and priests," but this is clearly applied to the phenomenon of martyrdom (cf. 5:10; Caird, *Revelation*, 17). There is no evidence that Hebrews, 1 Peter or Revelation depended upon one another for these usages.

24 Cf. Isa. 53:12, καὶ αὐτὸς ἁμαρτίας πολλῶν ἀνήνεγκεν. Although some (e.g., Bigg) see the phrase as a reference to the Levitical sacrifices, the similarity of wording to Isa. 53 leads Selwyn to regard it as 1 Peter's "true source."

25 Dodd, *According to Scriptures*, 34f.

26 *Ibid.*, 33f. ("There is nothing to suggest that he took it from

Paul, or from Hebrews''); see also Lindars, 50f., and Dunn, *Christology*, 109.

27 See Selwyn's table, 207.

28 The passive ὑποταγέντων appears to be independent of the Pauline usage.

29 See above, p. 101.

30 Cf. Hester, *passim*.

31 Macrae, 195, places 1 Peter and Hebrews in close proximity because of the claim that both use faith as the vehicle which ''shores up hope in the apocalyptic setting,'' but his presuppositions regarding ''the clearly Alexandrian context'' of *Auctor*'s doctrine of faith leaves him unable to consider Pauline theology of the kind recorded in Rom. 4 as a possible influence on the argument of Hebrews and 1 Peter on this point.

32 ''τύπος, κτλ.,'' 253.

33 See his table on 465.

34 See Beare, 48, and Barrett, ''Eschatology,'' 376. Barrett rightly differentiates the argument of *Auctor* and 1 Peter on this point: in 1 Peter ''they are resident aliens dwelling for a time in a foreign land while they hold their citizenship elsewhere. It is clear, however, from the language and imagery of Hebrews that more than this is involved.''

35 See also Lev. 4:2, 5:17, 6:1ff., etc. The reference in Hebrews is probably to the sins of ignorance for which the priest may make atonement (cf. Bruce, *Hebrews*, 90f.).

36 Bruce, *Hebrews*, 389.

37 See Longenecker, *Christology*, 80.

38 See Tinsley, 166ff.

39 See Flusser, ''Dead Sea Sect,'' 245, who notes that 1 Peter and *Auctor* both relate baptism to the notion of bodily cleansing and a clear conscience. This is a good example of the kind of superficial similarity already noted elsewhere. 1 Pet. 3:21 rejects completely the idea of a cleansed body (the baptism is not the ''putting away of the filth of the flesh, but the answer of a good conscience toward God''), while *Auctor* is interested in *both*, the one acting as a sign of the other (Heb. 10:22).

40 Delling, 42, admits rightly that in 1 Pet. 3:22 Ps. 110:1 and Ps. 8:6 represent only ''formally the brief confessional-type statement,'' while in 1 Cor. 15 and Heb. 2 ''we have a theological development of what is confessed.''

41 Cf. Wand, 25: ''No doubt the resemblances are partly due to the fact that both epistles share the same purpose, namely to strengthen the readers against persecution. This would explain the common emphasis upon hope and upon the connection of Christ's sufferings with His and our future glory.'' Robinson, *Redating*, 152, argues that the references to persecution in the two writings reflect differing situations.

Conclusion

1 *Hebrews*, 19.
2 This is in the main McCullough's conclusion in a generally competent survey of the issues. But his final statement (151) that the proper task for the future is to trace the background of Hebrews to "the religious pluralism and diversity within heterodox Judaism" is strangely pre-Hengel in its apparent acceptance of the old distinction between "heterodox" and "normative" Judaism.

BIBLIOGRAPHY

Primary sources

Old Testament
Biblia Hebraica. Ed. R. Kittel, 7th edn. (A. Alt, O. Eissfeldt and P. Kahle). Stuttgart, 1951.
Septuaginta, id est Vetus Testamentum Graece Iuxta LXX Interpretes. Ed. A. Ralphs, 8th edn., Stuttgart, 1965.

New Testament
Novum Testamentum Graece. Ed. Nestle-Aland, 26th edn., Stuttgart, 1979.
The Greek New Testament. Ed. K. Aland, M. Black, C. M. Martini, B. M. Metzger and A. Wikgren. 3rd edn., New York, London, Edinburgh, Amsterdam and Stuttgart, 1975.

English translations:
AV   Authorized King James Version, 1611.
RSV Revised Standard Version, 1952.
NEB New English Bible, 1961–70.

Other literature

Alexander, J. P. *A Priest Forever*. London, 1937.
Allegro, J. M. *Discoveries in the Judaean Desert*. Vol. V, *Qumran Cave 4*. Oxford, 1968.
   "Fragments of a Qumran Scroll of Eschatological *Midrašim*," *JBL* LXXVII (1958), 350–54.
   "Further Messianic References in Qumran Literature," *JBL* LXXV (1956), 174–87.
Allen, E. L. "Jesus and Moses in the New Testament," *ET* 67 (1955–56), 104–106.
Anderson, C. P. "The Setting of the Epistle to the Hebrews" (unpublished Ph.D. dissertation, Columbia University, 1969).
Arndt, W., and Gingrich, F. W. *A Greek English Lexicon of the New Testament and Other Early Christian Literature*. Chicago, 1957.
Ayles, H. B. *Date, Destination and Authorship of the Epistle to the Hebrews*. London, 1899.
Baaker, A. "Christ an Angel?" *ZNW* 32 (1933), 255–65.

Bacon, B. W. "The Doctrine of Faith in Hebrews, James and Clement of Rome," *JBL* XIX (1900), 12–21.

"Stephen's Speech: Its Argument and Doctrinal Relationship," *Biblical and Semitic Studies,* Yale Bicentennial Publications, (1901), 212–76.

Badcock, F. J. *The Pauline Epistles and the Epistle to the Hebrews in their Historical Setting.* London, 1937.

Barbour, R. S. Review of Montefiore's *The Epistle to the Hebrews, SJT* 20 (1967), 113.

Barclay, W. *Hebrews.* Daily Study Bible. Edinburgh, 1974.

Barfield, Owen. *Poetic Diction. A Study in Meaning.* London, 1962.

Barnard, L. W. "St. Stephen and Early Alexandrian Christianity," *NTS* 7 (1960), 31–45.

Barnett, A. E. *Paul Becomes a Literary Influence.* Chicago, 1941.

Barrett, C. K. "The Eschatology of the Epistle to the Hebrews," in *The Background of the New Testament and its Eschatology.* Festschrift for C. H. Dodd. Ed. D. Daube and W. D. Davies. Cambridge, 1956, 363–93.

From First Adam to Last. London, 1962.

"Stephen and the Son of Man," in *Apophoreta.* Festschrift für Ernst Haenchen. Beihefte zur *ZNW.* Berlin, 1964, 32–38.

Barth, M. "The Old Testament in Hebrews," *Current Issues in New Testament Interpretation.* Festschrift for O. Piper. Ed. W. Klassen and G. F. Snyder. London, 1962.

Batdorf, I. W. "Hebrews and Qumran: Old Methods and New Directions," in *Festschrift to Honour F. Wilbur Gingrich.* Ed. E. H. Barth and R. E. Cockcroft. Leiden, 1972, 16–35.

Beare, F. W., *The First Epistle of Peter.* Oxford, 1958.

Beasley-Murray, G. R., "The Two Messiahs in the Testaments of the Twelve Patriarchs," *JTS* 48 (1947), 1–12.

Bigg, C. *A Critical and Exegetical Commentary on the Epistles of St Peter and St Jude.* New York, 1905.

Bihler, J. *Die Stephanusgeschichte im Zusammenhang der Apostelgeschichte.* Munich, 1963.

Black, M. "The Qumran Messiah and Related Beliefs," in *The Scrolls and Christian Origins.* London, 1961, 145–63.

Blackman, E. C. *Biblical Interpretation.* London, 1957.

Blunt, A. W. F. *The Acts of the Apostles, in the Revised Version.* Oxford, 1951.

Bonsirven, J. *Exégèse rabbinique et exégèse paulinienne.* Paris, 1939.

Bornkamm, G. "Das Bekenntnis im Hebräerbrief," *Theologisch Blätter* 21 (1942), 56–66, reprinted in *Studien zur Antike und Urchristentum* (collected essays, Vol. II), Munich, 1959, 188–203.

Bowman, J. "Early Samaritan Eschatology," *JJS* 6 (1955), 63–72.

"Faith in Samaritan Thought," *BJRL* 40 (1958), 308–15.

"The Fourth Gospel and the Samaritans," *BJRL* 40 (1958), 298–308.

Hebrews, James, and I and II Peter. Layman's Bible Commentary. Richmond, 1962.

Braun, H. *An die Hebräer.* Tübingen, 1984.

"Qumran und das Neue Testament: Ein Bericht über 10 Jahre Forschung (1950–59): Hebräer," *ThR* XXX (1964), 1–38.

Brown, R. E., "The Messianism of Qumran," *CBQ* XIX (1957), 53–82.

Brooke, G. J. *Exegesis at Qumran: 4Q Florilegium in its Jewish Context.* JSOT Supplement Series 29. Sheffield, 1985.

"Qumran Pesher: Towards the Redefinition of a Genre," *RQ* 10 (1981), 483–503.

Brownlee, W. "The Cosmic Role of Angels in the NQ Targum of Job," *JSJ* 8 (1977), 83f.

The Dead Sea Manual of Discipline. BASOR Supplementary Studies, nos. 10–12, New Haven, 1951.

The Meaning of the Qumran Scrolls for the Bible. New York, 1964.

Review of K. Schubert's *Dead Sea Community, JBL* 80 (1961), 278f.

Bruce, A. B. *The Epistle to the Hebrews.* Edinburgh, 1899.

Bruce, F. F. *The Acts of the Apostles.* London, 1965.

Biblical Exegesis in the Qumran Texts. London, 1960.

A Commentary on the Book of Acts. London, 1954.

The Epistle to the Hebrews. London, 1964.

"The Kerygma of Hebrews," *Interp.* 23 (1969), 3–19.

The Spreading Flame. Exeter, Paternoster, 1970.

" 'To the Hebrews' or 'To the Essenes,' " *NTS* IX (1963), 217–32.

Buber, M. *Two Types of Faith.* Transl. N. P. Goldhawk. London, 1951.

Buchanan, G. W. "The Present State of Scholarship on Hebrews," *Christianity, Judaism and other Greco-Roman Cults,* Vol. I. Festschrift for Morton Smith. Ed. J. Neusner. Leiden, 1975, 299–330.

"To the Hebrews." Anchor Bible Commentary. New York, 1972.

Buchsel, F. *Die Christologie des Hebräerbriefs.* Gütersloh, 1923.

Bultmann, R. "ἀληθινός," *TDNT* I, 249f.

"Gnosis," *JTS* n.s. III (1952), 19.

Bultmann, R. and Lührmann, D. "φαίνω, κτλ.," *TDNT* IX, 1ff.

"Gnosis," *JTS* n.s. III (1952), 19.

Bultmann, R. and Weiser, A. "πιστεύω, κτλ.," *TDNT* VI, 174ff.

Theology of the New Testament. Vols. I and II. London, 1952, 1955.

Burch, V. *The Epistle to the Hebrews, its Sources and Message.* London, 1936.

Burrows, M., "The Messiahs of Aaron and Israel," *ATR* XXXIV (1952), 202–206.

More Light on the Dead Sea Scrolls. London, 1958.

Burtness, J. H. "Plato, Philo and the Author of Hebrews," *Lutheran Quarterly* X (1958), 54–64.

Caird, G. B. *The Apostolic Age.* London, 1975.

"The Development of the Doctrine of Christ in the New Testament," *Christ for Us Today.* Ed. N. Pittinger. London, 1968.

"The Exegetical Method of the Epistle to the Hebrews," *CJT* V (1959), 44–51.

The Language and Imagery of the Bible. London, 1980.

New Testament Theology. Completed and edited by L. D. Hurst. Oxford, 1991.

Paul's Letters from Prison. Oxford, 1976.

The Revelation of St. John the Divine. London, 1966.

"Son by Appointment," in *New Testament Age: Essays in Honor of B. Reicke*, I. Ed. W.C. Weinrich. Macon, GA, 1984, 73–81.

Cambier, J. "Eschatologie ou Hellénisme dans l'épître aux Hébreux," *Salesianum* XI (1949), 62–96.

Carmignac, Jean. "Le Document de Qumran sur Melkisédeq," *RQ* VII (1970), 348–78.

Chadwick, H. "St. Paul and Philo of Alexandria," *BJRL* XLVIII (1965–66), 286–307.

Charles, R.H. *The Apocalypse of Baruch Translated from the Syriac.* London, 1896.

The Apocrypha and Pseudepigrapha of the Old Testament. Vols. I and II. Oxford, 1913.

A Critical and Exegetical Commentary on the Revelation of St. John I and II. Edinburgh, 1920.

Childs, B. "Psalm 8 in the Context of the Christian Canon," *Interp.* 23 (1969), 20–31.

Cody, A. *Heavenly Sanctuary and Liturgy in the Epistle to the Hebrews.* St. Meinrad, 1960.

Coggins, R.J. "The Samaritans and Acts," *NTS* 28 (1982), 423–34.

Cole, A. *The New Temple.* London, 1950.

Colpe, C. "ὁ υἱός τοῦ ἀνθρώπου," *TDNT* VIII, 400ff.

"New Testament and Gnostic Christology," in *Religions in Antiquity.* Ed. J. Neusner. Leiden, 1968.

Colson, F., Whitaker, G. and Marcus, R. *Philo, with an English Translation.* 12 vols. Loeb Classical Library, 1929–62.

Combrink, H.J.B. "Some Thoughts on the Old Testament Citations in the Epistle to the Hebrews," *Neotestamentica* 5 (1971), 32.

Conzelmann, H. *Die Apostlegeschichte.* Tübingen, 1972.

Coppens, J. "Les Affinités qumrániennes de l'épître aux Hébreux," *NRT* LXXXIV (1962), 128–41, 257–282.

"Le Messianisme sacerdotal dans les écrits du Nouveau Testament," *La venue du Messie*, Recherches Bibliques 6, Louvain, 1962, 101–12.

Cross, F.M. *The Ancient Library of Qumran.* London, 1958.

Cullmann, O., *Christ and Time.* London, 1951.

The Christology of the New Testament. Philadelphia, 1963.

The Johannine Circle. London, 1976.

"A New Approach to the Interpretation of the Fourth Gospel," *ET* LXXI (1959–60), 8–12, 39–43.

Dahl, N.H., "The Story of Abraham in Luke–Acts," in *Studies in Luke–Acts.* Ed. L.E. Keck and J.L. Martyn. Philadelphia, 1966.

Daniélou, J. *The Dead Sea Scrolls and Primitive Christianity.* Baltimore, 1958.

Daube, D. "Alexandrian Methods of Interpretation and the Rabbis," in *Festschrift Hans Lewald.* Basle, 1953, 27–44.

The New Testament and Rabbinic Judaism. London, 1956.

"Rabbinic Methods of Interpretation and Hellenistic Rhetoric," *HUCA* 22 (1949), 239–64.

Dautzenberg, G. "Der Glaube im Hebräerbrief," *BZ* 17 (1973), 161–77.

Davies, J.H. *A Letter to Hebrews.* Cambridge, 1967.

Davies, W. D. *The Gospel and the Land: Early Christianity and Jewish Territorial Doctrine.* Berkeley, 1974.

Paul and Rabbinic Judaism. London, 1948.

Delcor, M. "Melchizedek from Genesis to the Qumran Texts and the Epistle to the Hebrews," *JSJ* II (1971), 115–35.

Delling, G. "τάσσω, κτλ.," *TDNT* VIII, 27ff.

Del Medico, H. E. "Melchisédec," *ZAW* LXIX (1957), 160–70.

Dey, L. K. K. *The Intermediary World and Patterns of Perfection in Philo and Hebrews.* Missoula, Mont., 1975.

Dibelius, M. "Der himmlische Kultus nach dem Hebräerbrief," in *Botschaft und Geschichte, Collected Essays,* Vol. II. Tübingen, 1956, 160–76.

Studies in the Acts of the Apostles. London, 1956.

Dimmler, E. *Melchisedek Gedanken über das hohepriestertum Christi nach dem Hebräerbrief.* Kempten, 1921.

Dodd, C. H. *According to the Scriptures.* London, 1952.

The Bible and the Greeks. London, 1954.

In *A Companion to the Bible.* Ed. T. W. Manson. Edinburgh, 1950.

The Interpretation of the Fourth Gospel. Cambridge, 1958.

Dods, M. "The Epistle to the Hebrews," in *The Expositor's Greek Testament,* IV. London, 1910, 221–381.

Doeve, J. W. *Jewish Hermeneutics in the Synoptic Gospels and Acts.* Assen, 1953.

Driver, G. R. *The Judaean Scrolls.* New York, 1965.

Dunn, J. D. G. *Christology in the Making.* London, 1980.

Unity and Diversity in the New Testament. London, 1977.

Eagar, A. "The Hellenistic Elements in the Epistle to the Hebrews," *Hermathena* XI (1901), 263–87.

Eccles, R. S. "Hellenistic Mysticism in the Epistle to the Hebrews" (unpublished Ph.D. dissertation, Yale University, 1952).

"The Purpose of the Hellenistic Patterns in the Epistle to the Hebrews," in *Religions in Antiquity.* Festschrift for E. Goodenough. Ed. J. Neusner, 207–26.

Ellis, E. E. *Paul's Use of the Old Testament.* Edinburgh, 1957.

Prophecy and Hermeneutic in Early Christianity. Tübingen, 1978.

Fairhurst, A. M. "Hellenistic Influence in the Epistle to the Hebrews," *TB* 7–8 (1961), 17–27.

Fensham, F. C. "Hebrews and Qumran," *Neotestamentica* V (1971), 9–21.

Fenton, J. C. "Respice Finem," *ET* 84 (1973), 244–47.

Ferris, T. E. S. "A Comparison of I Peter and Hebrews," *CQR* III (1930–31), 123–27.

Feuillet, A. "Les Points de vue nouveaux dans l'eschatologie de l'épître aux Hébreux," *SE* II (1964), 369–87.

Filson, F., "The Epistle to the Hebrews," *JBR* XXII (1954), 20–26.

"The Nature of Biblical Faith," *JBR* 27 (1959), 223–27.

Yesterday. London, 1967.

Fitzmyer, J. A. "4Q Testimonia and the New Testament," *TS* XVIII (1957), 513–37.

"Further Light on Melchizedek from Qumran Cave II," in *Essays on the Semitic Background of the New Testament.* London, 1971, 245–67.

"'Now this Melchizedek ...' Heb. 7:1; Ps. 110:4; Gn. 14:8ff.,'' in *Essays on the Semitic Background of the New Testament*. London, 1971, 221–43.

Review of Horton's *Melchizedek Tradition* in *CBQ* XXXIX (1977), 437.

"The Use of Explicit Old Testament Quotations in Qumran Literature and in the New Testament," *Essays on the Semitic Background of the New Testament*. London, 1971, 3–58.

Floor, L. "The General Priesthood of Believers in the Epistle to the Hebrews," *Neotestamentica* 5 (1971), 72–82.

Flusser, D. "The Dead Sea Sect and Pre-Pauline Christianity," *Scripta Hierosolymitana* IV (1958), 215–66.

"Melchizedek and the Son of Man," *Christian News from Israel* XVII (1966), 228–39.

Foakes-Jackson, F. J. 'Stephen's Speech in Acts," *JBL* 49 (1930), 283–86.

Foakes-Jackson, F. J., and Lake, K. *The Beginnings of Christianity. Part I: The Acts of the Apostles*. London, 1920.

Foerster, W. "Stephanus und die Urgemeinde," *Dienst unter dem Wort*. Gütersloh, 1953.

Fohrer, G., and Lohse, E. "Σιών, κτλ.," *TDNT* VII, 292ff.

Friebel, K. G. "Biblical Interpretation in the Pesharim of the Qumran Community," *Hebrew Studies* 22 (1981), 13–24.

Fritsch, C. T., "The So-Called Priestly Messiah of the Essenes." *Jaarbericht van het voorraziatsch-Egyptisch genootschap Ex Oriente Lux* VI (1967), 242–48.

"TO 'ANTITYΠON," *Studia Biblica et Semitica*. Festschrift for T. C. Vriezen. Ed. W. C. van Unnick. Wageningen: H. Veenman & Zonen, 1966, 100–107.

Fuller, R. H. *The Foundations of New Testament Christology*. Collins, 1976.

Gärtner, B. "The Habakkuk Commentary (DSH) and the Gospel of Matthew," *ST* VIII (1955), 1–24.

The Temple and the Community in Qumran and the New Testament. Cambridge, 1965.

Gaston, L. *No Stone on Another: Studies in the Significance of the Fall of Jerusalem in the Synoptic Gospels*. Leiden, 1970.

Gilbert, G. H. "The Greek Element in the Epistle to the Hebrews," *AJT* XIV (1910), 521–32.

Giles, Pauline. "The Son of Man in Hebrews," *ET* LXXXVI (1975), 328–32.

Gnilka, J. "Die Erwartung des messianischen Hohenpriesters in den Schriften von Qumran und im Neuen Testament," *RQ* II (1960), 395–426.

Goodenough, E. *An Introduction to Philo Judaeus*. Oxford, 1962.

Goppelt, L. *Christentum und Judentum im ersten und zweiten Jahrhundert. Ein Aufriss der Urgeschichte der Kirche*. Gütersloh, 1954.

"τύπος, κτλ.," *TDNT* VIII, 246ff.

Typos. Darmstadt, 1969.

Gordis, R. "The 'Begotten' Messiah in the Qumran Scrolls," *VT* VII (1957), 191–94.

Goulder, M. "The Two Roots of the Christian Myth," in *The Myth of God Incarnate*. Ed. J. Hick, London, 1977, 64–121.

Grant, R. M. *The Letter and the Spirit*. London, 1957.

Grässer, E. *Der Glaube im Hebräerbrief*. Marburg, 1965.
"Der Hebräerbrief, 1938–63," *ThR* 30 (1964–65), 138–236.
Gray, G. B. "The Heavenly Temple and the Heavenly Altar," *Expositor* VIII (1908), 385–402, 530–46.
Grotius, H. *Annotationes in Acta Apostolorum et in epistolas catholicas*. Paris, 1646.
Guilding, A. *The Fourth Gospel and Jewish Worship*. Oxford, 1960.
Guthrie, D. *New Testament Introduction*. London, 1966.
Haenchen, E. *The Acts of the Apostles*. Oxford, 1971.
Hanson, A. T. *Jesus Christ in the Old Testament*. London, 1965.
Hanson, R. P. C. *Allegory and Event*. London, 1959.
Harris, J. R. *Testimonies*, II, Cambridge, 1920.
Hatch, E., and Redpath, H. *A Concordance to the Septuagint*. Oxford, 1897.
Hay, D. M. *Glory at the Right Hand. Psalm 110 in Early Christianity*. Nashville, 1973.
Hengel, M. *Judaism and Hellenism*. Transl. J. Bowden. 2 vols. London, 1974.
The Son of God. London, 1975.
"Zwischen Jesus und Paulus. Die 'Hellenisten,' die 'Sieben' und Stephanus," *ZThK* 72 (1975), 151ff.
Héring, J. "Eschatologie biblique et idéal platonicien," in *The Background of the New Testament and its Eschatology*. Festschrift for C. H. Dodd. Ed. W. D. Davies and D. Daube. Cambridge, 1954.
The Epistle to the Hebrews. London, 1970.
The First Epistle of St. Paul to the Corinthians. London, 1962.
Hester, J. D. *Paul's Concept of Inheritance*. Edinburgh, 1968.
Hewitt, T. *The Epistle to the Hebrews*. London, 1960.
Higgins, A. J. B. "Priest and Messiah," *VT* III (1953), 321–36.
"The Priestly Messiah," *NTS* XIII (1966–67), 211–39.
Review of W. Manson's *Epistle to the Hebrews*, *JTS* n.s. 5 (1954), 97.
Hofius, O. *Der Christushymnus Philipper 2.6–11*. Tübingen, 1976.
Katapausis. Die Vorstellung vom endzeitlichen Ruheort im Hebräerbrief. Tübingen, 1970.
Der Vorhang vor dem Thron Gottes. Tübingen, 1972.
Hooker, M. D. "Philippians 2.6–11," in *Jesus und Paulus*. Festschrift for W. G. Kummel. Ed. E. E. Ellis and E. Grässer. Göttingen, 1975, 151–64.
The Son of Man in Mark. London, 1967.
Horton, F. L. *The Melchizedek Tradition*. Cambridge, 1976.
Howard, G. "Hebrews and the Old Testament Quotations," *NT* 10 (1968), 208–16.
Review of R. Williamson, *Philo and the Epistle to the Hebrews*, *JBL* 92 (1973), 465f.
Howard, W. F. "The Epistle to the Hebrews," *Interpretation* 5 (1971), 80ff.
The Fourth Gospel in Recent Criticism and Interpretation. 2nd edn. London, 1955.
Hughes, G. *Hebrews and Hermeneutics*. Cambridge, 1979.
Hughes, P. E. *A Commentary on the Epistle to the Hebrews*. Grand Rapids, Mich., 1977.
Hunter, A. M. *Paul and his Predecessors*. London, 1940.
Hurst, L. D. "Apollos, Hebrews and Corinth: Bishop Montefiore's Theory Examined," *SJT* 38 (1986), 505ff.

"The Christology of Hebrews 1 and 2," in *The Glory of Christ in the New Testament. Studies in Christology in Memory of George Bradford Caird.* Ed. L. D. Hurst and N. T. Wright. Oxford, 1987, 151ff.

"Eschatology and 'Platonism' in the Epistle to the Hebrews," *SBL Seminar Papers* 23, Chico, Calif., 1984, 41ff.

"How 'Platonic' are Heb. viii.5 and ix.23f.?" *JTS* 34 (1983), 156ff.

"Re-Enter the Pre-Existent Christ in Philippians 2.5–11?" *NTS* 32 (1986), 449ff.

Jeremias, J. "Μωυσῆς," *TDNT* IV, 848ff.

Jérôme, F. J. *Das geschichtliche Melchisedech-Bild und seine Bedeutung im Hebräerbrief.* Freiburg, 1920.

Johnson, M. D. *The Purpose of the Biblical Genealogies.* Cambridge, 1969.

Johnsson, W. G. "The Cultus of Hebrews in Twentieth-Century Scholarship," *ET* 89 (1978), 104–108.

"The Pilgrimage Motif in the Book of Hebrews," *JBL* 97 (1978), 239–51.

Johnston, G. Review of Montefiore's *Hebrews*, *JBL* 85 (1966), 97.

Jonas, Hans. *The Gnostic Religion.* Boston, 1963.

Jones, C. P. M. "The Epistle to the Hebrews and the Lucan Writings," *Studies in the Gospels. Essays in Memory of R. H. Lightfoot.* Ed. D. E. Nineham. Oxford, 1955, 113–43.

Jones, M. "The Significance of Stephen," *The Expositor*, eighth series, 1, 13 (1917), 161–78.

Jonge, M. de, "The Use of the Word 'anointed' in the Time of Jesus," *NT* VIII (1966), 132–48.

Jonge, M. de, and van der Woude, A. S. "11Q Melchizedek and the New Testament," *NTS* XII (1965–66), 301–26.

Käsemann, E. *The Wandering People of God: An Investigation of the Letter to the Hebrews.* Transl. Roy A. Harrisville. Minneapolis, 1984 (Orig. *Das wandernde Gottesvolk.* Göttingen, 1961⁴).

Kennedy, J. N. D. *A Commentary on the Epistles of Peter and Jude.* London, 1969.

The Theology of the Epistles. London, 1919.

Kilgallen, J. *The Stephen Speech.* Rome, 1976.

Kilpatrick, G. D. "Again Acts vii.56: Son of Man?" *ThZ* 34 (1978), 232.

Kistemaker, S. *The Psalm Citations in the Epistle to the Hebrews.* Amsterdam, 1961.

Klappert, B. *Die Eschatologie des Hebräerbriefs.* Munich, 1969.

Klijn, A. F. J. "Stephen's Speech – Acts VII.2–53," *NTS* 4 (1957), 25–31.

Knox, E. A. "The Samaritans and the Epistle to the Hebrews," *The Churchman* 22 (1927), 184–93.

Knox, W. L., "Pharisaism and Hellenism," chapter II of *Judaism and Christianity.* Ed. H. Loewe, London, 1937.

St. Paul and the Church of Jerusalem. Cambridge, 1925.

Koester, H. *Introduction to the New Testament.* Philadelphia, 1982 (Orig. *Einfuhrung in das Neue Testament.* Berlin, 1980).

Kosmala, H. *Hebräer – Essener – Christen.* Leiden, 1971.

Kuhn, H. W. "Die beiden Messias in den Qumrantexten und die Messiasvorstellung in der rabbinischen Literatur," *ZNW* LXX (1958), 200–208.

Kuhn, K. G. *Konkordanz zu den Qumrantexten.* Göttingen, 1960.
"The Two Messiahs of Aaron and Israel," *The Scrolls and the New Testament.* Ed. K. Stendahl. London, 1958.
Kümmel, W. G. *Introduction to the New Testament.* 14th edn., Nashville, 1966.
Kuss, O. *Der Brief an Die Hebräer.* Regensburg, 1966.
Lampe, G. W. H. and Woolcombe, K. J. *Essays on Typology.* London, 1957.
Patristic Greek Lexicon. Oxford, 1969.
Lane, W. R. "A New Commentary Structure in 4Q Florilegium," *JBL* LXXVIII (1959), 343–46.
LaSor, W. S. *The Dead Sea Scrolls and the New Testament.* Eerdmans, 1972.
"The Messianic Idea in Qumran," *Studies and Essays in Honor of Abraham A. Neuman.* Leiden, 343–64.
Laubscher, F. Du T. "God's Angel of Truth and Melchizedek. A Note on 11Q Melch 13b," *JSJ* III (1972), 46–51.
Lee, E. "Words Denoting 'Pattern' in the New Testament," *NTS* 8 (1962), 167ff.
Leonard, W. *The Authorship of the Epistle to the Hebrews.* London, 1939.
Lewis, C. S. *Studies in Words.* Cambridge, 1960.
Lewis, T. W. "'And if he Shrinks Back' (Heb. X 38b)," *NTS* 22 (1975), 88–94.
Liddell, H., Scott, R., and Jones, H. *A Greek–English Lexicon, with a Supplement.* Oxford, 1968.
Lightfoot, J. B. *Paul's Epistle to the Colossians and Philemon.* Macmillan, 1884.
Saint Paul's Epistle to the Philippians. Macmillan, 1927.
Lindars, B. *New Testament Apologetic.* London, 1961.
Liver, J. "The Doctrine of the Two Messiahs in Sectarian Literature in the time of the Second Commonwealth," *HTR* LII (1959), 149–85.
Lohmeyer, E. *Kyrios Jesus: Eine Untersuchung zu Phil. 2:5–11.* Heidelberg, 1928.
Lohse, E. "σάββατον, κτλ.," *TDNT* VII, 1ff.
Lombard, H. "Katapausis in the Letter to the Hebrews," *Neotestimentica* 5 (1971), 62ff.
Longenecker, R. N. *Biblical Exegesis in the Apostolic Period.* Grand Rapids, 175.
The Christology of Early Jewish Christianity. London, 1970.
"The Melchizedek Argument of Hebrews: A Study in the Development and Circumstantial Expression of New Testament Thought," *Unity and Diversity in New Testament Theology: Essays in Honour of G. E. Ladd.* Ed. R. A. Guelich. Eerdmans, 1978.
Luck, U. "Himmlisches und irdisches Geschehen im Hebräerbrief," *NT* 6 (1963), 192–215.
Lundberg, P. *La Typologie baptismale.* Uppsala, 1942.
Lünemann, G. *A Critical and Exegetical Handbook to the Epistle to the Hebrews.* Edinburgh, T. & T. Clark, 1882.
McCullough, J. C. "The Old Testament Quotations in Hebrews," *NTS* 26 (1980), 363–79.

"Some Recent Developments in Research on the Epistle to the Hebrews,"
IBS II (1980), 141–65.

MacDonald, J. *Memar Marqah: the Teaching of Marqah*. Beiheft zur *ZAW*
LXXXIV, Berlin, 1963.

"The Samaritan Doctrine of Moses," *SJT* 13 (1960), 149–62.

The Theology of the Samaritans. London, 1964.

Mackay, C. 'The Argument of Hebrews," *CQR* 168 (1967), 325–38.

"The Order of Melchizedek," *CQR* 138 (1944), 175–91.

McKelvey, R. J. *The New Temple*. Oxford, 1968.

McNeile, A. H. *New Testament Teaching in the Light of St. Paul's*.
Cambridge, 1923.

Macrae, G. W. "Heavenly Temple and Eschatology in the Letter to the
Hebrews," *Semeia* 12 (1978), 179–99.

Manson, T. W. "The Argument from Prophecy," *JTS* XLVI (1945), 129ff.

"ΙΛΑΣΤΗΡΙΟΝ," *JTS* XLVI (1945), 1–10.

On Paul and John. Ed. M. Black. London, 1963.

"The Problem of the Epistle to the Hebrews," *Studies in the Gospels and
Epistles*. Manchester, 1962, 242ff.

The Servant Messiah. Cambridge, 1953.

"The Son of Man in Daniel, Enoch and the Gospels," *BJRL* 32 (1949–50),
171–93.

Manson, W. *The Epistle to the Hebrews: An Historical and Theological
Reconstruction*. London, 1951.

Marchant, G. J. C. "Sacrifice in the Epistle to the Hebrews," *EQ* XX (1948),
196ff.

Marshall, I. H. "Palestinian and Hellenistic Christianity: Some Critical
Remarks," *NTS* 19 (1972–73), 274ff.

Martin, R. P. *Carmen Christi*. Cambridge, 1967.

Martitz, P. Wülfing von, *et al*. "υἱός, υἱοθεσία," *TDNT* VIII, 334ff.

Masterman, J. B. *The First Epistle of St. Peter*. London, 1912.

Mayer, G. *Index Philoneus*. New York, 1974.

Medibielle, A. *L'Epître aux Hébreux*. Paris, 1938.

Meier, J. P. "Symmetry and Theology in the Old Testament Citations of
Heb. 1, 5–14," *Biblica* 66 (1985), 504ff.

Ménégoz, E. *La Théologie de l'Epître aux Hébreux*. Paris, 1894.

Metzger, B. M. "Epistle to the Hebrews," in *Twentieth Century Encyclopedia
of Religious Knowledge*, ed. Lefferts A. Loetscher. Grand Rapids,
Mich., 1955.

Michaelis, W. "ὁδός, κτλ.," *TDNT* V, 42ff.

"σκηνή, κτλ.," *TDNT* VII, 368ff.

Michel, O. *Der Brief an die Hebräer*. 12 Auflage. Göttingen, 1966.

"Μελχισεδέκ," *TDNT* IV, 568ff.

"ναός," *TDNT* IV, 880ff.

Milik, J. T. "Milkî-sedeq et Milkî-resha' dans les anciens écrits juifs et
chrétiens," *JJS* 23 (1972), 95–114.

"4Q visions de 'Amram/et/une citation d'Origène," *RB* 79 (1972), 77ff.

Ten Years of Discovery in the Wilderness of Judaea. London, 1959.

Milligan, G. *The Theology of the Epistle to the Hebrews*. Edinburgh,
1899.

Minear, Paul S. "The Cosmology of the Apocalypse," *Current Issues in New Testament Interpretation*. Festschrift for Otto Piper. Ed. W. Klassen and G.F. Snyder. London, 1962, 23–37.

Mitton, C.L. *The Epistle to the Ephesians*. Oxford, 1951.

"The Relationship of I Peter and Ephesians," *JTS* 1 (1950), 67ff.

Moffatt, James. *A Critical and Exegetical Commentary on the Epistle to the Hebrews*. Edinburgh, 1924.

The First Epistle of Paul to the Corinthians. London, 1938.

An Introduction to the Literature of the New Testament. Edinburgh, 1911.

Montefiore, H.W. *The Epistle to the Hebrews*. London, 1964.

Montgomery, J.A. *The Samaritans*. New York, 1968.

Moule, C.F.D. *The Birth of the New Testament*. London, 1962.

"Commentaries on the Epistle to the Hebrews," *Theology* 61 (1958), 228–32.

"Once More, Who Were the Hellenists?" *ET* LXX (1959), 100ff.

The Origin of Christology. Cambridge, 1977.

The Phenomenon of the New Testament. London, 1967.

Review of E. Grässer's *Der Glaube im Hebräerbrief*. *JTS* XVII (1966), 147–50.

"Sanctuary and Sacrifice in the Church of the New Testament," *JTS* 1 (1950), 29–41.

Moulton, J.H. and Milligan, G. *The Vocabulary of the Greek Testament*. London, 1914.

Muilenburg, J. "Ezekiel," in *Peake's Commentary on the Bible*, ed. M. Black and H.H. Rowley, 1976.

Munck, J. *Paul and the Salvation of Mankind*. London, 1959.

Murphy-O'Connor, J. "Christological Anthropology in Phil. 2:6–11," *RB* 83 (1976), 25–50.

Nairne, A. *The Epistle of Priesthood*. Edinburgh, 1913.

The Epistle to the Hebrews. Cambridge, 1917.

Nauck, W. "Zum Aufbau des Hebräerbriefes," in *Judentum, Urchristentum, Kirche*. Festschrift for J. Jeremias. Ed. W. Eltester. Berlin, 1960.

Neil, W. *The Epistle to the Hebrews*. London, 1955.

Nixon, R. *The Exodus in the New Testament*. London, 1963.

Oepke, A. *Das neue Gottesvolk*. Gütersloh, 1950.

Oesterley, W.O.E. *The Jews and Judaism during the Greek Period*. London, 1941.

O'Neill, J.C. *The Theology of Acts in its Historical Setting*. London, 1961.

Owen, H.P. "Stephen's Vision in Acts 7.55–6," *NTS* 1 (1954–55), 224–26.

Pannenberg, W. *Jesus, God and Man*. London, 1968.

Peel, M.L. "Gnostic Eschatology and the New Testament," *NT* XII (1970), 141ff.

Perry, M. "Method and Model in the Epistle to the Hebrews," *Theology* 77 (1974), 66–74.

Peterson, D. *Hebrews and Perfection. An Examination of the Concept of Perfection in the Epistle to the Hebrews*. SNTS Monograph Series 47. Cambridge, 1982.

Pfeiffer, R. H. *History of New Testament Times.* New York, 1949.

Plummer, R. "The Samaritan Pentateuch and the New Testament," *NTS* 22 (1976), 441–43.

Plumptre, E. H. "The Samaritan Element in the Gospels and Acts," *Expositor*, Series I, Vol. 7 (1878), 22–40.

Pretorius, E. A. C. "ΔΙΑΘΗΚΗ in the Epistle to the Hebrews," *Neotestamentica* 5 (1971), 37–50.

Priest, J. F., "Mebaqqer, Paquid, and the Messiah," *JBL* LXXXI (1962), 55–61.

Procksch, O., and Kuhn, K. G. "ἅγιος, κτλ.," *TDNT* I, 88ff.

Pryor, J. P. "Hebrews and Incarnational Christology," *RTR* 40 (1981), 44–50.

Purdy, A. C. "The Epistle to the Hebrews," in *The Interpreter's Bible*, Vol. XI. Nashville, 1955.

   "The Purpose of the Epistle to the Hebrews in the Light of Recent Studies in Judaism," *Amicitiae Corolla: A Volume of Essays Presented to James Rendel Harris.* London, 1933, 253–64.

Rackham, R. B. *The Acts of the Apostles.* London, 1953.

Rad, G. von. "Ancient Word and Living Word," *Interp.* 15 (1961), 3–13.

Rawlinson, A. E. J. *The New Testament Doctrine of the Christ.* London, 1926.

Reese, J. M. *Hellenistic Influence in the Book of Wisdom and its Consequences.* Anal. Bibl. 41, 1970.

Reicke, B. *The Disobedient Spirits and Christian Baptism.* Lund, 1946.
   Glauben und Leben der Urgemeinde, Bemerkungen zu Apg. 1–7. Zürich, 1957.

   "Traces of Gnosticism in the Dead Sea Scrolls?" *NTS* I (1955), 137–41.

Reid, R. "The Use of the Old Testament in the Epistle to the Hebrews" (unpublished Th.D. dissertation, Union Theological Seminary, New York, 1965).

Reifenburg, *Ancient Jewish Coins.* Jerusalem, 1947.

Rendall, R. "The Method of the Writer to the Hebrews in Using Old Testament Quotations," *EQ* XXVII (1955), 214–20.

Richard E. "Acts 7: An Investigation of the Samaritan Evidence," *CBQ* 39 (1977), 190–208.

   "The Polemical Character of the Joseph Episode in Acts 7," *JBL* 98 (1979), 255–67.

Rigaux, B. *Saint Paul et ses lettres.* Paris, 1956.

Riggenbach, E. *Der Brief an die Hebräer.* Leipzig, 1913.

Robertson, A., and Plummer, A. *The First Epistle of St. Paul to the Corinthians.* Edinburgh, 1911.

Robinson, J. A. T., *The Human Face of God.* London, 1973.
   Redating the New Testament. London, 1976.

Robinson, J. M. and Koester, H. *Trajectories through Early Christianity.* Philadelphia, 1971.

Robinson, T. H. *The Epistle to the Hebrews.* London, 1933.

Robinson, W. *The Eschatology of the Epistle to the Hebrews.* Birmingham, 1950.

Ropes, J. H. "Bemerkungen zu der Rede des Stephanus und der Vision des Petrus," *TSK* (1930), 307–15.

Roth, C. *The Historical Background of the Dead Sea Scrolls.* Oxford, 1958.

Rowland, C. *The Open Heaven: A Study of Apocalyptic in Judaism and Early Christianity.* London, 1982.

Rusche, H. "Die Gestalt des Melchizedek," *MTZ* V (1955), 230–52.

Rust, E. C. *The Christian Understanding of History.* London, 1947.

Sanday, W., and Headlam, A. C. *The Epistle to the Romans.* Edinburgh, 1902.

Sanders, J. T. *The New Testament Christological Hymns.* Cambridge, 1971.

Schaeffer, J. R. "The Relation Between Priestly and Servant Messianism in the Epistle to the Hebrews," *CBQ* 30 (1968), 359–85.

Scharlemann, M. H. *Stephen: A Singular Saint.* Rome, 1968.

Schenke, "Erwägungen zum Rätsel des Hebräerbriefs," in *Neues Testament und christliche Existenz.* Festschrift for H. Braun. Ed. H. D. Betz and L. Schottroff. Tübingen, 1973, 421–37.

Schierse, F. J. *The Epistle to the Hebrews.* Transl. B. Fahy. London, 1969. *Verheissung und Heilsvollendung.* Munich, 1955.

Schille, G. "Erwägungen zur Hohepriesterlehre des Hebräerbriefes," *ZNW* LXIV (1955), 81–109.

Schlier, H. "δείκνυμι, κτλ.," *TDNT* II, 25ff.

Schmidt, K. L. "Jerusalem als Urbild u. Abbild," *Eranos-Jbch.* 18 (1950), 207ff.

Schmithals, W. *Paul and James.* London, 1965.

Schnackenburg, R. "Die Erwartung des 'Propheten' nach dem Neuen Testament und den Qumran-Texten," *SE* I (1959), 622–39.

Schneider, J. "τίμη, τιμάω," *TDNT* VIII, 169ff.

Scholem, G. *Major Trends in Jewish Mysticism.* New York, 1954.

Schrenk, G. "ἱερός, κτλ.," *TDNT* III, 221ff.

Schröger, F. *Der Verfasser des Hebräerbriefes als Schriftausleger.* Regensburg, 1968.

Schubert, K. *The Dead Sea Community.* Transl. J. W. Doberstein, London, 1959.

Schulz, S. "σκιά, κτλ.," *TDNT* VII, 394ff.

Schweizer, E. "I Korinther 15.20–28 als Zeugnis paulinischer Eschatologie und ihrer Verwandschaft mit der Verkündigung Jesu," in *Jesus und Paulus.* Festschrift for W. G. Kümmel. Ed. E. E. Ellis and E. Grässer. Göttingen, 1975.

"σάρξ, κτλ.," *TDNT* VII, 98ff.

Scobie, C. H. H. "The Origins and Development of Samaritan Christianity," *NTS* 19 (1972–73), 390–414.

"The Use of Source Material in the Speeches of Acts III and VII," *NTS* 25 (1979), 399–421.

Scott, E. F. *The Epistle to the Hebrews, its Doctrine and Significance.* Edinburgh, 1922.

Scroggs, R. "The Earliest Hellenistic Christianity," *Religions in Antiquity.* Ed. J. Neusner. Leiden, 1969. 176–206.

Selwyn, E. G. *The First Epistle of St. Peter.* London, 1946.

"St. Stephen's Place in Christian Origins," *Theology* V (1922), 306–16.

"The Two 'Messiahs' of the Manual of Discipline," *VT* V (1955), 77–82.

Silberman, L. "The Two 'Messiahs' of the Manual of Discipline," *VT* 5 (1955), 77–82.

Simon, M. *St. Stephen and the Hellenists*, 1958.

"Saint Stephen and the Jerusalem Temple," *JEH* 2 (1951), 127–42.

Smith, M. "What is Implied by the Variety of Messianic Figures?" *JBL* LXXVIII (1959), 66–72.

Snell, A. *New and Living Way*. London, 1959.

Sowers, S. G. *The Hermeneutics of Philo and Hebrews*. Zurich, 1965.

Spicq, C. "L'Authenticité du chapitre 13 de l'épître aux Hébreux," *Coniectanea Neotestamentica* II (1947), 226–36.

"Le Philonisme de l'epître aux Hébreux," *RB* 56 (1949), 542–72; 57 (1950), 212–42.

L'Epître aux Hébreux. 2 vols. Paris, 1952.

"L'Epître aux Hébreux, Apollos, Jean-Baptiste, les Hellénistes et Qumran," *RQ* I (1959), 365–90.

Spiro, A. "Stephen's Samaritan Background," Appendix to J. Munck, *The Acts of the Apostles*. Anchor Bible, New York, 1967.

Stacey, W. D. *The Pauline View of Man*. London, 1956.

Stadelmann, A. "Zur Christologie des Hebräerbriefes in der neueren Diskussion," *Theologische Berichte* II, Einsiedeln, 1973, 135–221.

Stanton, G. "Stephen in Lucan Perspective," *Studia Biblica* III (1978), 345ff.

Starcky, J. "Les Quatre Etapes du messianisme à Qumran," *RB* LXX (1963), 481–505.

Stendahl, K. *The School of St. Matthew and its Use of the Old Testament*. Philadelphia, 1968.

Stewart, R. A. "Creation and Matter in the Epistle to the Hebrews," *NTS* 12 (1966), 284–93.

Strack, H. L. *Einleitung in Talmud und Midrasch*. Munich, 1921.

Strack, H. L., and Billerbeck, P. *Kommentar zum Neuen Testament aus Talmud und Midrasch*. 5 vols. Munich, 1922–26.

Strathmann, H. "πολις, κτλ.," *TDNT* 6, 616ff.

Strugnell, J. "The Angelic Liturgy at Qumran – 4Q Serek Sirot 'Olat Hassabbat," *VT* Suppl. VII (1960), 318–45.

Swetnam, J. "'The Greater and More Perfect Tent.' A Contribution to the Discussion of Hebrews 9, 11," *Biblica* XLVII (1966), 91ff.

"On the Imagery and Significance of Heb. 9, 11," *CBQ* XXXVIII (1966), 153ff.

"On the Literary Genre of the 'Epistle' to the Hebrews," *NT* XI (1969), 261–69.

Synge, F. C. *Hebrews and the Scriptures*. London, 1959.

Taylor, V. *The Atonement in New Testament Teaching*. London, 1945.

Thackeray, H. St J., Marcus, R. and Feldman, L. *Josephus with an English Translation*. 9 vols. Loeb Classical Library, 1926–65.

Theissen, G. *Untersuchungen zum Hebräerbrief*. Gütersloh, 1969.

Thomas, K. J. "The Old Testament Citations in Hebrews," *NTS* XI (1964–65), 303–25.

"The Use of the Septuagint in the Epistle to the Hebrews" (unpublished Ph.D. Thesis, University of Manchester, 1959).

Thompson, J. W. *The Beginnings of Christian Philosophy*. CBQ Monograph Series 13, 1982.

Thornton, L. S. *The Common Life in the Body of Christ*. London, 1950.

Thornton, T. C. G. "Stephen's Use of Isa. LXVI.1," *JTS* 25 (1974), 432–34.

Thurston, R. W. "Midrash and 'Magnet' Words in the New Testament," *EQ* 51 (1979), 22–39.

"Philo and the Epistle to the Hebrews," *EQ* 58 (1956), 133ff.

Thyen, H. *Der Stil der judisch–hellenistischen Homilie*. Göttingen, 1955.

Tinsley, E. J. *The Imitation of God in Christ*. London, 1960.

Torrance, T. F. *Royal Priesthood*. London, 1955.

Traub, H., and von Rad, G. "οὐρανός κτλ.," *TDNT* V, 497ff.

Trotter, R. J. F. *Did the Samaritans of the Fourth Century Know the Epistle to the Hebrews?* Leeds, 1961.

Vanhoye, A. "'Par la tent plus grande et plus parfaite ...' (Hé 9,11)," *Biblica* XLVI (1965), 1–28.

Situation du Christ. Hébreux 1–2. Paris, 1969.

"Trois ouvrages récents sur l'épitre aux Hébreux," *Biblica* LII (1971), 62–71.

Vermes, G. *The Dead Sea Scrolls in English*. Penguin Books, 1965.

Jesus the Jew. Collins, 1973.

Scripture and Tradition in Judaism. Leiden, 1973.[2]

Villalón, J. R. "Sources vétéro-testamentaires de la doctrine qumrânienne des deux Messies," *RQ* 8 (1972), 53ff.

Waal, C. van der. "'The People of God' in the Epistle to the Hebrews," *Neotestamentica* 5 (1971), 83–91.

Waard, J. de. *A Comparative Study of the Old Testament Text in the Dead Sea Scrolls*. Leiden, 1965.

Wanamaker, C. A. "Philippians 2.6–11: Son of God or Adamic Christology?," *NTS* 33 (1987), 179ff.

Wand, J. W. C. *The General Epistles of Peter and Jude*. London, 1934.

Wcela, E. A. "The Messiah(s) of Qumran," *CBQ* XXVI (1964), 340–49.

Westcott, B. F. *The Epistle to the Hebrews*. London, 1889.

Williams, C. S. C. *A Commentary on the Acts of the Apostles*. London, 1957.

Williamson, R. "The Background of the Epistle to the Hebrews," *ET* 87 (1976), 232–37.

The Epistle to the Hebrews. Epworth, 1964.

"The Eucharist and the Epistle to the Hebrews," *NTS* 21 (1975), 300–12.

"The Incarnation of the Logos in Hebrews," *ET* 95 (1983), 4ff.

Philo and the Epistle to the Hebrews. Leiden, 1970.

"Philo and New Testament Christology," *ET* 90 (1970), 361–65.

"Platonism and Hebrews," *SJT* XVI (1963), 415–24.

Wilson, R. McL. *Gnosis and the New Testament*. Oxford, 1968.

Hebrews. The New Century Bible Commentary. Grand Rapids, Mich., 1987.

Wilson, S. G. *The Gentiles and the Gentile Mission in Luke–Acts*. Cambridge, 1973.

Windisch, H. *Der Hebräerbrief*. Tübingen, 1913.

Woude, A. S. van der. "Melchizedek als himmlische Erlösergestalt in den neugefundenen eschatologischen Midraschim aus Qumran Höhle XI," *Oudtestamentliche Studiën* XIV (1965), 354–73.

Die messianischen Vorstellungen der Gemeinde von Qumran. Assen, 1957.

Wrede, W. *Das literische Rätsel des Hebräerbriefs.* Göttingen, 1906.

Wülfing von Martitz, P., Fohrer, G., *et al.*, "υἱός, υἱοθεσία," *TDNT* VIII, 334ff.

Wuttke, G. *Melchisedech der Priesterkönig von Salem.* Beihefte zur *ZNW* 5, 1927.

Yadin, Y. "A Crucial Passage in the Dead Sea Scrolls," *JBL* LXXVIII (1959), 238–41.

"The Dead Sea Scrolls and the Epistle to the Hebrews," *Scripta Hierosolymitana* IV (1958), 36–53.

"A Midrash on 2 Sam. vii and Ps. i–ii (4Q Florilegium)," *IEJ* 9 (1959), 95–8.

"A Note on Melchizedek and Qumran," *IEJ* XV (1965), 152–54.

The Scroll of the War of the Sons of Light against the Sons of Darkness. Oxford, 1962.

Young, N. H. "The Gospel According to Heb. 9," *NTS* 27 (1981), 205f.

"ΤΟΥΤ' ΕΣΤΙΝ ΤΗΣ ΣΑΡΚΟΣ ΑΥΤΟΥ (Heb. X.20): Apposition, Dependent or Explicative?" *NTS* 20 (1974), 100–104.

Zimmermann, F. *Die Hohepriester-Christologie des Hebräerbriefes.* Paderborn, 1964.

Zuntz, G. *The Text of the Epistles.* London, 1953.

INDEX OF PASSAGES QUOTED

Intertestamental and other Jewish writings

New Testament

Other ancient and early Christian writings

GENERAL INDEX